DAVID DUBINSKY:

A Life With Labor

DAVID DUBINSKY

AND

A. H. RASKIN

SIMON AND SCHUSTER · NEW YORK

PUBLISHED BY SIMON AND SCHUSTER
A DIVISION OF GULF & WESTERN CORPORATION
SIMON & SCHUSTER BUILDING
ROCKEFELLER CENTER
1230 AVENUE OF THE AMERICAS
NEW YORK, NEW YORK 10020

DESIGNED BY EVE METZ
MANUFACTURED IN THE UNITED STATES OF AMERICA

1 2 3 4 5 6 7 8 9 10
LIBRARY OF CONGRESS CATALOGING IN PUBLICATION DATA

DUBINSKY, DAVID, 1892–
DAVID DUBINSKY: A LIFE WITH LABOR.

INCLUDES INDEX.
1. DUBINSKY, DAVID, 1892–   2. TRADE-UNIONS
—CLOTHING WORKERS—UNITED STATES—HISTORY.
3. TRADE-UNIONS—UNITED STATES—OFFICIALS AND
EMPLOYEES—BIOGRAPHY. I. RASKIN, ABRAHAM HENRY,
1911–   JOINT AUTHOR.
HD6509.D8A33   331.88′18′7120924   76-52414
ISBN 0–671–22437–9

CONTENTS

INTRODUCTION

YOU CAN'T SEE the Statue of Liberty from Seventh Avenue, but the venturesome spirit that made millions of poor, often persecuted, Europeans crowd into the steerage of ships steaming toward that symbol of freedom in the early years of this century is nowhere more boisterously alive than in the thousands of garment factories huddled in twenty mid-Manhattan blocks.

The shops that mass-produce the dresses, coats, pants and undergarments that women wear gross billions of dollars each year. But there is no General Motors among them, no United States Steel, no single tycoon who dominates. There are, in the garment center, many moguls whose success depends, season after season, on their interpretations of style. Twice a year each manufacturer gambles everything he owns and everything he can borrow—once on his spring line and again on his fall line. A wrong guess on fabric, cut, color or hemline and he is wiped out. Competition is savage, delivery dates inexorable. "It's today, not yesterday, not tomorrow; it's selling ice cream in a blast furnace," is the manufacturer's wail. So swift is extinction that the same employer can bob up in a half dozen corporate cloaks in a single year.

Building a union in this "rag jungle" required a special kind of leader, one who could civilize the industry at the same time that he lifted its workers out of the degradation of the sweatshops in which they originally toiled in the "lung blocks" of the old Lower East Side. For more than three decades that leadership was provided by David Dubinsky, president of the International Ladies Garment Workers Union, a five-foot-five dynamo who dominated Seventh Avenue in a manner never approached by such arbiters of fashion as Pauline Trigère, Halston, Christian Dior, Mollie Parnis or Yves St. Laurent.

When David Dubinsky became its president in 1932, the union was an insignificant enterprise facing bankruptcy. Its staff was unpaid; the elevator in its headquarters had to be stopped because there was no money to meet the electric bill. The new president Dubinsky and four fellow officers pledged all their personal assets as security for a $5,000 loan to start the union's first organizing drive under Franklin D. Roosevelt's New Deal. The union was a warren of brawling political factions rooted in Marxist doctrines of class struggle and made more contentious by virulent ethnic and religious antagonisms. An undertaker or an asylum superintendent seemed more appropriate than a new president.

By the time Dubinsky relinquished command in 1966, the garment union had been transformed into a flourishing welfare state, a pattern-setter for labor generally. The I.L.G.W.U. and its affiliated locals had a half billion dollars in pension, welfare and treasury reserves. Its membership had grown to 450,000, nearly twenty times the total in 1932 when he began, and it had become the principal stabilizing force in an industry still so volatile that half the union's membership quit and were replaced by others in the three years between conventions. Huge cooperative-housing developments, a palatial union vacation resort in the Poconos, towering health centers, theatrical and movie ventures that won wide critical praise and the distribution of forty million dollars to labor and charitable causes all over the world testified to the organization's concern for human values.

Although he had been a Socialist soapbox speaker in his early union days, Dubinsky gradually grew to believe that "unions need capitalism like a fish needs water." Under his auspices, the unmeltable alumni of the melting pot once became financial angels to the Rockefellers by investing heavily in a Rockefeller-sponsored housing project for Puerto Rican workers. This, a generation earlier, would have been comparable to Eugene V. Debs accepting a partnership in the House of Morgan. Yet, even after the modified socialism of the New Deal caused Dubinsky to abandon formal enrollment in the Socialist Party, he retained such an atavistic aversion to pulling down a lever on either the Democratic or the Republican line that he made his union the mainstay of an independent labor-liberal party in New York State—not primarily because it would give him great political clout (which it did) but because as an American by adoption he felt it was un-American not to exercise his franchise. His philosophy of industrial relations was simple: "First you get a whip and then when everyone knows you have it, put it in the refrigerator."

In the larger affairs of labor, Dubinsky played a prime role in unifying the American Federation of Labor and the Congress of Industrial Organizations after their twenty years of civil war. The principles and precedents he established helped shift the mainstream of labor into a new riverbed of probity and social responsibility. He served as conscience and goad for all labor in a no-surrender battle against corruption in union ranks, persevering until the merged Federation incorporated his precepts into the code of ethics that gave it the weapons to oust Dave Beck, Jimmy Hoffa and other union freebooters.

Honors and monuments piled up around David Dubinsky, this irrepressible little refugee from the Tsar's jails. Presidents, governors and mayors credited him with swinging votes to their election. But none of these badges of accomplishment, none of the trappings of power stripped him of the loneliness or the compassion that stems from a recognition of the enormity of human misery and social neglect. He could be cruel and overbearing, even autocratic; his rages were fearsome. Yet overriding this imperiousness was a radiance of spirit, a zest for life and, above all, an intimate concern for people that made him that rarest of leaders, a man who cared. Of all the qualities of heart and mind that carried David Dubinsky to greatness, the one that distinguished him most from the other strong men of labor was that, at the end, he could still weep.

Not that he was morose or given to introspection, much less self-doubt. On the contrary, even when he quit at age seventy-four, he remained so consumed with the pure joy of living that he often kicked off his shoes in exuberance and did a little twirling dance with a shuffling step of his own invention. He would alternate between periods of dieting (so rigid that one time he lost twenty-five pounds in a single month) and of Rabelaisian self-indulgence in which he assaulted his indestructible digestive system with huge baskets of onion rolls, highly spiced pickles and goose pastrami, all washed down with enough Scotch or rum to floor a truck driver.

Until his wife's slow, tortured slide into death, after his eightieth birthday, tore at his own vitality, age did little to take the fire out of his volcanic temper or the steel out of his rugged constitution. On his winter trips to Miami Beach as a vice-president of the A.F.L.–C.I.O., he used to get up at dawn to plunge into the ocean. He was happiest when there was a heavy surf and he could be pummeled by waves that kept his less hardy labor colleagues in their beach chairs. He whipped himself with an icy shower each morning and boasted that he got his best ideas then. Saturday afternoons were reserved for visits to a Rockefeller Center steam room, where he sought out areas hot enough to cook a side of beef. Sundays he pedaled from his home in a lower-Fifth-Avenue hotel to Central Park for a long spin on the bicycle paths. At sixty-five he learned to drive, turning the car over once in the process; ten years later he acquired a power boat and sped around Shinnecock Bay in Long Island, gleeful as a teen-ager, creating great spumes of spray in his wake.

A perfectionist in his union duties, D.D. devoted the same pains to effecting a ten-cent economy as he did to approving a ten-million-dollar investment. He collected tickets at union functions, adjusted the microphones, peeled off his dinner jacket to help the waiters roll out extra banquet tables, quarreled over the price of floor tile, and switched off the light in empty union offices, leaving behind a note with some such reproof as, "What's the matter, Edison gives it to you free?"

At union conventions his major speeches ranged across the mountaintops of social idealism, seeking to evoke the sense of a union grown to wealth and power, but richer still in the devotion of its rank and file. And a moment later, while the mood of exaltation remained strong in the hall, he would scold some hapless delegate for stirring from his seat. He was the fond papa, sometimes captious, sometimes domineering, but always able to infuse a note of high drama into every report and every talk.

When he spoke, you forgot how tiny he was. The back, hunched from years of bending over a cutting table, seemed straighter. The blurred Yiddish accent, a reminder of his youth in Lodz and Brest-Litovsk, faded in the poignancy of his delivery. His words came out a prose poem, bringing reassurance and rededication both to the union's pioneers, worried about the slippage of their authority to upstarts from the new I.L.G.W.U. locals in the Midwest, the South and the Pacific Coast, and to the restless newcomers who wondered why so many executive-board members still came from New York and bore in their speech the marks of birth in Russia or Italy.

He could switch with lightning speed from the gravity of a labor statesman to the irreverence of a Dead End kid; his ebullience refused to be stifled by the most august of surroundings. Received by Pope Pius XII in 1948 after the Communists had been edged out in a bitter contest for control of postwar Italy, in which both the I.L.G.W.U. and the Vatican had been secretly bankrolling the anti-Communist coalition of Socialists and Christian Democrats, Dubinsky broke the initial stiffness by chortling, "Father, you did a great job in the elections."

At the British Foreign Office one stifling afternoon, he was depressed by the mustiness of both the actual office and the civil servants who manned it (even with a Labour government in power). After waiting for some minutes in a windowless anteroom, bereft of fan or air conditioning, he threw wide the corridor door and bellowed, "It's time someone let a little fresh air into the British Foreign Office."

This book is David Dubinsky's own story, the accumulation of his enthusiasms and his hatreds, the letting of a little fresh air into neglected corners of American labor history. It is the way Dubinsky sees his life, as he dictated it to me in a hundred tape-recorded conversations from 1969 to 1972. The organization is mine, and so are many of the words; but the thoughts and appraisals are all his. This is not a balanced story, nor does it pretend to be. You will search it in vain for any acknowledgment of error, any sense of important failure, any questioning either of goals or of their fulfillment. It is D.D.'s version of history, and it is unabashed in its parading of virtue.

As one whose daily task it was in a quarter century of labor reporting for *The New York Times* to chronicle the feats and lapses of all the panjandrums of labor, I am well aware of how many blank spots he leaves in the record and, much more important, how terribly time, human frailty and institutional weaknesses in the garment industry, the labor movement and the over-all structure of an economy geared to private greed have eroded many of his proudest innovations.

By the time he stepped down in 1966—and even more now, a decade later—much tragedy had come into the brave dreams. In New York City, birthplace of the I.L.G.W.U. and still its heartland, the union membership keeps atrophying as manufacturers reach out over the world in search of contractors who will make their garments for less. That almost always means with cheaper labor—profiting out of lower wages, longer hours, inferior or nonexistent fringe benefits— because that is where the biggest and easiest savings can be made in a dog-eat-dog industry.

First the runaways went to shops in New Jersey, Pennsylvania and upstate New York; then to town-built factories in the antiunion South and Southwest; now they have gone global—to sanctuaries in Taipei, Bangkok and a thousand other exotically situated overseas hideaways, all reincarnations of the hellholes where immigrants once huddled over their sewing machines on the Lower East Side. Dubinsky fought this defection by strikes, in the courts, and before impartial umpires. He won injunctions and money damages for the union. He even constructed a union dress factory in the South and subsidized it in his determination to best one struck fugitive from Seventh Avenue. But none of this checked the migration and the whittling away of the labor standards so painfully established by the I.L.G.W.U.

The result was inevitable. The union came out of World War II with wage levels in many of its shops comparable to those in such heavy industries as steel and autos, an incredible achievement in a field where 85 percent of the union members were women and capital investment was nominal. Two decades later a yawning gap had opened between pay averages in garment shops and those in steel and autos, a gap which keeps widening year by year. Indeed, the union is hard-pressed these days to enforce scales twenty or twenty-five cents an hour above the federal minimum wage, the least Uncle Sam will let any employer pay.

The erosion has been crueler still in the areas where the Dubinsky-led I.L.G.W.U. made its most memorable breakthroughs, notably industrial pensions. In the early 1940s, when wartime wage controls limited the size of increases, he induced garment-industry employers to set aside some of the extra money they would have granted workers and put it in a pooled pension fund managed by the union. This entry into Social Security under a union label gave the garment workers an important new layer of financial protection for their old age, one that the unions in steel, autos and other basic industries were quick to copy after the war. And soon the retirement benefits of these unions dwarfed those of the innovators. In the United Auto Workers, people could retire as early as age fifty-five on pensions of $400 or $500 a month. In the I.L.G.W.U., when Dubinsky left, the standard monthly benefit at age sixty-five was still only sixty dollars a month, a figure that inflation had rendered meager to the point of insult.

Frustrations abounded everywhere. The membership became predominantly black, Puerto Rican and Mexican-American, and overwhelmingly female; the leadership remained predominantly Jewish and Italian, and overwhelmingly male. Bureaucratic smugness smothered both vitality and idealism in many locals. Corruption, exorcised by Dubinsky, refused to stay exorcised. In the garment industry and in labor generally, the moral armor he created has proved an imperfect shield against renewed racket penetration. Even the anti-Communism, which never ceased being a religion with him—a religion ingrained by the havoc Communist Party wreckers inflicted on the union in the 1920s and fortified by the Stalin-Hitler pact and other acts of Soviet villainy—has now become a butt for revisionist scoffing in an America weary of cold war.

But awareness of the flaws and the frustrations in no way diminishes the admiration due Dubinsky for the magnitude of his contribution to a better labor movement and a better America. From the day he flashed a borrowed diamond ring to impress a cloakmaker into hiring him as a cutter, he was a Seventh Avenue "original," more distinctive than any created in the ateliers of high fashion. Of all the great men of labor, he was easily the most engaging—impish, inventive, hyperactive ("You've got to be on your toes, not on your bottom"), eternally chomping an unlit cigar, the cherubic artlessness of his mien masking a mind as nimble and full of guile as that of a medieval sorcerer.

Perhaps the best way for me to encapsulate all the traits that I found so fascinating in this most complex of characters is to conclude this introduction to his own memoirs with one episode in the Dubinsky saga. He was furious, early in the Kennedy administration, when Representative Adam Clayton Powell of Harlem, then chairman of the House Labor Committee, initiated an investigation into the garment union on charges that it was denying equal opportunity to blacks and Puerto Ricans. Powell was an even more complicated character than Dubinsky—part dauntless battler for black rights in a white world, part demagogue, part playboy. But so far as Dubinsky was concerned, he was all racist mountebank, and the Congressional inquiry was solely an act of retaliation for the refusal of Dubinsky to back Powell with election funds.

It did nothing to soften D.D.'s mood when a nonunion manufacturer demanded that the I.L.G.W.U. call off a strike lest the manufacturer go before the Powell Committee and offer damaging testimony in support of its charges.

"No chiseling runaway employer can intimidate our union," Dubinsky shouted. "If you want to know the address of the Powell Committee, I'll give it to you."

President Kennedy invited him to attend a White House luncheon along with other members of the A.F.L.–C.I.O. Executive Council just before the hearings began. "I don't know whether you should have me here," Dubinsky told the President. "I'm accused of being a racketeer, anti-Negro and anti-Puerto Rican." Kennedy's reply was unhesitating. "If you're a racketeer, anti-Negro and anti-Puerto Rican, so am I," he declared.

As he left the White House Dubinsky encountered a guard he remembered from the Roosevelt days. "I've seen you here for twenty-five years, and you don't change," the guard said. "How do you do it?" Dubinsky shrugged, but there was nothing passive about his words. "I take care of myself, and I take care of my enemies," he said. At the hearings he took care of them so well that the committee never filed a report.

For weeks afterward he glowed with satisfaction at the discomfiture he had caused his interrogators through the solidity of his carefully documented testimony and the flamboyance of his delivery, the extent to which his exuberant personality with its swift switches from humor to rage had dominated the chamber, reducing the Congressmen to cowed onlookers. But Dubinsky the All-Conquering could not shut out that other Dubinsky, the union leader who cared—not about his image but about the realities of an industry that had come out of World War II with wage rates among the highest in any manufacturing field and now ranked well down the list.

He knew all the factors—jungle competition, gangster infiltration, insecure capitalization, coolie-labor imports, bankruptcies—that provided perfectly valid alibis for this relative deterioration in garment earnings. But these explanations gave him no comfort as he studied government figures showing thousands of his members in the $1.50-an-hour bracket, a level so low that many full-time workers needed to apply for supplemental relief from the public welfare authorities to keep abreast of the high cost of living.

While the sycophants were still shaking Dubinsky's hand and applauding him for humiliating his detractors, he was telling me: "Here is our union, a pioneer in pensions, welfare, paid vacations. We led everybody else in factory wages only a few years ago; now we are criticized because our wages are too low. And it is true, many of them are low. That has affected me deeply. Where did we go wrong?"

He wedded power to compassion. That is as much part of his legacy to American democracy as the D.D. stamp of social concern he put on a labor movement rooted in the bread-and-butter tradition of business unionism.

A. H. RASKIN

ONE

"Open the Door of Heaven"

WLADYSLAW STANISLAW REYMONT, a Polish winner of the Nobel Prize for Literature, called it "The Promised Land." He was not talking about America; he was talking about Lodz, the city where I grew up. The name was a grisly joke. The only thing Lodz promised for a poor Jewish boy was *tsouris*—"trouble"—lots and lots of trouble. It was the biggest industrial city in Poland when my family moved there from Brest-Litovsk in 1895, an ugly place, where the palaces of the millionaire factory owners stood on the main streets close to the factories out of which they squeezed their great wealth. In those factories workers toiled for twelve or fifteen hours a day at miserable wages, and the Cossacks were always ready to charge in to smash any workers' protest and drag the leaders off to jail.

Out of sight, behind the factories and the palaces, were mile after mile of slums where the workers lived, whole families in a single, tiny room. Everything in Lodz, a city of a half million people, was geared to serve the factories. They were the degraded cathedrals of privilege, around which all municipal services were organized. The gutters ran red, blue and green with the waste dyes dumped into them by the huge textile mills. There was no sewage system, so the rainbow of industrial waste swept along with all the rest of the city's filth. Anything good that was done the authorities did for the factories, not for the people. Cheap, fast transportation was important for getting workers to their jobs. So this city, which considered sanitation a luxury, rushed to put in electric trolley cars at the turn of the century. Warsaw didn't get them till many years later, but it wasn't dominated by its industries the way Lodz was.

Naturally, in such a community exploitation was a way of life. The rich exploited the poor, and the poor exploited one another. Jews struggled to keep alive as tradesmen. Many had small stalls, with a barrel of pickles, a few herrings and a big copper siphon of soda water. To start one of these holes-in-the-wall meant scraping together maybe five or ten rubles, but that microscopic investment had to yield enough income to support the entire family. That meant keeping the store open all the time, from early morning till nearly midnight, except on the Sabbath. For more ambitious shops, a Jew had to borrow from a usurer at scandalous interest rates. Waclaw Solski, a Polish writer, who was a boy in Lodz at the same time I was, recalls that Jewish merchants not only had to pay exorbitantly to get money but also had to mortgage themselves in the most real sense. The loan sharks were not interested in taking promissory notes because the collateral was never worth very much. Instead, they invented an iron-clad kind of promissory note called a "Lodzer." The borrower had to forge the signature of an endorser on his note and the lender had to be sure that it was forged, even if that meant insisting that the forgery take place in his presence. Then, if the note was not redeemed in time, the borrower could be sent to jail for forgery.

My father brought us to Lodz when I was almost three. I had been born in Brest-Litovsk on February 22, 1892, but nobody in the Dobnievski household knew I was sharing a birthday with George Washington. I'm not even sure they knew who George Washington was. I was the youngest of nine children, and it didn't take me long to learn that in our family it was the mother who wore the pants. My father, Betsall, had a small bakery in a basement that was also our home, but he was a religious man whose chief interest was in going to *schul* to pray three times a day. He hated to be bothered with the business. All he did was keep the books and order the flour. He knew very little else about the bakery or even about baking. He left most of that to the older boys. The real boss, the one who ran the bakery and ran the family, was my mother.

As the youngest child I was her favorite, but because she had too many other things on her mind she had no time to give me any special attention. One day when I was four years old I got hurt and came crying to cling to her apron. Somehow my hand found its way into her pocket and I felt a few groschen there. I tried to say the Yiddish word for take —*nemmen*—but in my childish mumble it came out "memmen" and my mother couldn't make out what I was talking about. When I pulled my hand out, five or six groschen came with it. Each one was a half-kopeck, the equivalent of about a quarter of a penny. To me it was a small fortune and I raced off to the candy store to buy some sweets with little strips of paper in them that snapped when you pulled them. As soon as my brothers saw them, they asked where I had got the money. Right then any resemblance that I might have had to George Washington evaporated. I told them I had gone to the store with a bunch of boys and we had grabbed the snappers. When one brother said he would go himself and grab some more, I told him they were all gone.

Then just before my eighth birthday, my mother died and the house was given over to mourning. As was the custom, for a whole year there would be a *minyan*—ten men—to pray in the morning, the late afternoon and the evening. One of the regular visitors was an extremely devout man we called Rebbe Isaac. He was in the house so often that he and my father became close friends. One day, when they were taking time out from praying, my father confided that he was thinking about getting married again as soon as the year was over. Rebbe Isaac was aghast. "What do you need a wife for?" he asked. "You already have so many children." My father explained that he needed somebody to boil the soup and mend the stockings. And sure enough, almost before the last prayer was over, my father had gone back to his old home in Brest-Litovsk and returned with a new wife. By the time Rebbe Isaac visited our house again a couple of years later there were two new babies playing on the floor. He looked at my father and said in Yiddish, *"Rebbe Tsall, dis ist bei dir ein soup und dis ist bei dir ein shkarpeke?"*—which means, "This is what you call a soup and this is what you call a stocking?"

We all roared because we had developed a great hate for our stepmother. Maybe I was influenced a little in that by my older brothers and sisters. They were grown up and eager to be independent, and they resented having a stranger come in and take over. She dominated my father, and that made her the boss even more than my mother had been. She made our life a hell and we did the same for her in every way we knew how. She had a habit of fainting so she could get some cordial that she was very fond of. One day when she passed out, my brother stuck a pin into her to see if she was faking. My father came in and hit him. The next time she keeled over I was in the room. She was moaning, "Water, water." I went to the sink and pissed into the glass. She drank it and said, "You saved me."

The bakery had a little drawer where coins were kept and whenever I saw an opportunity I would snatch out a couple of groschen so I could go to a store and buy a hard-boiled egg. One day when I was about ten I had quite a few groschen and I needed some place to hide them, so I put them in the sweatband of my hat. But before I went out of the house several boys came to our kitchen window and began teasing me. I got so angry that I wanted to hit them through the open window. The only weapon I had handy was the hat and I tried to sock them with that. The money flew every which way. My eldest brother, who was the master baker, got furious. "Where did you get the money?" he demanded. "They threw it at me," was my feeble answer. It was so ridiculous that he gave me the name "Die Gonavey," because he didn't think just plain *goniff* ("conniver") was strong enough. So far as he was concerned, I was a cross between a conniver and a crook.

But most of the time I behaved. I was quite serious about going to school, not just the Hebrew school, where I started to learn to write Polish and Russian as well as Yiddish, but, when I got to be twelve, the semiprivate school, where I wormed my way in. There were in Lodz a few schools that had been endowed by the rich industrialists and I was determined to get into one of them, because I knew I could get a better education there. The best of all was the Poznansky School, named for the city's outstanding textile manufacturer, but I couldn't take a chance on applying just to that school. Also I couldn't hope for any help from my father, who was much too busy praying, or from my stepmother, who had no use for me. So all by myself I got on the trolley and went to four different schools. I registered at each one under a different name. The only one at which I used my right name was the Poznansky School, and luckily that was where I was accepted.

Ever since I attended Hebrew school, I had worked as the delivery boy for my father's bakery. The bread and rolls were all baked at night, and at six o'clock every morning I distributed them to the stores, before going to school. Sometimes they were in a bag, sometimes a basket, which I balanced with difficulty on my shoulders; the load was so heavy that it has left me with a permanent hunch. When I was almost fourteen and had been at the Poznansky School for just two years, my precious schooling came to an end. It all happened because my eldest brother, the master baker, was a card player. One night when he was losing he insisted on playing on and on and never did come in to work. I was sleeping in the kitchen back of the ovens, and my father woke me up and said I had to take my brother's place. I told him I wasn't sure I could do it. "It's my bakery," he said, "and on my beard you can learn how to be a barber." It may not sound like much in English, but in Yiddish it's a very reassuring expression.

My father had two professional bakers whose job was to knead the dough and shape the rolls and the *challahs,* the braided bread that was our chief stock in trade. Then it was the job of the master baker to put them in the oven. The trick was to load up ten boards with ten loaves each, push one after another through the narrow door of the oven, then get them all out without any being underdone or burnt. The two old-timers both watched me, tiny as I was, and they were amazed. Not a single loaf was spoiled. I had practiced on my father's beard without cutting his throat.

From then on, there was no more school. I was now a baker—a master baker yet. And if I was a baker I had to join the Socialist union, the Bund. Even while I was a schoolboy I had been thrilled by the Russian revolution of 1905. I remember going with another boy to a mass meeting, a very crowded meeting, and being filled with excitement by the revolutionary speeches. I considered myself a Bundist at heart; joining the bakers' union made me one in reality. The fact that I could write not only Yiddish but Russian and Polish helped me to move up in the union right away. By the time I was fifteen, I had been elected assistant secretary. My first assignment was to write a call for a strike that shut down my father's bakery along with all the rest.

We won the strike, but it was not much of a victory because that very night the police came and arrested all the organizers. When they came for me at three o'clock in the morning, my father gave me a few coins to use if I needed something from the jailors. That was the only language they understood. At the police station I was locked in a big cell with more than sixty other strikers, but before I was docketed my father bribed me out by paying twenty-five rubles to the police chief. There was one condition: I had to get out of town and not come back.

I was sent to Brest-Litovsk to stay with an uncle, a well-to-do businessman who ran a dry-goods store. He was not glad to see me. To him I was a criminal, a disgrace to the family. But he did open a little shop for me to sell candy and soda opposite the girls' high school. That's where I got cheated for the first time in my life. I still can't understand how it could happen. Somebody gave me a fake five-ruble gold piece and I gave him change for it. The most amazing fact is that I had that much change; it was as much money as I took in in a week. When my uncle learned I had been swindled, he denounced me as a *shlemiel*. After that, things got worse and worse between us, until another relative of my mother stepped in and told my uncle that she couldn't stand the way he was mistreating me. "You wouldn't treat Shayne Malke [an idiot girl] that way," she stormed. She gathered up my belongings and put me and them into her wagon. We traveled all night to her home in Korbrin, about twenty miles away. There I worked for several weeks as a baker, but I earned only three rubles a week. It was a miserable life. I couldn't make enough to live on, and my relatives were too poor to help.

The only answer seemed to be to go back to Lodz, but if the police stopped me on the street, asked for my passport, and saw I was David Dobnievski I would be back in jail again. So I decided to go back to Brest-Litovsk, where I was born, and try to get a passport under another name. I told the officials there that I had lost my passport and needed a new one. They replied that under the law they could not give me one unless I advertised in a newspaper for three days to see if anyone had found the lost passport. I took the ad and got a new passport. But I was still afraid to move around freely in Lodz for fear some policeman would recognize me and clap me back in prison. I moved from one relative to another each night, so no neighbor would get suspicious about a "stranger" and report me.

It was in that period of furtively moving around Lodz that I experienced one of the greatest disappointments of my life. I was walking along a street when I met a man I knew only by his party name of Ivan, a Russian-Jewish intellectual, who had been the main representative of the Bund in leading our strike. I had come to worship him; he typified everything I thought was brave and noble about the movement; the proudest part of my being assistant secretary of the local was that I was associated with such a splendid chief. The minute I spotted him in the street, I forgot all my own fears and called out happily, "Ivan." He kept right on walking. I felt maybe he didn't recognize me so I hurried after him and tried again. "Ivan, it's me, David, David Dobnievski, don't you know me?" His reply was brusque, "No, I don't," and he hurried off, leaving me dumbfounded.

The explanation for his odd behavior was given to me by others of my old comrades. Ivan, the great revolutionary, had deserted the cause. The arrests had scared him and he had cut all his ties with the Bund. He was afraid even to talk to anyone on the street lest the police think he was still active and put him behind bars. The more I thought about his cowardice, the more anger and contempt I had. And the more suspicious I became of all intellectuals and their devotion to the working class. Evidently Ivan had always looked down on us miserable workers, and when I realized that, I thought, well, if that was what intellectuals are like, the Bund can do very well without them. And so can the workers. But it didn't take me long to discover that there was more to intellectuals than I had learned from Ivan.

On January 8, 1908, a month before my sixteenth birthday, I decided to risk going to a meeting of the bakers' union where they were supposed to elect officers. The police had issued a permit, and there was no reason to expect trouble. The chairman was the head of the union, an active figure in the Bund, whose party name was Noach. Under the election rules, whenever an officer was nominated, he was supposed to step out of the main hall into an adjacent office. That way when the members voted by show of hands the candidate would not see who voted for him and who voted against. Noach was the first to be placed in nomination. When he went into the next room, which was the headquarters of the hosiery workers' union, the president of that union warned

him that the police were setting a trap. They had surrounded the hall and were planning to arrest us all. Noach
was told he could get away through a back door if he moved
fast. He had been arrested before, because he was a key man
in the revolutionary movement. To be arrested now would
mean God-knows-how-many years in prison or summary exile to Siberia or torture—perhaps even death. But Noach
didn't hesitate for a second. He refused to abandon his members. When he came back into the hall, he whispered the
story to me, said he would put my name in nomination for
secretary, and told me to escape when I went into the next
room while the members were voting on me. I was too ex-
hilarated by his decision to stay to even think about running
away. Here was Noach, an intellectual like Ivan, willing to
sacrifice himself for the workers. He could have walked
through the door to freedom that night. If he wanted to
think only of himself, he could have been a rich and respected man in the professions or in business. Instead, he
chose to rot in jail. "I'm responsible for this meeting, and I'm
going to stay here," he had said. How could my decision be
any different. Fifteen minutes later we were all under arrest.

This time going to jail was no lark for me. I was classed as
a political prisoner, one who had returned to Lodz without
permission. The interrogation was long and exhaustive;
sometimes the questioning was brutal, sometimes there
would be a quick switch to softness in the hope of breaking
down my guard and getting me to incriminate others. One
interrogator made a particular effort to win me over by pretending total sympathy. At the start of every talk he would
assure me that he was a secret revolutionary and wished me
nothing but good.

"If you are a revolutionary," I asked, "how do you explain
that you are sitting there behind your desk and I am here
before you as a political prisoner?"

"Well, I'll tell you," was the reply, "it's like this: you and I
believe in the revolution, but I think it is too soon. I have to

see to it that the revolution does not come too soon because that would be a calamity. I have to protect against that happening."

The warden in charge of the Lodz prison was a barbarian; six times prisoners tried to kill him, and so when I was there he wore armor to shield his body. Our existence was so miserable that the prisoners used to chant a prayer for deliverance. Over and over we would sing, "Open the door of heaven." The door never budged. I got gentler treatment than the other "politicals," because I was so young. And also because my sister once brought the warden a tasty fish. He was a venal brute, always eager to have his hand greased or his stomach stuffed.

One of the privileges I was given was an assignment to be a messenger between the prisoners and the outside world. Several times a week parents or other relatives were allowed to send food, which they would give to the guard on duty at the gate, along with five kopecks for the guard. I would take the food to the prisoners and sometimes I would bring back notes to be delivered to the families. I became the go-between to such an extent that the guards made a practice of giving me cigarettes to sell to the prisoners. Soon I was walking around with pockets full of money; and then the warden found out and put me in solitary for a while. He still considered me smart and sometimes useful, and I never knew when he sent for me whether it was to hit me with the billy club he carried or to use me as special courier for some racket of his own. One day I got word that he wanted to see me and I was so sure it was for a beating that I took my little leather knapsack and put it under my shirt to protect me when I was hit. It turned out that the warden had no interest in punishing me that day. He wanted me to go to the women's section of the jail and escort Freda, the best-known of the women prisoners, a Socialist from a rich family, to the room for visitors. On the way, I kept wondering why the warden was asking me to do this instead of a guard. The answer became clear: he counted on me to tell Freda's wealthy friends that a little remembrance for the warden would not be amiss. He couldn't trust that kind of mission to the guards. He got his graft, and my stock went up with him. The other prisoners did not mind it a bit because the more freedom I got the more I could act as a communications link to make life easier for them.

I was marked for exile to Siberia, and for eighteen months I moved from prison to prison in Poland and Russia on my way to the wasteland on the other side of the Urals. In an important way it was the richest part of my education, for some of the Tsar's jails were a kind of labor college where I could learn Socialist principles and practice from men of great brilliance. It is true that often my cellmates were professional thieves, even killers, hardly men of culture. But I was struck by the special friendliness these tough criminals invariably showed me. They told me that they admired and respected the "politicals" because they were ready to sacrifice themselves for people who had nothing.

Such respect from so unlikely a source—hardened criminals, men whose whole life was a repudiation of idealism—impressed me profoundly. I began to see that it was not enough for a union to be concerned only with getting more for its own members. What gave the Bund meaning was that it sought freedom and opportunity for everybody. I had already seen how complicated even the simplest part of that effort could get. When we called the strike of bakers just after I started in the union, the need was clear. The bakers did not earn enough to live on, so they had to fight for more. But whom were we fighting? Not long after my father agreed to the raise, he had to close his shop and go to work for a more prosperous baker. The same thing happened to many other small bakers. Obviously, it was not fair to blame them that workers got paid so badly. Noach had told me that, but only now, in prison, did I begin to read the books that would help to give me some understanding of the interaction of social forces and of how a despotic government held everybody in check except the rich and favored.

In the Paviak penitentiary in Warsaw and the Butyrki in Moscow, I was incarcerated with a brilliant group. Even the bedbugs in those jails were intelligent. There were whole armies of them in the dirty straw mattresses. To get away from their embrace, we prisoners would sleep on the stone floor of our cell and put a circle of water around us to keep the bedbugs from getting through. That didn't discourage them for long. They would crawl up the walls to the ceiling, come across until they were directly over a sleeping prisoner, then drop down on him. The bugs made sleep so uncomfortable that we talked to one another, and talked, and talked, until just before daybreak when the bugs would disappear. For me the whole thing was inspirational even when the bedbugs were biting.

From Moscow I was sent to Samara, the jumping-off point by train for exile in Siberia. The custom was to handcuff prisoners to one another on such journeys, but the guards had a problem with me. My hands were so small that no handcuff they put on me would stay on. In a few minutes I was always out of the cuffs. Finally, they gave up. All they asked was that whenever the chief guard came along I pretend that I was chained to the man next to me. Before they loaded all of us on a prison train bound for Chelyabinsk, we were searched from head to toe. But we were ready for the guards. Whatever little money we had we folded lengthwise and put under our upper lip. That way it couldn't be seen even when we talked.

Our train stood on a siding for a long time in Samara. I leaned out of a window with a Russian officer still in uniform, also a political prisoner, with whom I had become friendly. We noticed two pretty girls about my age standing alongside the tracks. We smiled at them and they smiled back. The prettier of the two, a stunning brunette, blew a kiss in our direction. My companion insisted it was meant for me. "It's funny how a Jewess can always tell a Jew," he said. I wasn't disposed to argue. I was too smitten. The girls came closer to our car and the one who had thrown the kiss asked: "How do the guards treat you?"

My heart beat even faster. That question meant that the girls were "politicals," for only politicals knew how important the attitude of the guards was to all political prisoners. They had it in their power to make life miserable without half trying; things went a lot easier if they had a little humanity. Our guard was standing only a few feet away so I decided to be diplomatic. "The guard from Warsaw to Moscow was terrible; the guard from Moscow to Samara was much better but the guard we have here on this train is the best of all," I shouted.

The girl nodded her head and smiled. We didn't say another word for many minutes, just stared fondly at one another and kept smiling. Finally I broke the silence by asking where she was from. I knew Jews were not permitted in Samara and I suspected that the girls might be political escapees. But I did not dare ask that question directly for fear it might get them in trouble. Asking where they were from was the closest I could think of to getting a clue. The reply was Siedlce in Poland, and that was all the confirmation I needed of their status.

The two girls whispered something to one another; then, shouting a promise to come back, they disappeared. A few minutes later they returned with a big bag of oranges and they sent it to me with a guard. I gave the oranges to the Russian officer to distribute among the other prisoners while I went back to the window to moon at the girls. In a few minutes the officer, this supposed gentleman, pushes me aside and yells to the girls, "There aren't enough oranges. Bring some more quick." I was so embarrassed at his rudeness that I fell to the floor in a dead faint. When I recovered consciousness and looked out the window again, they had vanished.

That made me extremely melancholy. I had not talked to a girl for more than a year, let alone flirted with one. I did not want it all to end so abruptly. I suddenly remembered a story that Ilya Reich, a Jewish poet, who was a fellow prisoner in Moscow, had told me about being on a train near Samara with a good-looking girl with black eyes. The guard had made a pass at her and Reich took her part—which earned him a beating, but the guard left the girl alone. I began putting two and two together and convinced myself that this must be the same girl. I scribbled out a note in Yiddish and gave a guard fifty kopecks to try to find the girls and deliver it. The note asked whether they had ever known Ilya Reich or been on a prison train. The guard came back after twenty minutes, unsuccessful. That made me even more depressed. Night and day, as the train chugged toward Chelyabinsk, I saw that lovely face before me, her smile always a little more loving. I vowed that whenever I regained my freedom, I would go to Siedlce and search her out. I never did, of course; but I never gave up the idea of meeting her again. After I came to the United States I discovered that she too remembered. I was sitting in a cooperative cafeteria on Thirteenth Street arguing with an anarchist about Siberia, when a girl came to the table and asked, "Were you ever in Samara?"

"Yes."

"Did you get a bag of oranges?"

I didn't need to hear any more. The story of that incident was so holy to me that I had never confided it to anyone, always hoping that some day, some place, I might meet that girl again. And here she was. Her name was Esther Minkus. She had a husband, but they were separated. We became the fastest of friends on the spot. More than friends. She and her baby girl moved in with me, and we lived as brother and sister. Her little girl grew up in my arms.

When the prison train reached Chelyabinsk, not far from the Russian border, we prisoners were divided into small groups and sent out on foot to villages deeper in Siberia. I discovered that some old friends from Lodz had been allowed to remain in Chelyabinsk itself, so I sent a letter to the local governor asking for permission to do the same. Before any response could come, I was being marched off with other exiles to a tiny village I had never heard of. We marched from eight o'clock in the morning till six o'clock in the evening, covering twenty or thirty miles each day. In Lodz everyone had the idea that it was always cold in Siberia, so all the clothes I had on my back and in my gunny-sack were heavy. But this was midsummer and the heat was murderous. All we had to eat was black bread and water. After ten days of marching in a bath of my own sweat, I decided to try to escape.

I maneuvered my way to the tail end of the ragged line and, by way of testing the guards, lagged farther and farther behind the rest of the group. Finally one guard came over and said, "What are you up to? Are you trying to escape?" His tone reassured me and I winked at him. "Don't try to get away here," the guard advised. "You'll have a better chance if you wait till we get to the next village." He told me there was a medical assistant there, a Polish Socialist political exile, who might help me. He promised that he would arrange to let me see the man as soon as we arrived, and he kept his promise.

The medical aide was happy to suggest a plan for getting away. There was a railway station close by, but it would be a mistake to go there, because that would be the first place the guards would look if I ran away. The right place to go, he felt, was another train stop twenty miles away. After getting directions on how to make my way through the woods to the second station, I rejoined my guard and he brought me back to the prisoners' hut.

I was the only "political" in the whole group; the rest had all been arrested and exiled for various crimes from rape to robbery. A particularly tough character named Krynin had established himself as the leader of all the other prisoners. I knew I had to get him on my side if I was to escape. Early in the morning I gave him all my extra clothes, keeping only what I was wearing. He didn't ask me why I was doing it. In fact, neither of us said a word. But he understood what I was up to.

I stuck my cap under my shirt and waited until the guards sat down to breakfast. Then I slipped out of the hut and walked away as quietly as I could. I had arranged a cover story in case a guard did try to stop me. I would tell him that I was going back to the hospital to see the Polish medical assistant, who had promised to confirm my alibi. But no one challenged me. The other prisoners hadn't given the alarm about my escape. Perhaps the guards had not noticed me going, but I doubt it. From what I later came to know about the attitude of guards in general, I don't think they were ever too eager to capture escaped prisoners. Guards received nine kopecks a day to cover the rations for each prisoner; when one died or ran away they kept that money for themselves.

I walked very slowly at first to avoid attracting attention, but when I got some distance away I ran at top speed. Soon I was out of breath and had to rest, no matter what the danger. I saw a haystack in a nearby field and crawled into it to rest. When I ventured forth several hours later and started through the forest, I heard a horse behind me. Trying to appear totally unconcerned, I kept right on walking. The rider reined in the horse as he came alongside and said, "You're an escaped prisoner." It was a statement, not a question, but I still tried to brazen it out. "What makes you say that?" I demanded with all the outrage I could muster.

"The straw on your shoulder," the man on horseback replied. "If you weren't a fugitive, why would you be sleeping in a haystack?"

I looked down at my clothes and saw that I was covered from head to toe with wisps of straw. I also noticed that the rider seemed to be a peasant, certainly not a soldier or a guard. So I told him my story and he listened all the way through without saying a word. Finally, he asked whether I could ride a horse.

"No, I can't," I said. "Why?" The truth is I was a bit afraid of him. I didn't know where he might take me. He explained that I didn't look strong enough to go on, but he told me how to get to the next town. When I got there, I knocked at a door and introduced myself to the peasant who answered. Without any pretending, I told him that I was a runaway political prisoner. He went to the corner of the room, where an ikon was hanging, and knelt before it to pray for my safety. A little while later a neighbor came in and asked the peasant who I was. "Oh, he's an architect from Poland. I'm planning to build a new house and he's here to make the plans." When the neighbor left, my new friend fed me and advised me to get some sleep because the only safe time to make a getaway would be late at night. When he woke me, he offered to give me his gun. He figured that as a revolutionist I would have access when I got home to a new Browning rifle, which was then the latest thing in guns. He wanted to arrange a swap: his old-fashioned gun now in exchange for my sending him a Browning later on. I had to tell him the truth. I didn't know the first thing about guns, old or new, and didn't want to learn.

He still seemed ready to help me, and told me to lie on the floor in the back of his wagon. We drove through the night to a whistle stop where I could flag a train without as much danger of arrest as there would be if I went to a station. He gave me money for a ticket and a couple of rubles to spare, said another prayer and loaded me on the train to Chelyabinsk. When I got there it was still pitch dark and I took a droshky to the address of a political exile from Lodz, Yussel Rosenberg, an old friend of my family. When I was trying to get permission to stay in Chelyabinsk on my arrival from Samara, I had sent him and his wife a letter telling them of my hope to be with them. Now maybe it would come true.

But the driver could not find the address. He left me in a dark alley and told me their house must be somewhere close by. There were no lights in any window, no people about to ask for directions. Having no passport, I decided the smart thing would be to sleep between two piles of stones in the alley, using a little package I was carrying as a pillow. By this time I could sleep anywhere, and I was so sound asleep early the next morning when the town crier started whirling his wake-up siren that I didn't hear it till he pushed me with his foot. He told me to get moving before I got arrested as a beggar. He said the police were very strict about begging in that district.

Just then a woman came to the door of the house at the head of the alley. I asked her where Yussel Rosenberg lived. She said he had lived in that very house but the whole family had moved out only a few days before. Then she startled me by adding, "You're David Dobnievski, aren't you? We've been expecting you." It developed that the letter I had mailed to the Rosenbergs four weeks before had not been delivered until the very day before I slept unknowingly on the doorstep. You can see how high a priority mail from prisoners got in the Tsar's Russia.

The woman invited me in and fixed me a big breakfast. She explained that the Rosenberg family had been sent to another part of Siberia, but that there were plenty of political prisoners still around and I was welcome to stay. In that house were a couple of girls about my age. They were friends of Yussel, from Bialystok in Poland. Both were prisoners, but they had been allowed to stay in Chelyabinsk to work as dressmakers. They advised me to go to the synagogue and see the *shamus*, the caretaker, who acted as mentor to all the political exiles. When I introduced myself, the shamus clapped his forehead and said, "Are you Tsalke's son?" That was the diminutive for my father's name of Betsall. Once again I had stumbled on an old family friend. The shamus had come from Brest-Litovsk, and was more than eager to help me. He sent a telegram to my father in Lodz, telling him I was free and giving my address; and within a few hours—even though it was Saturday, the Sabbath—came a return telegram with a money order for twenty-five rubles. Such a sum then was the equivalent of $500 these days. You can't imagine how my prestige rose. The shamus rushed to introduce me to his pretty daughter. Every one else in the exile colony quickly got the word that I must be very special. It was not so much the twenty-five rubles that impressed them, but rather that my father, a very religious man, had violated the Sabbath to send money. When I returned to Lodz months later, I learned how it happened. My father had called the whole family into council when he got my message from Chelyabinsk. "We've got to send Dovidel twenty-five rubles," he said. One of my brothers interjected, "Tatte, it's *shabas*." That didn't stop my father. "According to the Bible," he said, "you can do it to save a life."

I moved in with the family of a butcher, and I slept on a couch in the living room. The butcher's daughter did her studying there at night to the accompaniment of my snores. I didn't want to squander my money, so I found a job as a baker, earning three or four rubles a week. That made me feel so rich that I bought a pair of flared whipcord breeches of the kind officers wore, along with some long boots and a warm jacket. But most of the time I would go along with some of the other exiles to a few small stores outside of town, where we could get food and other things cut-rate. I thought for a while about taking up the tailor's trade, instead of baking. The tailor I went to was keen on making me an apprentice, but he showed me why he couldn't. He took me into his workroom, and there were all five of his journeymen tailors stretched out under the cutting tables dead to the world. The day before had been payday and the men were still so drunk they couldn't stay awake. "I have nobody to teach you," the master tailor explained.

There was a lot of friendship in the six months I spent in Chelyabinsk. The girls especially, they always took care of me. There was no love affair, but we would go swimming together when the weather was warm. Often we would go to concerts or bicycling or for long walks. And always we would talk. As a revolutionary, I was supposed to be an expert on everything from social theory to prison plumbing. I can't pretend that I ever tried to discourage anyone from believing I knew all the answers. But what I had learned was less from books than from people whose whole life was a struggle against despotism. If you went into jail in those days half—or even a quarter—a Socialist, you were likely to come out a dedicated revolutionary. You were ready to make whatever sacrifices were needed to move things a little bit forward toward improvement in society.

Finally, once more I decided I had to go home, no matter what the risk. There were dozens of underground organizations at that time that provided help and new passports to escapees in trying to get back from Siberia to Russia or Poland. I couldn't get a train ticket, but I could hide under the seats. The other passengers would try to cover me up, but three times the conductor discovered me and threw me off the train. Once I got in the engine cab, near the boiler, and rode from one place to the next. Twice I stopped at cities and got a few rubles from the relief organizations there so I could buy some food.

When I reached Bialystok, where I had an uncle, himself a baker, his first question was, "When are you leaving?" His two daughters were friendlier. One fixed a bed for me on the couch, with a fluffy, feather comforter. Just before turning in, I wrote two letters and left them on the table unsealed. One was to the Governor General in Warsaw, telling him that I was a young boy who had gone through hell in jail and Siberia and pleading for a pardon. The other was to my father telling him that my uncle's first question had been how soon I was leaving.

When I finished the letters I turned to the wall and pretended to be asleep. I soon heard a tumult in the room; it was the daughters giving my uncle the devil for his rudeness. They had read the letters and felt what he had done was outrageous. After that, my life in Bialystok was a picnic. I became pals with the bakers and the girls; and everybody, including my uncle, treated me like a lord. But after a few weeks homesickness crept up on me again, despite all the kindness, and I returned to Lodz. Once there I had to change my sleeping place every night to dodge the police, but I did get a job during the day working for an express company loading and unloading textiles. On Friday nights I also worked as a master baker on *challahs,* saving money so I could go off to America.

My oldest brother, the gambler, had already gone to New York, and he sent me a steamship ticket. With another brother I was smuggled across the border. That was an established business, like bootlegging in America during Prohibition. You paid somebody. They got you out. There was no heroism to it. Once outside Russia, we didn't need passports or visas. Those were the days when anyone who wanted to live and work in America was welcome.

TWO

Amerikanski Cutters versus Greenhorns

A PATCHY FOG hung over Manhattan as the S.S. *Lapland* cast anchor off Ellis Island on New Year's Day, 1911. It was a Sunday, and we had to wait until the next day to disembark. Most of my seven hundred companions in steerage were from Eastern Europe—Jews from Poland and Rumania, peasants from the Ukraine, heavy-muscled Hungarians and Slavs bound for the steel mills and coal mines of Pennsylvania. We had sailed from Antwerp and had been on the water for eleven days; they had been bumpy, rough days, and we were a subdued crowd as we leaned over the foredeck rail trying to catch a glimpse of our new homeland.

I stood in an overcoat, ten sizes too big, that swept the deck. Most of the men around me were at least a head taller, and I was glad when the supper gong sounded and they all went down to eat. I stared through the mist as the lights came on in this fabled city, hoping for some clue to what it could all mean for me. A nudge in the ribs from my brother Chaim ended my reverie. "You missed supper, Dovidel. It's all over, but I saved some food for you. Let's go down."

The next day my eldest brother, Godel, who was already a business agent in the Bakery Workers Union and had Americanized his name to Dubinsky, came to pick us up. As we left the pier, one thought kept pounding through my head: "At last I am free." It was no let-down when we got to Godel's apartment at 14 Clinton Street on the Lower East

Side to find that he had only two rooms and a kitchen, no inside toilet. It seemed a palace to us, and Chaim and I gladly slept in the kitchen. Walking through the chilly streets of the Lower East Side was a special joy all by itself. The people, the smells, and especially not worrying about the police, whether they're following you, that perhaps you're walking suspiciously. That was the greatest thing: seeing people walk free, not being molested, not fearful.

The first night Godel decided he would give me a big treat. He took me to Cook's, a famous restaurant on Essex Street, which was a hangout for politicians, union leaders, Yiddish actors and writers. In later years it became the Café Royal on Second Avenue. My brother, as a union big shot, wanted to impress me, so he took me there and ordered me a dish I had never heard of, a breaded veal cutlet. The next day I went alone and sat down at the same table. When the waiter, Pinkowsky, came over, I said, "Remember what I had last night? Give it to me again." He looked at me. "Wait, I'll go in the kitchen and see if they didn't throw it out." Sixty years later, I watched the Rowan and Martin television comedy show and there was the same joke. Some things never get thrown out.

Godel was ambitious for me and thought I should be a doctor. But that was not what I wanted, nor did I want to go back to baking. My first job was as a dishwasher and bus boy in a restaurant about four blocks from my brother's place. I had needed some clothes because I was falling out of my trousers, and my brother bought me a second-hand suit on Rivington Street for three dollars. That was exactly my weekly wage as a dishwasher, and I could see there was no future in that. What could you get out of a dirty dish? With help from a friend of my brother's, I went to work in a knee-pants factory in Brooklyn, across the Williamsburg Bridge.

At first I was an apprentice to an experienced operator, and I was paid nothing. Then after a few weeks I was back to earning three dollars a week. With all that money, I could buy rolls for breakfast. Even in a restaurant you could get six rolls for a nickel, and I loved rolls, especially the big onion rolls. I was always surprised that my brother, the baker, would eat only one roll. When I asked him why he ate so little when I ate so much, he said, "Wait, when you'll be here a few years, you'll eat one roll, too." It never happened.

I had to be in the shop by seven o'clock, so I took the trolley across the bridge in the morning and walked home at night to save the three-cent fare. Two weeks after I started working I went to East Broadway to join the Socialist Party. But I was just a listener at its rallies until the horrible fire in the Triangle Shirtwaist Company, just off Washington Square; it killed 146 girls on March 25, 1911. The only exit doors to the factory were locked to keep out union organizers; the lone fire escape ended in mid-air; the three upper floors of the "fireproof" building where Triangle had its factory became an incinerator. Locks had been put on the doors two years earlier when the seven hundred Triangle girls had joined in the famed "Revolt of the Twenty Thousand," the great strike of waistmakers that was to become so important an element in the tradition of the International Ladies Garment Workers Union. But, for the Triangle workers, the strike had only brought misery. The pickets were beaten by both the police and the owners' hired thugs; many of the girls were hauled off to court and fined; some got jail terms. They had to go back to the factory without union recognition or any improvement in conditions. On the day of the fire the same policemen who had once beaten them back into the factory helped pick their charred bodies off the pavement and load them into the dozens of wooden coffins the city had sent. Like everyone else on the East Side, I was deeply touched by this shameful tragedy and by the wretched exploitation that had brought it about. I marched with tens of thousands of others in the funeral parade, a day in which even the heavens wept, hours and hours of cold rain. I tore out of the *Jewish Daily Forward* and kept for years the dirge written by Morris Rosenfeld, the poet laureate of the slums:

Neither battle nor fiendish pogrom
Fills this great city with sorrow;
Nor does the earth shudder or lightning rend the heavens,
No clouds darken, no cannon's roar shatters the air.
Only hell's fire engulfs these slave stalls
And Mammon devours our sons and daughters.
Wrapt in scarlet flames, they drop to death from his maw
And death receives them all.

Sisters mine, oh my sisters; brethren
Hear my sorrow:
See where the dead are hidden in dark corners,
Where life is choked from those who labor.
Oh, woe is me, and woe is to the world
On this Sabbath
When an avalanche of red blood and fire
Pours forth from the god of gold on high
As now my tears stream forth unceasingly.
Damned be the rich!

Moved as I was by this whole episode, I was not yet a member of the I.L.G.W.U. or of any other union. The knee-pants factory in Brooklyn was a nonunion operation. My brother had a guilty conscience about bringing me over to work at such insignificant wages in a shop where there was no future. Since I wouldn't become a doctor, he and his wife decided the most exalted line of work for me would be to become a cutter in a women's coat-and-suit house. In their eyes and in mine too, a cutter was the equivalent of a physician, a genuine aristocrat.

Aside from the big established shops, most of the jobs in the garment industry in those days were rotten, except for those in the cutting rooms. Men and women used to trudge from one loft building to another looking for a pasteboard sign with the notice "Operator Wanted" or "Finisher Wanted." If you found a sign, you would climb three or four dirty flights of stairs; and often when you got to the top you would find an angry foreman yelling that he didn't want any help. If he did want you, his first question would be, "Do you have a machine?" Those who didn't would have to go out and rent one at two dollars a month and then hire a pushcart to trundle it to the shop. Once there the sewing machine had to be lugged up the stairs, put together, cleaned and oiled and finally the operator had to supply his own needle. Even then he might still not have the job. If he was a skirtmaker, the foreman would give him a single skirt to make for a quarter. That would be put on a dummy and examined, after which the foreman could tell the worker he was no good and he would have to cart off his machine and start the search all over again.

I remember Julius Hochman, who many years later became my associate as an international vice-president and manager of the New York Dress Joint Board, telling me how bad it was in those sweatshops on Greene, Mercer, Delancey and Center Streets—the neighborhood of my brother's apartment—on the Lower East Side. Each man would work amid masses of rags and filth in a cavern of a room lit by a flickering gas jet. "No matter how early you arrived," he used to recall, "workers were already at their machines. No matter when you quit, some were still at work. At the height of the season, workers would sleep on their bundles to snatch a few hours of slumber between days of endless labor."

As the youngest worker in the plant, Hochman would be sent to the corner saloon for beer and pretzels to keep the workers going into the early morning hours when there were rush orders to get out. "The pay at the end of the week was just what we used to call it—starvation wages," Hochman said. "You didn't get paid in cash, and very often the checks came back from the bank marked 'insufficient funds.' On payday the saloonkeeper would cash your check at a charge of 3 percent. But the worst part of all was the demoralization of the workers. When a needle had gone clear through a man's finger, no one came to his assistance. The workers were all absorbed in their work and did not dare leave their machines. We had to supply new needles and continue to work without first aid."

My family was determined that I should not join most of our young neighbors in that kind of existence. If I became a cutter, I would be all right. Godel's wife, Ruchscha, who made money as a midwife, had a *landsman* named Danziger, who worked as head cutter for the Boston Cloak Company on West Twenty-fourth Street, between Broadway and Sixth Avenue. She took some of her money to arrange with him to have me admitted as a cutter about a month after the Triangle fire. Danziger insisted that I would have to pay twenty-five dollars for the privilege of learning how to cut canvas. Not money for himself, you understand, but money to reimburse the firm for the expense of canvas that would be wasted or spoiled because of my ignorance of the trade. When I reported to join the eight or ten cutters working under Danziger's supervision, I came in clutching five five-dollar bills. As soon as I introduced myself, I gave him the money and he made a great show of walking to the door with the bills in his hand and then going across the hall to give it to the boss. By that time, I had become sophisticated enough to keep my eyes on him. No sooner was he out the cutting-room door than he stuffed the cash into his pocket. He did go into the boss's office, but I am sure the money was never turned over. That was my first exposure to "the deals." When I came home I was seething. I told my sister-in-law that I was paying for my job, not for material I might spoil. She wasn't shocked at anything, except perhaps at my innocence. "You'd better keep quiet if you want to work there," she said. "Forget about it."

The cutters were great exclusionists and especially those in the coat-and-suit business. At the start the cutting of material was done by women with long shears working alongside the sewing-machine operators. But in the late 1860s the short knife, which could cut through several thicknesses of cloth at one time, was used. In the 1880s the knives were long enough to cut stacks of material six inches high. At the same time the jigger knife was invented. It had a curved blade that could be guided against the cloth by motion of the wrist. You didn't have to apply the full weight of the body to back up the arm, but the work did entail a degree of strain that soon knocked women out of the trade and established a male monopoly in cutting departments.

In January 1884 the old Knights of Labor chartered the Gotham Knife Cutters Association of New York and Vicinity to make sure that this monopoly remained ironclad. At first it functioned as a local assembly covering cutters in all types of garment factories, but after two years a separate charter was granted to a group operating exclusively in the cloak shops. Neither group had much use for the "greenhorns," who were pouring into New York from the ghettos of Eastern Europe, people unfamiliar with the language and customs of America. Many of the union cutters were native born; almost all the others had come here with their parents well before the 1880s tidal wave of Jewish immigration. They were mainly of Irish or German stock, and these "Amerikanski cutters" conducted their meetings in English, not in Yiddish as did other unionized groups of garment workers. In general, their pay and conditions were better, and they intended to keep them that way by keeping out the rabble.

Some idea of the elitist philosophy that ran through the Cutters Union in these early days is evident in the frayed minutes of the meetings. The officers, elected every six months, had such august titles as Master Workman, Worthy Foreman, Almoner, Worthy Treasurer, Unknown Knight, Inside Esquire, Venerable Sage and Judge Advocate. Initiations took place in a sanctuary, with a globe, a sword and inner and outer veils used as symbols of the holiness of labor and the power of the Knights to enforce their commandments. Members could be fined for teaching anyone to be a cutter without the association's consent. They could also be fined for using long or jigger knives, since under the rules "the short knife, the machine and the shears" were the only recognized tools of the trade. As with all such rules, however, this attempt to veto progress was widely disregarded by the cutters.

Not long after the I.L.G.W.U. was formed in 1900 and chartered by the American Federation of Labor, the New York cutters joined it. But they never changed any of their exclusionist ideas or felt any more cordial to the "immigrants" who made up most of the garment work force. In fact, even among the cutters there was a decade of conflict because of the unwillingness of the old-line leadership to take in the so-called "downtown" cutters—those who worked in shops making women's blouses and children's coats, where wages were low and conditions much worse than in the established coat-and-suit houses uptown. Through their influence with the foremen who did the hiring, the old-timers were able to learn first when the good jobs were available. Their resistance to opening membership to the downtown cutters was so strong that at one point they resigned from the I.L.G.W.U. rather than submit to a convention order to accept the downtown group as a sublocal. It was not until a year before my coming into the trade that the breach was healed and Cutters Union, Local 10, returned to the fold. But the local still put no welcome mat out for greenhorns.

The first hurdle I had to leap in getting into the union was to prove that I had at least six months' experience as a cutter. That was a little hard, since I had been in the United States only four months and had not spent even one day of that period as a cutter. However, Danziger, with the twenty-five dollars in his pocket, was not going to let a minor thing like that get in the way. And neither was I. My brother Godel, through his work as a Bakery Union business agent, knew Sol Metz, then head of the Cloakmakers Union. He prevailed on Metz to put in a good word for me with Jesse P. Cohen, the manager of the Cutters Union and one of the old guard. Cohen said he couldn't do a thing unless I had documents showing I had worked as a cutter for six months. When Metz assured him that I could produce the proof, he said, "O.K. Send him down."

Again a little fakery was necessary. My sister-in-law went to a ladies' tailor who made her clothes and arranged to use his letterhead. On it she wrote that I had been employed cutting garments for six months, and I presented the letter to Cohen as prima facie evidence that I met the union's experience standard. That wasn't quite all, however. I still had to go before an admission board to answer a few questions. The chairman asked me exactly what I did in the shop where I worked. I started out bravely enough: "I put out the patterns and make markings." Then he asked what I made the markings with, and I couldn't think of the word *chalk*. After I had floundered for a bit, the chairman said in exasperation: "What do you mean? A man is in this country six months and he still can't say 'chalk.'" Luckily Danziger had talked to another member of the board beforehand to smooth the way for my getting in. That member came to my rescue by saying, "Don't forget there are a lot of greenhorns who take a long time learning English but they're still good mechanics." That got me past the union's front door.

It didn't take me long to pick up a cutter's skill. The designer at the Boston Cloak Company was a young Russian who was eager to help me in every way, and with his help I became an expert canvas cutter within two months. Under the union scale that entitled me to a wage of twelve dollars a week. But I knew I could make more than double that as a regular cutter of fabric for coats and suits. I also knew that it would take me a long time to advance to the full twenty-five-dollar scale if I stayed at Boston, because they knew how little experience I really had. So I decided to up anchor and look for another job.

In those days the only way to get a job was to stand on the corner of Twenty-fifth Street and Sixth Avenue, in the heart of what was then the market, and wait for an employer to pick you out. It was the height of the season, and few cutters were looking for work. When I took up my station on the corner, there were only two old men there with me. Finally someone came up and asked one of the other men whether he could recommend a cutter. "Here you have a young boy," he said, and I was hired. The firm was Aaron Levine & Co. at 4 West Sixteenth Street, directly across the street from what later became my office as president of the international union.

Levine suspected that I didn't know as much about cutting as I should and he paid me only twenty dollars a week, five dollars below the union scale. The work week was fifty hours —five nine-hour days during the week and five hours more on Saturdays. I didn't protest the underpayment, because I knew this was all part of my education. After a few weeks the slack period arrived and I was laid off. This time I had a long wait in the market before anyone tapped me for another job. Now many people were waiting to be hired and no one seemed interested in a young half-pint like me. Only after the corner was empty of job-seekers did a foreman come up to take me. He represented Simon Cohen, later to gain fame as the "rainwear king," whose factory was on Twenty-seventh Street.

This time I was determined not to be shortchanged on wages. Just to make sure that I would be received with proper regard, I decided I would show up on my first day at the new job with that classic badge of the successful cutter, a diamond ring. I borrowed my brother's ring and kept flashing the diamond all around the shop. It worked. They put me on the payroll at twenty-five dollars a week, with no questions asked. In fact, the foreman took my competence so much for granted that he gave me a full assignment right away and didn't bother to look over my shoulder to see whether I knew what I was doing. The training at Aaron Levine's stood me in good stead; I was more than able to do my share. That first payday, when they put five crisp, new five-dollar bills in my hand I felt like a miniature Rockefeller.

Alas for dreams of affluence. In a few weeks there was

another slack and I was back on the corner. As the last cutter hired, I was the first to be fired. Weeks passed before the shop got busy enough again to call me back. By the time I returned I had forgotten about my passport, the diamond ring. I gave it back to my brother as soon as I was laid off. But no sooner did I return to Simon Cohen than one of the other cutters, a smart man who recognized how little skill I really had, asked, "Dave, what happened to your diamond ring?"

"Well, you know we had a long slack with no money coming in," I said. "I had to take the ring to a pawnshop." That made everything all right again. I was put on the most exacting jobs, and with double pay for overtime, I was making as much as fifty dollars a week. But making money and making soapbox speeches at night for the Socialist Party all over the Lower East Side didn't keep me busy enough, and I began to get active in the union.

The arrogant practices of the Local 10 old guard were causing more and more membership discontent. Finally a Committee of Fifty was organized late in 1913, calling on oppositionists to challenge the leadership in an election. Elmer Rosenberg, a young cutter who had joined Local 10 only four years before and attracted attention as a brilliant writer and speaker, was elected president by a narrow margin over an old-timer, John C. Ryan. Even though the conservatives swept all the rest of the offices, our rebel group was encouraged enough to set up a Good and Welfare League dedicated to a long-range struggle for change in union policies and leadership.

The leadership of Local 10 had grown increasingly unrepresentative of the new elements in the membership. That, of course, is always a problem in a union where ethnic or racial composition is changing rapidly. It happened later in the whole union when we were faced, especially in New York, with a shift from a predominantly Jewish and Italian rank and file to one that was largely black and Puerto Rican. All I want to say now about how we coped with that subsequent change is that much of my awareness of the need for an active union policy of encouraging the broadest involvement in positions of responsibility stemmed from my remembrance of how blind and stupid the old guard in the Cutters Union had been in slamming the door on new ideas and new leaders in those early years.

By the time the Good and Welfare League was formed, the newcomers outnumbered the old-timers by almost four to one. Most of the Jewish immigrants had to be content with jobs in shops where turnover was greatest and wage chiseling worst. The bulk of the leaders were gentiles, and even the few who were Jewish were more gentile than the gentiles. Politically, they were for Tammany Hall and conservatism; we were mainly Socialists with a sprinkling of every other brand of radicalism. The central point in our program was equal division of work, which the old-timers promptly rechristened "equal destruction of work." To us this proposal was the key to abolishing favoritism and discrimination in employment, and it became the principal battle point between the reformers and the old guard.

Equal division of work was just the opposite of the seniority principle, which many unions even today regard as the foundation stone of unionism. Our idea was that, if there was not enough to go around, you did not lay anybody off. Instead, all the workers shared equally in whatever work there was. Suppose you had twelve cutters in your shop and you had only enough work to keep four busy. Then, according to our concept of equal division, four would work one week, four others the second week and the remaining four the third week. Under the usual idea of seniority, the four cutters who had been in the shop longest would get all the work until things got busy enough to bring the others back. Even then they would come back on the basis of seniority, with the newest man in the shop waiting till last.

The old-timers organized a Loyalty League to fight our Good and Welfare League. They had the local fragmented into three branches, one for cloaks, one for dresses and one miscellaneous. That helped them maintain control until

1917, when our group was aided by the general strength of the Socialists, capitalizing on antiwar sentiment shortly before the United States entered World War I. In 1917 the Socialists had elected ten Socialists to the New York State Assembly, one of them our own Elmer Rosenberg. Our group took command of the local at about the same time and made a clean sweep of all the offices in 1918. My own first election to the local executive board came in 1919, and in 1920 I moved up to vice-president and the next year to president.

Despite the fact that I was an extremely ardent Socialist and strongly opposed to the war, I did not let my politics affect the affairs of the Cutters Union. I felt it was extremely important that any decisions I made in the union be made solely on the basis of what was good for the union, even if that meant going against some of the ideas I was preaching at night as an antiwar speaker for the party.

Just after the United States entered the war the question arose as to whether Local 10 should buy Liberty Bonds. The Socialist position was no. That was also the position of the *Jewish Daily Forward,* which had great influence with our group. I took the floor to argue that we were not there to represent the Socialist Party or the *Forward.* We were there as trade-unionists, and the obligation of a union when the country was at war was to support the country. My position made a great impression on the old-timers and helped to compose the hostilities inside the union. But I did not do it for that reason. I knew that to oppose buying Liberty Bonds when the United States was fighting for its life would have hurt the union and hurt its members. That had to be my first concern.

Actually, my position was the same one that Meyer London, the great Socialist Congressman from the Lower East Side, was taking in the House of Representatives—at great personal cost to himself. He felt he had to vote for military appropriations, even though that meant voting against the dictates of the Socialist Party. He acted out of the same sense that I had of what was needed for America's survival. In his case the vote cost Meyer London the nomination and election next year. In mine it solidified my position in the local and contributed to my advancement with support from both factions.

Another event that unified Local 10 was the great 1919 strike victory that brought many gains, including employer acceptance of the principle that work should be divided equally in slack periods.

The responsibility demonstrated by our group paid dividends in terms of respect from the general labor movement. At the outset of the fight, the leadership of the State Federation of Labor and the Central Trades and Labor Council was wholeheartedly behind Local 10's old-guard elements. After all, they were partners in Tammany Hall and in economic conservatism. More important still, they were "Americans" and we were part of the "great unwashed." At one stage James Holland, the State Federation of Labor president, accused me of fronting for the Bolsheviks in an effort to kick out the true democrats in the Cutters Union. Not long afterward Samuel Gompers, who had no great love for Socialists but who knew something about the care we were taking to keep party and union interests separate, came to New York to talk to the Capmakers Union. When he met Holland on the platform, the A.F.L. president said: "Now listen, Jim, I know people have called you a son of a bitch for your statement about Local 10. I'll just call you a damn fool. Who gave you that stuff about the Dubinsky group being all Bolsheviks and wanting to turn Local 10 into the Third International? You don't know what you're talking about."

In December 1921 the increased unity in Local 10 enabled us to take a long-needed step toward more effective administration. The separate executive boards for the cloak, dress and miscellaneous branches were merged into one, and a single general manager was elected instead of the three the local originally had. I was designated as the candidate of the Good and Welfare League for the new post. Much to everyone's surprise, I was challenged not by one of the old guard, but by a respected member of our own group, Max Goren- stein, a former trade manager and vice-president of Local 10, who had been assigned by the international union to duties in Boston. Eager to return to New York, he let his name be put in nomination, even though his candidacy was viewed by the League as a breach of solidarity and group discipline.

It was soon clear that the majority of the members were with me; Gorenstein's support was confined to a handful of left-wingers. In desperation, he had circulars printed saying: "All Cutters Want Gorenstein." I checked the union label and discovered that the circulars were printed in Boston. So I came out with the reply: "The Boston Cutters Want Goren- stein but the New York Cutters Want Dubinsky." He was dead before, but that really killed him. Not only did I win, but the whole slate was swept in by a good margin. This marked the final rout of the old-guard elements in Local 10. Not long afterward, at the Cleveland convention of the I.L.G.W.U. in May 1922, I was elected to the General Execu- tive Board for the first time as a vice-president. That choice was more than a recognition of the strategic role Local 10 played in the New York market as a unit in both the Cloak Joint Board and the newly organized Dress Joint Board. It was also a sign of the International's confidence that we had resolved our internal struggle in a constructive fashion. No longer was old-timer pitted against newcomer; no longer did cloak cutter and dress cutter mistrust each other. By remov- ing the dividing lines we also ended a good deal of the fric- tion between groups of members.

But union affairs did not always go my way. In 1924, I proposed a 10-cent increase in the 35-cents-a-week dues, which were too low to finance the organizational activities and other services that Local 10 was engaged in. My proposal was duly ratified by the executive board, but when it was put before a membership meeting, it was overwhelmingly re- jected.

A few weeks earlier I had suffered a similar rebuff. One of

my subofficers had been prevented from taking his regular two-week vacation because of a strike. When he requested permission to take the vacation later, I asked the executive board to go along, but it turned down the request. So did a membership meeting. I felt this was so outrageous that I offered to let him take a vacation that was due me. The opposition packed the meeting and defeated me on that too.

The fact that this defeat was followed so quickly by another on the much more important issue of providing the union with the financial life blood it needed to represent its members left no doubt in my mind that we were slipping back toward a situation in which demagogues were seeking to exploit all the old divisions and re-create chaos in the local. Since these efforts were succeeding so well, I decided that the smartest thing for me would be to pack up and go back to working in the shop. The day after the membership rejected the higher dues, I went to the Henry Rosenzweig firm, then the largest in the coat-and-suit industry, and arranged to be hired as a cutter.

As soon as the word spread that I had drawn a working card and was planning to start on the job the next week, many cutters came to beseech me to stay as manager. One whose plea touched me most deeply was Sam Massower, the local's half-pint sergeant at arms, who came to my office with tears in his eyes. "Dubinsky, you can't leave us," he said. "Never mind the politics and the insults. You have a duty to stay with the union. Our union comes to an end when Dubinsky's out." By the time he finished we were both bawling. So many others came saying the same thing that I finally said, "I'll stay on one condition. I have learned now that with idealism alone you can't go too far. You've also got to be political-minded. Well, I've been through the mill as part of the Socialist movement. If the opposition wants politics, let's give them politics. I can do it with your support."

So we called another meeting and mustered all our forces. This time the 10-cent increase was approved by a very heavy margin, perhaps 80 to 85 percent. That gave me a tremendous lift. It also taught me the importance of local politics. Without mastery in that area, you can have the most wonderful program and wind up nowhere.

During all this time union politics were not my only concern, nor was the Socialist Party. Not long after I started as an apprentice at Boston Cloak Company I joined nine friends (all Socialists) in starting a cooperative restaurant on Tenth Street, between First and Second Avenues. We each contributed ten dollars to get started and we served meals for a quarter each. Leon Trotsky would often come in for lunch. We had a lot of customers, but I paid special attention to two who came in quite regularly. They became mainstays of a literary club we organized that met in the restaurant to read and discuss books. They were both good-looking girls who worked as operators in a shop making undergarments; one was named Emma Goldberg and the other Molly Farbyash. I used to go out with both of them, but always as part of a larger group—six or eight people—rowing, fishing, parks, concerts. I was known as the one who always ran ahead to pay the nickel subway fare for everybody or who paid the dime admission to the movies. The others objected, but it was my pleasure to be the host. I had another motive, too. I didn't want anyone to suspect that I had a favorite between Emma and Molly, so having the group always around offered protection even if it cost me extra money. Most of my friends thought I was in love with Molly, but Emma was always the one I really cared for.

When my twenty-first birthday was getting close, I knew I had to declare myself. That was hard, because the two girls worked together and also lived together in a room on Twelfth Street. They were inseparable. It was harder still, because, bold as I was about everything else, I was very frightened of opening my mouth about how I felt toward Emma. I wasn't even sure that she knew she was the one, not Molly. I finally decided on a no-risk way of finding out how much real interest she had in me. One night we managed to lose Molly and I took Emma to the Palace on Broadway, the showplace for all the best in vaudeville. She was wearing a velvet suit and it made her look particularly nice. Sometime between the seals and the acrobats, I told her that I would be seeing her for only a few more months, then I would have to go back to Russia to report for compulsory military service.

She got very upset. "No, you are not going back," she said. That was the music I wanted to hear. Now I knew she did care. Not long after, when we were holding hands on top of the Statue of Liberty, we formally declared ourselves as sweethearts. I lived then with the girl from Samara, Esther Minkus, and her baby on the top floor of a house on Tenth Street. Emma moved into a windowless room next door. We were very intimate, but Emma insisted that, for the sake of her family, we had to have a formal Jewish wedding. As a Socialist without interest in religious ritual, I would have been happier to skip that, but I had no intention of giving up Emma just to show my rejection of dogma. We were married by a rabbi in her aunt's dry-goods store on Pitkin Avenue, in Brooklyn, with her family there, not mine. We took an apartment in the Bath Beach section. Years later, in 1937, at the I.L.G. convention in Atlantic City, Emma gave me my proudest moment. She was called on to say a few words after I had been re-elected to my fifth year as president. "I do think that both you and I have got the right man," was all she said.

THREE

Fight for Life

No BATTLE against the worst of our employers in the early sweatshop years compared in fierceness or danger with the battle we had to fight for the very life of the I.L.G.W.U. in the 1920s. Our opponent was a disciplined outside political force dedicated to the philosophy of rule or ruin—the Communist Party. More than four decades have passed since the Communist Party was a threat to our union, but the passage of time has not made me less sure that our success in rooting out of places of power those whose first allegiance belonged to Moscow was the key to our survival and growth.

That battle ended with the union almost shattered, our hard-won working conditions nullified, our membership cut to less than half, a healthy treasury eaten up and replaced by a red sea of debts. But survive we did, and the story of how we did it, why we did it, and what we did afterward to assure that the I.L.G.W.U. would function as a united, constructive organization able to pioneer in advances not only for its own membership but for the general labor movement and for all American society is worth recounting in a period when too many have forgotten—or never knew—the intensity of the Communist push to infiltrate the American labor movement, with the I.L.G.W.U. as the springboard for its onslaught.

It was logical that our union would be the first target for Communist infiltration. After all, the I.L.G.W.U. was born on the Lower East Side in the years when the Lower East

Side was a hotbed of radical intellectual theories. Every concept had its high priests. The disciples of Karl Marx, of Bakunin, of Kropotkin, of Daniel De Leon, and of a dozen others, along with the Anarchists and the Wobblies, all gathered on the Lower East Side to drink tea and remake the world. The I.L.G.W.U. was the first big union created by these people, many of them working in the shops by day and going to school at night but still finding time to argue, to agitate and to plot.

After the Bolshevik Revolution in Russia in 1917, a quite new flavor came into all this aimless revolutionary palaver. Suddenly, the talk in radical circles was, "What's the use of studying? Who the hell needs a diploma? The world is in a revolutionary stage; this is the time to get in on the ground floor of the American Revolution." With thousands of garment workers, women even more than men, there was a common restlessness, an itch for quick change, for making a rotten society pure. These were mostly Jewish immigrants, but the spirit that moved them was not very different from that which animated the youngsters who flocked to the banner of Senator Eugene McCarthy in the early stages of the 1968 campaign or those who rallied to support Senator George McGovern early in 1972.

What made the operation different, however, from those later movements was the increasing autocracy that came into the Communist Party under Stalin. Even in the early days of 1918 and 1919, the Communist Party did not encourage free speech if it involved any dissent from party doctrine or any criticism of Russia. But there was still enough room for argument to make it possible for the Communists to work together with the Anarchists and other radicals. At that time the Industrial Workers of the World (the I.W.W., or "Wobblies") were popular on the Lower East Side, and their basic line was that none of the unions in the American Federation of Labor, including the I.L.G.W.U., was any good; they were all too reactionary and bureaucratic, in the opinion of the Wobblies.

The Communists shared that opinion, but they had a basic difference on what to do about it. Where the aim of the Wobblies was to organize "one big union" in opposition to all the A.F.L. groups, the C.P. under the leadership of William Z. Foster was committed to the concept of gaining control by boring from within the established unions. That idea brought them into conflict with the Anarchists, who rejected the whole notion of running for union office. They didn't believe in voting at union meetings, in signed contracts or in anything else that involved formal structure. As a result they came to meetings and fought over issues, but when it came time for a vote they just sat on their hands. Under the Communist approach, everybody was supposed to do just the opposite. The Communists advocated that their party loyalists take an active role in every aspect of union affairs and especially that they run for office and get into the leadership.

There would be nothing wrong with that if the Communists had stuck to concern for the needs of the membership—not solely their narrow needs as workers in the shop but the whole broad scope of their concerns as people. In essence, that was what we had done in the Cutters Union when we formed the Good and Welfare League to challenge the old-line leaders. The trouble with the opposition move generated by the Communists was that it tended more and more to be directed from the outside toward goals that served the interests of the party rather than those of the I.L.G.W.U.

The left-wingers capitalized on the emotions stirred by the overthrow of the Tsar and the establishment of a proletarian state in Russia. They found a fertile field for indoctrination among the girls in the waist- and dressmakers' shops. It was this group that, through the "Revolt of the Twenty Thousand" in 1909–10, had created a solid, militant tradition —a strike that so stirred the conscience of the city that many of New York's leaders in society and finance rallied to their support. One product of this uprising, and of the strike of 60,000 cloakmakers four months later, was the celebrated Protocol of Peace drafted by Louis D. Brandeis, the most civilized document for establishing harmonious labor-management relations ever produced in any industry.

Now in the 1920s a new generation of waist- and dressmakers, many of them fresh from the rebellion-charged atmosphere of Tsarist Russia, listened raptly to the Communist spellbinders and found in their denunciations of the entrenched union leadership an exciting outlet for their surplus energies and their revolutionary fervor. Down with the bureaucrats, was the left-wing cry. And who can ever be against that? The first focus was on trying to organize Workers' Councils (later called Shop Delegates' Leagues) on a pattern that had begun to spread from Russia to Great Britain. It was all part of a brave plan to have workers take over the running of industry, but it didn't last long in the Soviet Union, where Lenin abandoned it as soon as it became apparent that it was neither effective nor productive. The British experience resulted in a quick loss of enthusiasm among workers there, and the record in the I.L.G. was equally empty.

But the flop of the Shop Delegates' Leagues in the period immediately after World War I caused no slump in enthusiasm for the new Workers Party through which the Communists began to operate. They gained control in locals that had roughly 70 percent of our members in New York, and they also had considerable strength among the officers of several locals in Chicago, Boston and Montreal. Their task was made easier when the Third Congress of the Comintern in Moscow in 1921 swung away from the policy of smashing all capitalist institutions to the Trojan-horse method of boring from within. In line with that policy, the Workers Party set out to "win the masses" within the A.F.L. The spear carrier in this effort was the Trade Union Educational League (T.U.E.L.), headed by William Z. Foster, leader of the great steel strike of 1919.

The increased pressure on the I.L.G.W.U. Communists to follow each new Kremlin directive led to an increasing polarization within the union. The first showdown between the Foster group and the non-Communists came at the 1922 convention in Cleveland, when the General Executive Board sponsored a resolution demanding the release of Socialist and other non-Communist political prisoners in Soviet jails. The proadministration forces won overwhelmingly, despite frenzied opposition from the Communists. At that convention, as secretary of the Credentials Committee, I was cast in the role of district attorney presenting the case against three prominent New York delegates who were denied seats on the basis of disruption and of subservience to a foreign power. From then on I was discredited as far as the Communists were concerned.

For Benjamin Schlesinger, who had been president of the I.L.G.W.U. since 1914, the tensions of the battle with the Communists were extremely taxing. He was a tall, sensitive man with a striking physical resemblance to Abraham Lincoln, but he hated internal conflict so much that it undermined his health. At a meeting of the General Executive Board in Montreal in January 1923, he began to talk fretfully of resigning. I was a brand-new international vice-president at that time and it seemed to me that Schlesinger's remark was not a serious one. Rather, he wanted to be coaxed to stay. But most of the G.E.B. members felt he was too inclined to temporize in the fight with the left wing, that a stronger hand was needed.

So, as soon as Schlesinger hinted that he wanted to quit, Joseph Breslaw, the leader of the New York Cloak Pressers Union, said, "If you want to resign, put it in writing and we'll act on it." Breslaw was a blunt, hard-boiled man with none of Schlesinger's softness. The pressers were the "tough guys" of the union, accustomed to slugging it out with hoodlums on the picket line. They were more than eager to take on the Communists, and not just because most of them were girls. When it became plain that Breslaw was not alone in his demand that Schlesinger either act or resign, the president reluctantly took out a sheet of paper and wrote a twelve-word resignation.

I was the only board member who voted against acceptance when the resignation was put up for a vote. I had been on the board only seven months, but I felt that Schlesinger was a man of dignity and capacity, entitled to respect rather than rejection. No sooner had he gone back to his old post as business manager of the *Jewish Daily Forward* than I discovered why the sentiment for letting Schlesinger go had been so strong. Almost half the members of the board wanted to be president themselves.

Since I had no such ambitions, I persuaded the executive board of the Cutters Union, Local 10, that we had to take the initiative in making sure that the rivalries inside the G.E.B. did not engender a civil war over the Schlesinger succession of a kind that could only be helpful to the Communists. We concluded that the best way to defuse all the potential candidates was to call back out of retirement another respected leader, Morris Sigman, who had been general secretary-treasurer when Schlesinger started as president. The two had not got on well together, and Sigman found greater happiness in switching over to a post as manager of the Cloak Joint Board. In 1920 he was elected first vice-president, but his differences with Schlesinger made him decide to pack up and retire to his farm in Iowa.

He was a down-to-earth fellow even before he went back to the soil, an early organizer of the I.W.W. and a man who liked nothing better than to *schmooze* with the cloakmakers. I knew he was a fighter and a believer in fundamental union reform, just the kind of leader whose sincerity would appeal to the rank and file, and defeat the fakery of the Communists. Moreover, he was a giant in the history of the union and would dwarf the petty aspirants for Schlesinger's mantle. The cutters lined up strongly in support of a draft-Sigman effort.

Local 10 sent him a telegram urging him to accept nomination for the presidency. It was a surprise, since the cutters had traditionally held aloof from I.L.G.W.U. politics. All the would-be candidates for the top job decided to close ranks behind Sigman, and he was formally elected at a special convention in Baltimore a month after our telegram.

Sigman proved a "clean broom" with a vengeance. He could not stomach the Communists with their slavishness to outside masters. But neither could he stand the right-wing bureaucrats who controlled some of the most powerful locals fighting the Communists. He was still a Wobbly at heart, impatient of politicians and power seekers—whether they were reactionaries or Communist *apparatchiks*. Even though his attitude meant that he was always fighting on two fronts, he had a stubborn honesty and a total dedication that made him an invaluable leader in this period of strife.

In August 1923, at his instigation, the General Executive Board declared open war on Foster's T.U.E.L. by declaring it a dual union and outlawing all its cells in the I.L.G.W.U. Nineteen members of the executive board of the Dressmakers Union, Local 22, in New York, were tried by the board and convicted of conspiracy to destroy the union. Some were expelled outright and others barred from office for five years. Sigman also moved to clean house in Chicago, Philadelphia, Boston and other centers. These actions were confirmed at the 1924 convention in Boston, but to little avail—the Communists kept control everywhere they had crept in. When Sigman tried to break their grip by requiring that all candidates for local office swear that they did not belong to the T.U.E.L. or accept Communist domination, the lefties cheerfully perjured themselves and got elected.

In Sigman's eyes, the main task of the union remained the representation of its members at the bargaining table. He recognized that the strong Communist hold on the New York locals would complicate the bargaining in the cloak industry, the traditional pattern setter for the whole metropolitan market; he would have to be looking over his shoulder every minute to see what knife was going into his back from his own "team." But that danger did not lessen the union's need to deal with the increasing headaches caused by runaway shops (those manufacturers leaving union-controlled cities) and by the irresponsibility of here-today, gone-tomorrow contractors. Accordingly, Sigman presented to the employer associations a program that he hoped would solidify union attention on economics instead of fratricidal politics. Its aim was to make the jobbers, usually the most stable and best-financed element in the industry, responsible for the payment of wages and other benefits to workers in the shops of their contractors. In the so-called inside shops, where designing, cutting and manufacture were done under one roof, the Sigman proposals included a guaranteed minimum period of work (a forerunner of the guaranteed annual wage), a cut in the work week from forty-four hours to forty, an increase in minimum-wage rates and an industry-financed unemployment-insurance fund (a pioneering demand a full decade before the federal government adopted unemployment insurance as part of Franklin D. Roosevelt's New Deal).

The program contained fourteen demands, which the Communists promptly ridiculed by likening them to Woodrow Wilson's Fourteen Points for inclusion in the Treaty of Versailles a few years earlier. When the three New York employer associations rejected the whole program, the union prepared for a general strike. To make sure it didn't happen, Governor Alfred E. Smith, who had grown up with many of the union's leaders on the Lower East Side, appointed a special advisory board to study all the issues and make recommendations for a settlement. George Gordon Battle, a distinguished lawyer, was chairman and one of the members was a banker and philanthropist named Herbert H. Lehman, whom we were to come to know well and admire greatly in later years.

The board came up with an excellent report. It favored the call for an unemployment-insurance fund and for greater responsibility on the part of jobbers. It also held out a number of other improvements important to the union, including the appointment of Raymond V. Ingersoll, a progressive reformer, as impartial chairman of the industry. Sigman and the non-Communist majority in the G.E.B. were enthusiastically for acceptance of the report. The jobbers did not like the recommendations, but they reluctantly agreed to go along. However, the Communists would have no part of the proposed settlement. They denounced it as a sellout.

In the middle of the whole conflict, on May Day 1925, the three big left-wing locals in New York held a joint rally at the old Metropolitan Opera House, with Dr. Moissaye J. Olgin, editor of the Communist Jewish *Daily Freiheit*, as chief speaker. He wound up his address with "Long live a Soviet America!" The cheers that greeted his call so infuriated Sigman that he preferred charges against the officers and executive boards of the three locals for "violating the I.L.G.W.U. constitution" by flagrantly collaborating with the Communists. It was scarcely the ideal issue on which to draw the battle lines, but unfortunately I was visiting my parents in Lodz at the time, so I had no chance to try to talk Sigman out of pressing his point.

The three left-wing-controlled locals were suspended, but their officers refused to recognize their removal and the Communists managed to keep physical control of the building owned by Dressmakers Local 22 on West Twenty-first Street. As a device for hanging on to power, the rebels formed a Joint Action Committee under the chairmanship of Louis Hyman, the manager of Cloak Finishers Local 9, a fellow traveler, who had served his apprenticeship in the British Labour Party in the days of Keir Hardie and Ramsay MacDonald. The secretary was a brilliant youngster named Charles S. Zimmerman, who had just come back to Local 22 after bumming around the country as a Wobbly.

The Joint Committee started acting like a dual union right away. It collected dues, adjusted shop grievances and pressured employers to recognize it rather than the International. To show that it really did have the workers—which it did, outside the Cutters Union and the two big Italian locals of cloakmakers and dressmakers—the committee called a mass meeting to be held in Yankee Stadium on July 11, 1925. It got a turnout of somewhere between 30,000 and 40,000 people. They roared approval for a "demonstration stoppage" intended to shut down the garment district for the afternoon of August 10. It had the double purpose of showing that the rank and file was militantly in support of more internal democracy and also of better contract terms than the Battle commission had recommended. When August 10 came, so many workers left the shops that it took a dozen East Side halls to hold the rallies dominated by left-wing speakers.

Meanwhile, Sigman went right ahead with his campaign against the three dissident locals, but some of us on the General Executive Board who realized that we were on shaky ground enlisted the help of our respected chief counsel, Morris Hillquit, and persuaded him that a truce was in order. Even Abe Cahan of the *Forward*, that most resolute of anti-Communists, advocated an accommodation with the leftists. After several weeks of internal jockeying, Sigman was induced to confer with the opposition; the result was an agreement that the I.L.G.W.U. would "tolerate political differences" and that the left-wingers would be allowed to resume their old offices pending the holding of new elections.

There was also agreement that a special convention would be held in Philadelphia at the end of the year to consider taking a referendum on left-wing demands for a system of proportional representation that would give big locals a voice in conventions and in joint boards commensurate with their membership. Up to then small locals had exactly the same total representation as big ones, a system that made it easy for the administration to dominate things through its manipulation of "rotten boroughs." A genuine democrat at heart, Sigman sympathized with the left in their pressure for reform of this inequitable voting structure. Fortified by these concessions and several lesser ones, the pro-Communist group won overwhelmingly in the new local elections in New York shortly before the special convention. Hyman became general manager of the New York Joint Board and Zimmerman head of its dressmaking department.

Sigman's somewhat naïve hope was that the reforms would provide a basis for prying the nonideologues in the Communist group away from party domination and thus enable the I.L.G.W.U. to function as a unified trade union once again. The emptiness of that hope was demonstrated at the Philadelphia convention, where the left-wing delegates found themselves converted into servile pawns of the party commissars. Instead of giving my own version of that dismal episode in the degeneration of our union, I asked Zimmerman, the floor leader on the other side, to tell the story in his own words. The conversation we had in my office on West Fifty-second Street in 1971, in which he recalled his own Communist Party activities and the heartbreak that followed, represented the first time he and I had ever talked frankly about that period of civil war.° Through all the years of close association and mutual respect that we have had since the war with the Communists, that period remained a closed book— one which neither of us wished to open in talks with one another. To me, the Philadelphia convention wound up a disaster, an occasion for heating up the divisions in the union, not healing them.

Inevitably, the price for Communist infiltration had to be paid in a submergence of the needs of the rank and file to the vagaries of a party line governed by other than union considerations. The next year, in May 1926, the Governor's special advisory board headed by George Gordon Battle rendered its final report on a contract for the cloak industry. It again upheld the union on the central issue, increased responsibility by jobbers for seeing to it that their contracting shops fulfilled all requirements for payment of union wages and maintenance of union working conditions. The *quid pro quo* for the employers was the right to "reorganize" in the

---

° I have made the Zimmerman recollections, along with some incidental interpolations of my own, the next chapter in this book because I believe his words are more revealing than any of my own might be.

interest of efficiency, which meant they could dismiss as much as 10 percent of their work force in the course of a year.

Sigman wanted to accept the report as a basis for negotiation. So did I. On the left-wing side, Hyman and Zimmerman had the same view, but their voices were not the controlling ones. The party leadership decreed that even to talk about a management right to fire workers was an unacceptable form of "class collaboration." All the good things in the report were tossed aside, and the Joint Board called a general strike for July 1, the start of the fall season in the coat-and-suit shops. The right-wing locals quit work and otherwise gave the strike full support, despite their certainty that it was a party-dictated mistake. The International officers also got on the solidarity bandwagon. They persuaded the Central Trades and Labor Council, representing the citywide labor movement, and the national A.F.L. to pledge complete backing for the walkout. The Communists reciprocated by freezing all the non-Communist elements out of any role of meaningful participation in strike policy or in negotiation. In defiance of precedent, President Sigman was denied chairmanship of the strike committee. Hyman took his place. Because the Communists didn't dare ignore the strategic role of the cutters in the industry, I was given an important-sounding title as secretary of the strike settlement committee, but it didn't mean a thing in actual practice. The lefties took care to keep me from having any say in running the strike or in how to end it.

Their general plan was to stage a blitz that would force the employers to give up on the "reorganization" issue in a few days. But the manufacturers dug in for a siege. Both sides were soon engaged in the wholesale hiring of gorillas. The employers hired gangsters from Jack "Legs" Diamond; the Communists got their strong-arm men from Louis "Little Augie" Orgel. In addition, the Joint Board reportedly paid $2,500 a week in graft to detectives on the Police Department's Industrial Squad. All that the rest of us knew was that the union's money was disappearing fast, with only the loosest accounting for where it was going. Among the funds that were wasted was $800,000 in security deposits turned over to the union by employers as a guarantee of faithful contract performance. None of the money went into the pockets of Hyman, Zimmerman or the other left-wing leaders—all of them scrupulously honest when it came to the union's resources—but there was plenty of mismanagement, waste and even outright larceny.

The use by the Communists of muscle men—*balagoulas,* we used to call them—had begun as soon as Sigman moved to oust the left-wingers from control of their local headquarters before the truce. Our cutters had been instructed not to work with people who did not have work cards from the kosher branch of the union—the locals recognized by Sigman—and naturally that produced some bitter fights in which our people were beaten up and sometimes stabbed. One shop we stopped off was under direct gangster protection, and I was warned that, as head of Local 10, my life was not safe. I decided I needed a gun, even though I didn't know how to use it. The police didn't like the idea, but they finally issued a permit. The only time I ever drew the revolver was when one left-wing tough pulled a knife on me when I was going into one of their headquarters to try to evict them from union property. You should have seen him run at the first sight of my gun. At night when I took the subway home to our apartment at 176th Street and Southern Boulevard, in the Bronx, I used to switch the pistol from my pocket to my sleeve so it would be handy if the leftists arranged an ambush. But they never did, and by the time the 1926 strike was on we were all nominally working together again.

The speed with which the strike treasury was being exhausted and the leftists' inability to slow down the outflow prompted them to look desperately for someone on the industry side to throw them a lifeline. They turned to a retired manufacturer, A. E. Rothstein, whose philanthropic activities and basic decency had earned him great respect. This scholarly man had a son Arnold, who had established himself in New York's underworld. He was in every racket from white slavery to dope. Despite his great power, his brothers and sisters would have nothing to do with him; but the father would let him come to his home occasionally to visit, hoping perhaps that he might eventually reform.

When the Communist strike leaders came to the elder Rothstein, he said he was too removed from activity in the employer association to be of great help as a peacemaker. But he put them in touch with one of the most prominent manufacturers, who minced no words in telling them that the man they ought to see was not the father but the son. The younger Rothstein was more than happy to help. Maybe he thought his father would be pleased that he was doing something constructive for a change. More probably, this astute manipulator saw a chance to muscle in on the garment industry. That was exactly what his lieutenants, Louis "Lepke" Buchalter and Jacob "Gurrah Jake" Shapiro, did after Rothstein himself was murdered in a midtown hotel barbershop in 1928.

In the strike, Rothstein's first assignment was to persuade the Legs Diamond gang to stop working for the employers in helping to smash picket lines and intimidate the union members. A telephone call took care of that. With the industry's goons gone, the Joint Board decided it could stop paying off Little Augie's mob. But Little Augie had other ideas, until he too got a phone call from Rothstein. That took all the mobsters out of the picture. At that point Rothstein demonstrated that he had a lot of muscle not only with the hoodlums but with the employer associations as well. He got the bosses and the Joint Board together, and in a short time the essence of a settlement had been worked out. It provided for some softening of the hated "reorganization" clause along with most of the other provisions recommended by the Governor's committee. The strike had been on for about ten weeks, and Zimmerman and Hyman felt it would be smart to accept the tentative deal. But again political one-upmanship among the Communist commissars got in the way and everything went downhill from that point on.

By then most of the fall season was past and the manufacturers had little interest in getting their shops reopened in a hurry. So they pulled back on some of the concessions they had been ready to make in mid-September. They wanted to renege entirely on the most important issue of all, the setting of limits on the number of contractor shops that the jobbers could use in farming out their work. Such limitation represented a form of protection that was necessary to keep jobbers from undercutting union standards by playing off one contractor against another. Despite efforts in the Communist press to picture these watered-down settlement proposals of the employers as tremendous victories for the Joint Board, the workers could not be fooled. They knew that their leftist leaders had missed the boat.

The International moved back into active command in mid-December, when the strike was clearly in danger of collapse. The left-wing leadership was ousted and Sigman himself took over as head of the Joint Board. By this time the Communists had signed a miserable contract with one group of manufacturers; many other employers had signed individual agreements, all on terms substantially below those proposed before the strike by the George Gordon Battle commission. Sigman got the rest of the contractors and jobbers to come into line, but it was impossible to overcome the disastrous pattern of the earlier settlements.

The union was left with two million dollars in unpaid debts, internal chaos and a system of shattered relations within the industry and outside with the community. For more than a year Sigman tried to effect a sound reorganization in New York, the heartland of the Communist rebellion, and in the many other cities where Communism had spread —Chicago, Montreal, Boston, Baltimore, Los Angeles and San Francisco. But it soon became apparent that this resolute "Iowa farmer," who had provided such uncompromising leadership in the fight against the Communists, was not the right man to supervise the delicate task of reconstruction. It was not only that Sigman was a symbol of irreconcilable battle to the left wing, he also had a knack for alienating many important right-wingers by his stubbornness. Essentially, he was an unreconstructed rank-and-filer in the old Wobbly mold. He was too quick to spot "bureaucracy" in any design for organizational stability, and he rightly resented those among his vice-presidents who were trying to build their own miniature Tammany Halls inside the union. The result of his two-front battle with the rightists and the leftists was that the union was kept in a state of continuous conflict at the very time when Sigman's goal was the creation of unity and concord. The same qualities that made him a good field commander made him a poor angel of peace.

My own relations with Sigman remained extremely cordial. As manager of Local 10 I took pride in the fact that we had been in the vanguard of those who summoned him back out of retirement. We also took pride in the fact that our local, with its pivotal place in the industry, had been the rock on which the Communist drive to take over the I.L.G. had foundered. They met their Verdun in the Cutters Union; had we succumbed, the International would have had to surrender in short order. But the satisfaction I derived from our role and the admiration I had for Sigman's leadership against the Communists did not blind me to the fact that it would be better if he went back to the farm and let someone with a more conciliatory approach take over.

This was especially true since there were some signs from Moscow that the Communist line toward labor was changing in a way that might cause intense disenchantment among some of the party's converts in the I.L.G. and other American unions, thus making it easier to bring them back into the fold of genuine trade-unionism. Stalin, having won his fight against the "left opportunism" of Leon Trotsky, was now declaring war on the "right opportunism" of Nikolai Bukharin. As part of the new line, the Profintern—the Kremlin's instrument for controlling world labor—was discouraging the tactic of "boring from within" established unions and encouraging the organization of rival trade-union centers. I was quite sure that people like Zimmerman and Hyman would never be happy with such outright sabotage of unions like ours. The test for us was whether we could put our own house in such order that workers would turn back to us and away from the Moscow-inspired Communists.

With that in mind, I told Sigman three months before the I.L.G. national convention in Boston, in May 1928, that I felt it would be helpful to have his predecessor, Benjamin Schlesinger, involved once more in the leadership. The ex-president had always been notable for his flexibility, his diplomatic skill and a remarkable flair for public relations in the best sense—an identification of the union with the welfare of the community. My idea that Sigman should step down and allow Schlesinger to replace him was a bombshell that caused a fresh split in the General Executive Board. The opposition did not come from the left wing; that bloc had ceased to be a factor, since practically all its leaders had been expelled as part of Sigman's poststrike reorganization. But there were plenty of hard-liners on our side who wanted to carry on a war of extermination against the very substantial number of garment workers still lined up with the Communists in secessionist locals outside the I.L.G. fold. There were also some right-wing chiefs who were ambitious for the presidency themselves and were unwilling to give it to Schlesinger.

The last thing I wanted at this stage in the union's history was to see the dominant right-wing forces bring a new civil war to the union. My first thought was that the way to solve the problem was to have the new international officers elected through a referendum, instead of through vote by convention delegates. Even with the modest changes that Sigman had agreed to at the time of the left-wing demand for proportional representation, the convention was still dominated in undemocratic fashion by the small locals. Unions with 20 percent of the total membership were still in position to control the outcome of a convention vote if they all banded together against those with 80 percent. So I made a passionate speech at the Boston convention, pointing up how unfair this system was and urging that the entire membership be given a voice in choosing the new leaders through a referendum.

But, realistically I knew that this was pure politics, not a matter of justice at all. The Sigman forces would have been outraged if we had forced a referendum that would have left them badly defeated by the rank and file. It would have broken Sigman's heart, which he did not deserve—least of all from me, his devoted ally through the excruciating fight with the Communists. Caucuses went on day and night, until seven o'clock every morning, to try to resolve the situation. I would take a cold shower, grab a quick breakfast, and plunge into the next day's round of conferences. Abe Cahan of the *Forward* came to me with a compromise proposal. The slate, he said, should be Sigman again for president with me as secretary-treasurer and heir apparent. He would guarantee me ten illustrated feature articles in the *Forward,* all intended to make me known with the members and the general labor movement as the hero of the battle to restore genuine rank-and-file democracy in the I.L.G.

I told Cahan I appreciated the great honor he wanted to confer on me but the answer was no. I had no personal ambitions at this stage. The important thing was to bring about a transfer of power from Sigman to Schlesinger without leaving another burden of ill-will to dim still further the future of our union. In the end it occurred to me that the safest way to defuse tensions at the Boston convention was to ask our general counsel, Morris Hillquit, to act as mediator. Hillquit was a man whose devotion and resourcefulness throughout the years of struggle had earned him universal respect among the board members. He proposed that Sigman be re-elected by acclamation but that a new post of executive vice-president be created—with Schlesinger to quit his post as general manager of the *Forward* and come back in the new capacity. Sigman realized instantly that he was expected to step down soon and leave the presidency for Schlesinger. But he was exhausted by the strains of the past turbulent years and he knew that the next few years would not be any easier; and so he accepted Hillquit's alternative.

In October, five months after the convention, Sigman and the General Executive Board locked horns over one of his pet projects for internal union reform. He had merged a local representing cloakmakers with a smaller one representing the makers of children's coats. The action was one of the building blocks in his concept of "one big union" inside the I.L.G., in place of the craft units that provided power centers for many princelings on the G.E.B. When the board voted to undo the merger of the two locals, Sigman took it as a vote of no confidence. He packed his bags and went back to the farm, leaving the field open for Schlesinger's reaccession to the presidency.

Schlesinger's immediate task was to bring the union's finances back to the black, a monumental assignment considering that the membership was in disarray and the union owed money to the employers, the banks and to its own unpaid staff. The unorthodox manner in which he attacked the finances taught me a lesson that profoundly influenced my whole future career. One of his first acts was to authorize a contribution of $5,000 to the Federation of Jewish Charities. I was working closely with him at the time and I was aghast to see him giving priority to a philanthropic contribution when the union couldn't pay its electric bills and had to keep its own organizers and clerks waiting for their pay checks. I never forgot his explanation.

"We are a union that is part of the community and that has scored its greatest gains because the decent people in the community regard us as responsible for something more than looking out for ourselves. Even though it means giving the last penny we have in the treasury, we have to give. This is more important than having salary for our people. My only regret is that we have so little to give." And very soon I discovered that the Schlesinger philosophy of community obligation as the foundation of good public relations paid off, even though no other New York union considered it necessary to behave in the same manner. Schlesinger could go to three of the wealthiest members of the Jewish community and get from them interest-free loans to start our bankrupt union back on the way to solvency. Julius Rosenwald, the founder of Sears, Roebuck, loaned $50,000. Herbert H. Lehman and Felix M. Warburg advanced $25,000 each. That helped get the I.L.G. machinery running again. It also made it easier for Schlesinger to get support inside the union and among such friendly associated groups as the Workmen's Circle for a $250,000 issue of union-reconstruction bonds. I made myself a one-man team campaigning for the success of the bonds, because I was so impressed by the vigor with which Schlesinger was moving.

In the spring of 1929 the union was still in a disordered state. The cloak employers still had the right to discharge 10 percent of their workers every year under the reorganization clause they obtained as part of the 1926 strike settlement. That clause made job security a myth for our members; the manufacturers could pick and choose in the most arbitrary manner. But life was not too rosy for the employers either. Chiseling bosses of every description were operating without regard for any union standards. The decent manufacturers were just as much victims of their piratical methods as our members were.

From the standpoint of both the union and the bona fide elements in the industry, drastic surgery was necessary to root out the cancerous sections. Unfortunately, Schlesinger's health was beginning to fail and so he assigned to me most of the responsibility for developing a remedy. The union was weak, but it had one advantage. The chief spokesman for the manufacturers with the biggest shops—the so-called inside shops, where all the operations from designing and cutting through finishing of the garments were done under a single roof—was a man who wanted to get away from the tradition of perpetual dog-eat-dog conflict, a man who recognized that a strong union was essential for stabilizing conditions and enforcing uniform conditions.

His name was Samuel Klein. In his younger days he had been a member of the Socialist Labor Party, a disciple of Daniel De Leon. When he became executive director of the association representing the better shops in the early 1920s, it was still called the Protective Council of Cloak and Suit Manufacturers. The name made clear its purpose: to protect the manufacturers from the union—and most of the protection was strong-arm stuff, strikebreaking, planting *agents provocateurs*, paying off the cops to harass the union. But Klein saw no future in murder and more murder; he wanted to build a better relationship, instead of trying to capitalize on the chaos the Communists had left after their strike. He changed the name of his group from Protective Council to Industrial Council as a signal that a new philosophy was operating in at least some sections of the industry.

I thought I could trust Klein to work cooperatively with us in trying to end the demoralization and disorganization in the industry, for the mutual benefit of the workers and the manufacturers. But I knew I had to proceed with great care, because of the inherent suspicion of the industry. The union's Communists were still hoping for a comeback and were doing everything in their power to discredit the present administration. Employers were still disgusted over the 1926 strike and at the breakdown in the union's capacity to keep the cutthroat operators from undercutting the wages that the more ethical employers were required to pay.

In the spring of 1929 I called Klein and told him I wanted to meet him under conditions of total secrecy; I asked him to bring along the president of his association, I. Grossman. A few days later the three of us climbed into a taxicab and rode around Central Park for hours while I outlined my plan for restoring stability (the bill came to $40, which Klein paid). Even after all these years, I have to admit that what I was asking them to support took quite a bit of gall, but I was never short on *chutzpah*. I told them I thought the industry needed another strike. With everybody still suffering from the last disastrous strike and the union itself in hock, their first reaction was to look at me as if I were crazy.

But I explained to them that what I had in mind was no ordinary strike. The union would not be out to raise wages but to solidify its organization so that it could police the standards it wrote into its contracts, thus assuring its members of greater long-term job security and earnings by ending the chiseling that had made a joke of contract enforcement. I emphasized the great stake the reputable employers had in a secure, clean union as a shield against Communists, crooks and industrial scavengers. They needed assurance that when they made an agreement with the union they would have not only immunity from strikes during the life of the contract but also a dependable promise that all their competitors would be paying the same scale and living up to the same shop requirements.

What I wanted from Grossman and Klein was a promise that the members of their association would not fight the strike by bringing in goons or scabs, but instead would cooperate in drafting an agreement that would guarantee effective enforcement of union standards in all shops and thus rule out competition at the expense of labor.

"We're weak and you're in trouble," I told them as we rode through the park. "You need a union as much as the workers do. We're going to call a strike to rebuild this organization, and we're not going to ask for more money. All we ask is that you keep your shops closed and let us solidify our ranks."

They both agreed on what I was trying to accomplish, but Grossman had doubts about how much faith manufacturers could put in my promise that the union would not insist on higher wages once the shops were shut down. I gave him the only answer I could: "I can't go to a notary public; I can promise you nothing but my word that I will fight with everything in my power to stand by that assurance." I am not sure I would have persuaded him, if Klein, who knew me through his experience as executive director of the Industrial Council, had not underwritten my commitment. "Dubinsky's word is better than any written guarantee," he told Grossman. "I've dealt with him. He is honorable and trustworthy." That was all the convincing the association president needed; I had made my sale.

The strike lasted only a few days; the major employers did not fight it and the others could not hold out; the workers went back on the strength of a tentative settlement that stressed union security and industrial stabilization, but gave the workers no immediate money gains. The Communists, looking for ways to make a comeback, promptly began a drive to turn the agreement down at a ratification meeting that weekend.

Schlesinger, still weak from his illness, came to our headquarters to confer with me. I told him of the personal commitment that I had made to the employers. He was doubtful about the wisdom of ending a strike with nothing more in the pay envelope. "How in the world can we send the workers back without higher pay?" he asked me. "Why aren't we able to ask for more money?" Before answering, I walked to the fourth-floor window at the front of Schlesinger's office. "You'll be able to ask for it," I said in my quietest voice, "but only after I jump out this window." That ended the discussion.

Schlesinger wasn't present at the ratification meeting, and so I had to defend the new agreement alone. "All I bring you is a union," I told the workers. The applause was thunderous. Instead of rebelling, the strikers carried me out on their shoulders. Now, for the first time, there was solid basis for hope that we could put the union back together. The cloakmakers had demonstrated their confidence in the non-Communist leadership. The Communists had not only been repulsed in their attempt to upset the agreement, but their ranks were being fragmented by internal splits and purges caused by Stalin's new separatist line. As for the employers, the respect the union had shown for its pledged word vastly increased their readiness to work with us toward mutual stability. Under the new three-year contract, we set up a joint commission composed of prominent citizens and union and management representatives who would explore methods of controlling the substandard shops. Herbert Lehman, now Lieutenant Governor, and Mayor James J. Walker joined us in signing the pact as a symbol of the community's interest in the health of our industry.

These moves toward a firmer foundation for the union came just in time. Less than three months after the signing of the agreement, the stock-market crash ushered in the worst depression in the country's history, a time of tribulation for even the most unified labor organizations. The signs of economic distress were already clear when the I.L.G. met in Cleveland in December 1929 to hold its biennial convention. Abraham Baroff, who had been secretary-treasurer through most of the period since 1915, resigned because of poor health. Schlesinger, whose designation as president was formally confirmed at the convention, wanted me to replace Baroff. So did the rest of the General Executive Board, but the idea didn't appeal to me. I preferred to stay with Local 10 and help out the General Office whenever a special emergency arose as it had done in the cloak strike. My reluctance to leave the local was so great that I stayed away from the convention hall to escape those who would persuade me.

Finally, Morris Hillquit, the one man to whom I could never say no, told me that my duty was to take the secretary-treasurership. I accepted his judgment as having the weight of the Torah that Moses carried down from Mount Sinai. My new job was made easier by the convention's brave decision to vote a $3.50 tax on each member as a means of paying off some of our debts and restoring the union's capacity to finance organizing drives. But I did not delude myself that collecting the money would be simple, since no industry was more vulnerable to an economic slump than women's wear. As if the depression-born fall-off in sales volume and employment weren't handicap enough, I quickly found that I had another obstacle to overcome in collecting the tax. The followers of Sigman still harbored resentment against the 1928 "compromise" that led to his retirement. They took out their anger by refusing to pay the new levy. That was too much! Just when the first wave of disaffected Communists were coming back into our ranks, we were going to have to fight a rearguard rebellion by some of our most militant anti-Communists.

I was as tough as I had to be. Retrenchment was the order of the day and the year for every union activity. The staff was cut, and those who remained didn't get paid. Just when I was beginning to see a little daylight ahead, the I.L.G.-sponsored International-Madison Bank and Trust Company, to which the union owed $140,000, was taken over by the State Banking Department. All loans were called, and we had to impose another levy on the membership to pay off part of the debt. Even Charles Ponzi would have been astonished at some of the deals we made as we moved money from here to there and back again to liquidate our most pressing obligations—always at cut rates. By the time of our next convention, in Philadelphia in May 1932, I was able to report that we had cut our indebtedness by nearly one million dollars. We did it by actually paying out roughly $470,000 and persuading our creditors to write off the rest.

The convention helped to end the feud between the Schlesinger and Sigman forces. It was obvious to all present that Schlesinger was a dying man. For months before the delegates gathered at Philadelphia he had been so frail that I had had to discharge all the functions of his office as well as my own. During the convention he was spitting blood and had to absent himself from the platform for hours at a time to lie on a couch in an adjacent room. Many of my associates urged me to accept nomination for the presidency in his place, but it was plain to me that Schlesinger still wanted re-election. A delegation woke me at two o'clock one night to demand that I run for the top spot. "Get out of here," I screamed at them. "You have a candidate—only one, Schle-singer."

When I announced that I would personally put Schle-singer in nomination for another term, he reacted in the best tradition of the Yiddish Art Theater. He would not accept the unanimous vote of the delegates. It was only when Morris Hillquit added his voice to those begging him to take the office again that he let himself be persuaded. Even then he insisted on reading a letter of resignation to be read at the convention, with the clear understanding that it would be shouted down. He was recalled to the rostrum amid vast acclaim and made an acceptance speech second only to the Gettysburg Address for eloquence.

Three weeks later this pioneer from whom I had learned so much of the techniques of patience and persuasion and of constructive public relations died of a heart attack in a Colorado Springs tuberculosis sanitarium. Only eleven months before, Morris Sigman had died at his Iowa farm. Both were in their early fifties, yet their careers had left our union a great legacy of conflict and compassion. In a sense both were combat victims, their lives shortened and often embittered by the cruel demands of building a union in this stormiest of industries.

In mid-June of 1932 the General Executive Board met to choose a new president. I had just passed my fortieth birthday, but to most of the board members I remained a youngster—a youngster who still had to prove himself in battle. Most of the board were in favor of moving me up to the top spot, but I could see that several of the most influential members had reservations. They were determined to put in a strong secretary-treasurer—more to monitor me than to help me—and I was not about to take the presidency on that basis. My own experience with Schlesinger had convinced me that, even without problems as gigantic as those that were facing the bankrupt and faction-torn I.L.G. in the Great Depression, a division of authority was a major block to efficient administration.

The evidence to support this gloomy conclusion went back to the union's earliest days. From 1905 to 1914 the real power in the union was exercised by its forceful general secretary, John Dyche, with the amiable Abraham Rosenberg a figurehead in the president's chair. The explosion came when two dynamic leaders were chosen in 1914—Schlesinger as president and Sigman as general secretary. Their efforts at co-existence failed after a year, and Sigman left the General Office for the more congenial environment of the Cloak Joint Board. His place as general secretary was taken by Baroff, an unobtrusive, unambitious man, who lasted until 1929 mainly because he made himself almost invisible.

I would never have been able to work with Schlesinger had he not been away sick so much of the time. He was a leader of great vanity, given to posturing and shows of power, and his illness made him particularly crochety and suspicious. And I am sure I was difficult to get along with. I had the impetuousness of youth and wanted to do everything myself. From cutting down on use of paper clips to running a strike, I was sure I knew more than anybody else and I wasn't always as diplomatic as I should have been in paying attention to other people's ideas—even when the other person happened to be the I.L.G. president.

If becoming president in my own right meant that I was going to have handcuffs on me because of friction with the new secretary-treasurer, they could keep the job. I would rather stay as secretary-treasurer or go back to being manager of the Cutters Union. Nobody could think of a solution for the problem, so, as had become our well-settled habit, we turned to our sagacious counselor, Hillquit, and once again he did not fail us. He drafted the following statement, which was unanimously approved by the board:

Mr. David Dubinsky has been induced to accept the office of President upon the following conditions for which we have given him our assurances: (1) That he will have the wholehearted support of every member of the GEB, not only in his election but also and particularly in the forthcoming negotiations and struggles in the cloak industry; (2) That the election of Secretary-Treasurer will not create any division but will be postponed until such time when there will be substantial unanimity in the Board about a candidate; (3) That in the meantime he (Dubinsky) will continue to perform the functions of Secretary-Treasurer.

A quarter century was to go by before the two posts were separated again. In accepting the double responsibility the G.E.B. had entrusted to me, I made no effort to minimize the difficulties ahead. "Neither you nor I can underestimate the burden of assuming the leadership of a union bled white in recent years, first by the bitter internal struggle we experienced and now by the industrial crisis, which have cost us nearly two thirds of our membership," I told the board. "Our union is at a low ebb. Its very life may be uncertain. If it is destined that I be its undertaker, well, I am and always have been a good soldier—I shall not try to duck my fate."

FOUR

View from the Other Side

To GIVE A FULLER PERSPECTIVE on the grueling battle with the Communists and on the subsequent reconciliation, I asked Charles S. Zimmerman to come into my office and tape his recollections of the 1926 strike and the developments that made him first an insurrectionist inside the union and eventually persuaded him to abandon Communism and return to a position of leadership inside the I.L.G. In the forty years from his return until his retirement as an international vice-president and manager of the Dress Joint Council in July 1972, no man played a more commendable or constructive role in our union than Sasha Zimmerman. When he spoke frankly about some of the mysterious turns and twists of the party line, I could not restrain myself from jumping in with a few memories of my own. And so what follows is the taped text of our exchange, with his remarks in direct statement and my interpolations in italics.

CHARLES S. ZIMMERMAN: Toward the end of World War I, opposition groups took shape in the I.L.G. concentrating on the need for reform in its internal structure and fighting against bureaucracy. These groups represented a coalition of Socialists and Anarchists, whose primary goal was to rebuild the union on the basis of control by delegates elected in the shops. Many of the more progressive officers in the union were part of this movement, because they felt that the union was too bureaucratic and that a shop-delegate system would bring power closer to the people.

The inspiration came from Great Britain, where the shop-steward system had much more meaning than in the United States, so much so that the national officers of unions rarely had much influence over the shops. It was unclear how this system could be translated into the I.L.G., but despite that many of us considered it an ideal system that needed adoption here. When the Communist Party began organizing in 1919 and the early 1920s, it began paying attention to the reform movement in the needle trades, and it organized factions of its own to operate inside that movement.

At first the party had no well-defined policy for its activities in the trade unions. All it wanted was to sign up individual members. But William Z. Foster, who had led the steel strike of 1919, came in 1921 and proposed a new line. It was very different from that of the Wobblies and the other old radicals, who basically considered the unions part of the capitalist system and incapable of reform or basic change. Foster advocated change from within, and he set up a Trade Union Educational League to infiltrate all unions of the American Federation of Labor and try to take them over.

In New York he called a conference of factions—not of unions, but of the party units in the various unions—and a branch of the league was formed, with me as its first secretary, and Foster's son-in-law as director and chairman. The objective was still to reform unions from within. The Communist Party played an important part, but we worked with the Anarchists and those who were not primarily political but wanted to be part of a general reform movement.

Then, in 1922, the party's Central Executive Committee issued a directive that the Trade Union Educational League was to affiliate with the Profintern, the Red International of Trade Unions, which had headquarters in Moscow. After that the Anarchists split away because they did not want to become part of the Profintern and also because they could see that the Communists intended to dominate the reform movement and make it subject to outside orders.

I had been working as a sewing-machine operator in the dress industry, and belonged to the famous Waistmakers Union, Local 25, spearhead of the famous 1910 strike, the "Revolt of the Twenty Thousand." It was both the dominant local among the dressmakers and the one with the strongest Communist Party faction. In fact, the left opposition succeeded in electing all its candidates to the local executive board. They elected a majority the first time and then a bigger majority the second time. But the fight inside the union was already on and the General Executive Board under Schlesinger suspended first seventeen of us, and then nineteen, for various infractions. With so many charges brought, there was tremendous turmoil inside the local. In 1921 I was brought up on charges of slandering the I.L.G.W.U. in a leaflet I had written and distributed. I was suspended for a year and went off on a hobo trip to the Pacific Coast.

I missed the I.L.G. convention in Cleveland in 1922, where the fight over the issue of shop delegates first surfaced. The Communists had support from some key non-Communist delegates and from the Anarchists, but their resolution was defeated. The convention provided the impetus for the call in 1923 for Morris Sigman to return as president. The majority felt he would take a strong hand against the Communists, but the Communists were convinced that nothing could stop their drive to take over by organizing the shop delegates. Characteristically, however, they promptly got into trouble internally over such issues as how many delegates should come from small shops and how many from large shops—none of which they ever solved.

The idea was very vague, but it was distinctively different from the joint boards that were a central part of the union structure. The institutional purpose of the joint boards was to give the different crafts an opportunity to keep their separate identity but also to work together on common problems with the employers or the community. The Communist idea was to get a bigger voice for the rank and file. They established Workers' Councils; the membership card for these councils had a figure of a man in chains breaking his bonds, and the preamble of the councils was taken from a similar section in the Constitution of the Soviet Union.

This split was part a general fight against bureaucracy in the union and part a fight for a system which the Communists advocated as the moral basis for reorganizing the union.

INTERPOLATION BY D.D.: *The 1922 convention was the one at which I was first elected a vice-president. The entire administration headed by Schlesinger realized what was developing, and the entire opposition was centered in New York, even the non-Communist allies, men like Julius Hochman of the Dressmakers and Sam Shane of the Cloakmakers, both of whom later became vice-presidents. But the bulk of the voting strength in the convention came from out of town, so it was easy to defeat them. Also we had already voted to unseat a number of Communists and fellow travelers on the ground of loyalty to outside forces, rather than to the union. Schlesinger, who was always a strong adherent of the* Jewish Daily Forward, *brought its founder and editor, Abraham Cahan, in on two occasions—once to address the entire convention and the second time to address the opposition group. Cahan was confident that his prestige and authority would enable him to persuade them, but it didn't work.*

ZIMMERMAN: The fact is that there were many things wrong with the union structure. A local with three hundred members could have the same convention representation as a local with twelve thousand. Naturally, as a means of maintaining control, bogus locals were created—paper locals—and no matter how small they were they could overrule the

big locals in the Joint Boards and in the International convention. There was one vice-president named Jack Halpern
who headed the Out of Town Department. He controlled so
many convention votes that he could decide all by himself
which way the convention would go on any issue. He used to
come in with scores of locals at his command, and nobody
could check up on how many members they had—or even if
they had any. There were no membership audits, local by
local, of the kind we have now. The unfairness of that
system was a big issue, one on which many people went
along with the left wing. Let me stress again that originally
the left-wing movement was not a Communist movement. It
was a movement of dissatisfied garment workers looking for
more progressive methods of representation and other reforms to make the union better. When the Communists came
in later, they brought with them the conviction that it was
all right to lie—as Lenin had written in his pamphlet on
leftism—so, when candidates for local union office had to
sign a statement that they did not belong to the Shop Delegates' League, which had been declared a dual union, the
Communists did not hesitate to sign.

They kept gaining strength, and in the annual elections at
the end of 1924 and the beginning of 1925 they controlled
the executive boards of three important New York locals, 1
and 9 in Cloaks and 22 in Dress. Part of their success came
from inducing ambitious right-wingers to join their slate and
thus divide the administration forces. Actually, we Communists also were helped by the brazenness of the administration. One of the things Morris Sigman did to control our
power was to merge the Cloak and Dress Joint Boards into
one Joint Board, so we could not take over either division.
And when delegates were being elected for the 1924 convention, one of their managers came by as we were distrib-
uting leaflets outside the old Joint Board headquarters at
Twenty-fifth Street and Lexington Avenue. He sneered at us.
"You're wasting time giving out those circulars. The election
has been decided already. We completed it just now." In his

cynical, brazen way he was telling us they had stuffed the ballot boxes. And they did, but we managed somehow to get through one or two of our people.

At the 1924 convention the preliminary bouts were fought before the Joint Action Committee fight, and they were really good. Dubinsky was secretary of the Credentials Committee, and Joseph Breslaw, the most uncompromising of the administration hard-liners, was chairman. Every day the committee would bring in a report and then a supplementary report and then a supplement to the supplementary report, and each time more of our people would be unseated. But we had mobilized, and our fight was backed up by a big faction in the galleries.

The party representative who stayed at the hotel—the Bradford Hotel—was James P. Cannon, who later became national leader of the Trotskyites. None of our people knew he was there, and I always wondered afterward who was the contact with him. There was no doubt that he was directing the party's forces at the convention. It was he who called the shots in an open fight on the floor when the administration started unseating already seated delegates.

After that convention, the pressure kept building. In March of 1925 there was a by-election in Local 22 and a half dozen of us were elected to the executive board. It was the first time I had been elected to any office in the union. By that time the Communists were becoming more insistent on their policy and their party line. We had a big May Day rally at the Metropolitan Opera House in that year and Moissaye J. Olgin, the editor of the Communist daily, *Freiheit*, was the principal invited speaker.

The General Executive Board under Sigman took this, along with other events in the same period, as a basis for suspending the three executive boards and reorganizing the locals. The first thing the International did was to send a letter to all the banks closing the local accounts so that we would be cut off from all access to union funds. They took over the buildings of the two Cloak unions at dead of night, but as soon as we learned what was happening we organized a patrol to turn the building of Dressmakers Local 22 into a fortress. That building, at 16 West 21st Street, could not be touched.

The Communists were now in full command of this building. Hundreds of active members came after work each day and stayed all night. Every night the building was filled with people ready to defend the local at any cost, a situation that went on for months. In the meantime, the executive boards that were under suspension met to plan a coordinated strategy—to decide what to do and how to do it. Louis Hyman, the manager of Local 9, a big, rangy man with a wry sense of humor, proposed that we organize ourselves around the proposition of rejecting the suspension but not resisting it in a way that would insure our total defeat. He put it this way: "If I have a dispute with you, we have a fight. You hit me, and I can hit you back. But suppose I am walking down the street and I meet Jack Dempsey and he hits me. Shall I hit him back? Does that make any sense?"

So we listened to Hyman and decided to organize the Joint Action Committee, with him as chairman and me as secretary. We started the battle with the stand that we were the genuinely elected officers of the genuine Joint Board and we refused to recognize the suspensions as legitimate. We had the support of most of the members of all three locals; they resented and resisted the suspensions, and they went to surprising lengths in their willingness to sacrifice to show their resentment. Many of them sacrificed good jobs where they had worked for years, and they had an almost religious conviction about what was right.

The leading faction in all these developments was made up of Communists like myself. We would meet all the time with Ben Gold of the Furriers and others from what we called the Needle Trades Committee to discuss our activities and strategy. Our idea was to utilize the strong support by the membership to build up our action so that each protest would be bigger than the one before. We had several meetings in Cooper Union, then we called one in Yankee Stadium. Hyman was opposed to such an enormous venture; he doubted that many people would travel to the Bronx and thus the meeting would be a public failure. But we had a tremendous crowd—more than 30,000 people. I was chairman and Hyman spoke and Rose Wortis, who was our La Pasionara—long before there was a La Pasionara in Loyalist Spain.

Then we had a big fight inside our own ranks on whether we should follow up this success by calling a stoppage of the industry in New York for a day or two. We thought we would take three or four halls, but the response was so great that we filled seventeen halls. We took every hall on the Lower East Side. It was another remarkable success. Everybody stopped, and it was clear that we had worked up sentiment to a point where we had the shops with us and practically the entire membership. The only major exception was the Cutters Local 10, Dubinsky's local, though we did have a group there. The Italian Cloakmakers Local 48 was split, but in Local 10 alone we couldn't get a real foothold.

INTERPOLATION BY D.D.: *The key local. They couldn't win it.*

ZIMMERMAN: In September, three months after the suspension, peace feelers for negotiations began to go out. But let me backtrack a bit. I and five others had been elected in a Local 22 by-election which gave us a tactical edge we were able to exploit against the International. When they suspended the officers of the three locals, they took the names from the regular election ballot and sent them to the bank as the officers who no longer had the right to draw funds from the Local 22 account. But there was no blacklist on those elected in the by-election. So I called a meeting, and the six of us elected a chairman of the board and a secretary. We authorized the bank to recognize their signatures and demanded that the $80,000 in the local account be turned over to them. When the International challenged us, what would you expect us to do as Communists? We got the most distinguished firm on Wall Street to represent us in court and we won. The capitalist courts gave us the money.

But we weren't as lucky in a fight that really mattered more: our challenge of the International's right to take over Local 22. We had as our lawyer, our champion, Louis B. Boudin, the dean of the left-wing bar. Morris Hillquit, chief rabbi as well as counsel for the International, the man they looked up to more than any other, was the lawyer for the administration. That was a match. Boudin and Hillquit were always at odds in the Socialist movement about political theory and philosophy, so they obviously enjoyed being on opposite sides in this battle. But in the end we lost. The International took over the local and held on to legal control from that point on.

INTERPOLATION BY D.D.: *You omitted one important aspect. At Yankee Stadium you said that Israel Feinberg and Louis Perlstein must go. To you they were evidently the main culprits. Perlstein had been brought in from Cleveland to take over Local 2 (the new number for the old Local 1), and Feinberg was general manager of the combined Joint Board. The demand that these two people resign was made the popular issue, and it was upheld by many members. Sigman asked Hillquit for his advice, because the situation had become very critical; Hillquit advised that both resign, but Sigman was against that. As a compromise he suggested that only Perlstein resign, because he was a general organizer, whereas Feinberg was the top man as general manager. Sigman wanted to keep Feinberg, but Hillquit told him that would not solve the problem. "If you give them one, you've got to give them both." And it turned out that*

Sigman sacrificed Perlstein, and it didn't mean a damned thing. Ultimately, Feinberg had to go, too.

ZIMMERMAN: And Breslaw also went. So at that time people began mediating, trying to make peace. Some were rank-and-filers identified with non-Communists in the Joint Action Committee and some were people from the outside interested in stability in the industry. We met with Sigman to seek a settlement and finally we did reach a compromise which called for a modified system of proportional representation in the Joint Board, in place of the old system of five delegates from each local, regardless of size. For instance, Local 2, the Cloak Operators, had 12,000 members. Local 82 had 200 members. Local 64 had fewer than 100 members. Yet each had five delegates to the Joint Board, all with full voting rights. The result was that five locals having altogether 2,000 members had 25 delegates while Local 9 and Local 2, with a total of 18,000 members, had ten delegates. Sigman agreed to reform the system and gradually improve the representation.

It is true that it was not altogether proportional, but it was fairer than the original, so we agreed to it as a compromise and so did Sigman. We agreed on new elections to choose officers in all the locals and we also agreed on a special convention to be held in Philadelphia in December, a couple of months after the local elections.

We scored a clean sweep in the local elections: Perlstein was already out; Feinberg was out; Breslaw was defeated; Hyman became the manager of the Joint Board and I became the manager of its dress division. Not only did we elect a majority of the officers in all the locals but also a majority of the delegates to the special convention. We also had quite a representation of delegates from Chicago, Philadelphia, and Cleveland to this special convention.

After the peace negotiations were concluded, we discussed whether we could work with Sigman against the right wing. In a sense, he was in the middle, because he was not only fighting us, he was also fighting right-wing elements in the union, especially Breslaw, Jacob Heller and Isidore Nagler, whom we considered the master bureaucrats and reactionaries. Sigman himself had once belonged to the I.W.W., and we regarded him as a genuine trade-unionist fighting for clean unionism. So, in spite of all the nasty things we had said about him during the internal fight—and we said plenty—we knew he was a decent trade-unionist. Finally we agreed to talk to Sigman about forming a united front to fight against the Naglers and the Breslaws and the others of the right wing. We drew up a lengthy program and Hyman and I went to talk to Sigman.

He agreed with us on almost all points. The one point on which we were in fundamental disagreement was the formation of a labor party, and the whole thing broke up on that issue. To us this was a most important demand, but Sigman, as an old Wobbly, was cynical about it, and thus the united front collapsed. The fact that we would not bend on this issue when it was clear that Sigman could never go along indicates to what degree our actions already were determined by C.P. policy. The party felt very strongly on having a labor party in the program—everything else was secondary to that. William Z. Foster and Charlie Ruttenberg were at that time the chief definers of party policy. Jay Lovestone was not yet an important leader although he was in the C.P. national office.

Well, the Philadelphia convention came, and we tried to stick to the basic peace agreement, but it was a turbulent convention with numerous debates. Some of the fiercest were on the International's policy of settling disputes with employers through arbitration, which we denounced as a form of class collaboration harmful to the workers. The minutes do not reflect the discussion very accurately because Max Danish, the editor of *Justice*, cut them so drastically that we constantly protested. The discussions reached a climax when we got to the question of amending the constitution to change the method of representation in line with the agreement we had worked out with Sigman. Our interpretation of the agreement was not the same as the administration's. They insisted they were carrying out the understanding; we disputed them. Suddenly, in the midst of the debate, Hyman got disgusted and said, "Come on, let's walk out."

The idea that we would walk out of the convention had never been part of our plans, but suddenly everybody in our group left the hall and went back to our own hotel to caucus. That's where the party's representatives were staying. They were Benjamin Gitlow, who later became a star witness against the Communists before the House Un-American Activities Committee, and William Dunne, later editor of *The Worker*. We consulted with them all the time, and they knew everything that was going on, even though they never went near the convention.

When they heard we had walked out, Bill Dunne barked out an order. "You'll go back to that convention, even if you have to crawl back on your bellies." That was an expression we never forgot. "You'll crawl back on your bellies." But how do you go back? We had to find a way. So I went as an emissary to a special session of the convention that night to seek a point of clarification. You can understand how I felt going back there with some cock-and-bull story about our wondering whether we understood the whole matter right, that there might have been some misunderstanding. But those were the orders and I did what I was supposed to.

Julius Hochman, the most sophisticated of the administration leaders, understood what I was doing, and he got up and made a big speech quoting the policies of the Profintern, the Trade Union Educational League and the Communist Party. All of them stated it was the duty of Communists in the unions not to split any union, not to walk out, but to stay inside no matter what. On that basis, he said, we had to come back in a hurry. He put it on the line. He didn't try to spare our feelings, even a little bit. I don't remember what

Sigman said, but I came back and reported that I had got a satisfactory answer and we could now all go back to the convention. I am not sure that there was even the smallest gesture in our direction; I think Sigman tried to make it a bit easier for us, but I am not at all sure.

INTERPOLATION BY D.D.: *After they came back, the question of representation was again discussed and I hoped we could work out some accommodation.*

A committee that I was part of was set up and we straightened out the matter with another compromise. We modified the old constitution in a way that didn't give them exactly what they wanted, but it brought substantially better representation.

One other thing deserves mention in connection with the presence in Philadelphia of Gitlow and Dunne. Gitlow had been in jail in New York just before the convention, and Sigman sponsored a petition to the Governor, Alfred E. Smith, to free him. Sigman went personally to the Governor and it was through his intervention that Gitlow was released. Then he addressed the convention. It all came under the head of peace gestures. Gitlow came from jail to speak to the delegates, then he set up headquarters in another hotel to direct strategy for the Communists. Much later on he stepped out of the party and fought it.

ZIMMERMAN: After the representation battle, the administration appointed another subcommittee to meet with us and try to arrange a slate of new officers—how many vice-presidents we should get on the General Executive Board and whom could we agree on for president and secretary-treasurer. We didn't get anywhere, so it was decided there would be an open election. Since they had the majority at the convention, they would decide among themselves whom of us they would elect. Hyman ran against Sigman for president and I ran against Abraham Baroff for secretary-treasurer. Naturally, we were defeated.

As a youth in Lodz, Poland.

Picnic with East Side friends at Jersey Palisades about 1915.

Command performance of *Pins and Needles* for President Roosevelt in East Room of White House. March 3, 1938. I.L.G.W.U.–JUSTICE PHOTO

With Emma at close of 1937 I.L.G.W.U. convention in Atlantic City when she told delegates, "We both chose the right man."

With Eleanor Roosevelt and Rose Schneiderman at 1938 performance of *Pins and Needles*.

D.D. dines with John D. Rockefeller, Jr., once labor's Public Enemy No. 1 for his role in "Ludlow massacre" in Rockefeller-owned Colorado coal mines.

Mayor Fiorello H. LaGuardia auctions off paintings by members of Local 22 for benefit of World War II China Relief Agency. Left to right, Charles S. Zimmerman, head of local; F. H. Wood, agency chairman; LaGuardia and D.D.

William Green, president of American Federation of Labor, returns original charter issued to garment union in 1900 to mark its 1940 decision to return after having quit to join C.I.O.

D.D. looks younger than members at 1938 season opening of Unity House, union's resort.

Belly to belly with John L. Lewis, founder of C.I.O., at President Truman's Labor-Management Conference in 1945.

D.D. confers with Wendell L. Willkie, whom union had opposed whe he ran against F.D.R. for President in 1940. Willkie's death in 19. blocked Dubinsky's plan for Willkie to run for Mayor of New York Ci on Liberal Party ticket.

ll is surface harmony after D.D. upsets stay-away strategy of Vice
President Henry A. Wallace at 1944 Liberal Party rally in Madison Square
Garden to support Roosevelt–Truman ticket. Left to right, D.D., Wallace,
Senator Harry S. Truman and Senator Robert F. Wagner, Sr.

Ninetieth birthday
of John Dewey
brings best wishes
from D.D. In
center, Professor
William H. Kil-
patrick of Colum-
bia University.
October 20, 1949.

Founding convention of International Confederation of Fr
Trade Unions in London in November 1949. Matthew Wo
George Meany and William Green are in front row. Jay Lov
stone (wearing glasses) is behind Dubinsky in third ro
I.L.G.W.U.–JUSTICE PHOTO

Dave Beck, president of Teamsters Union, promises cleanup of racketeering in union at hearing before A.F.L.–C.I.O. Ethical Practices Committee. Cleanup never materialized, and Teamsters were expelled from federation. Left to right, Beck; D.D.; Arthur J. Goldberg, committee counsel; and A. J. Hayes of Machinists Union, chairman. September 5, 1957.

Hit on the head. D.D. brings oversize gavel down on head of James B. Carey, secretary-treasurer of C.I.O. at A.F.L.–C.I.O. merger convention in New York in 1955.

Employers turn tables by picketing Dubinsky at Unity House outing early in 1950s.

The family. Left to right, Shelley Appleton, I.L.G.W.U. vice president; Mrs. Dubinsky; granddaughter Ryna Appleton; daughter Jean Appleton and D.D. May 10, 1959.

Seventh Avenue bike ride with granddaughter Ryna, passing Macy's in 1959.

In litter-strewn Atlantic City convention hall with his secretary, Hannah Haskel, and chief aide, Louis Stulberg. 1959. PHOTO–BURTON BERINSKY

Smoky settlement. D.D. puffs on cigar as Julius Hochman, strike chairman, reports terms of settlement at Manhattan Center ratification meeting ending first strike in quarter-century, 1958.

With John F. Kennedy and Adlai E. Stevenson, then U. Ambassador to the United Nations, at 1960 Liberal Party dinner in New Yor
PHOTO—BURTON BERINSKY

Beaming as J.F.K. speaks at Seventh Avenue rally of garment workers near close of 1960 campaign. PHOTO— BURTON BERINSKY

With Jacob S. Potofsky, presi dent of Amalg; mated Clothin; Workers of An ica, at John F. Kennedy's inau ration in 1961.
PHOTO—BURTON BERINSKY

With Robert F. Kennedy when he visited D.D.'s office while serving as Attorney General in 1962. PHOTO–BURTON BERINSKY

D.D. and George Meany study resolutions at I.L.G.W.U. convention in Miami Beach in 1961. PHOTO– BURTON BERINSKY

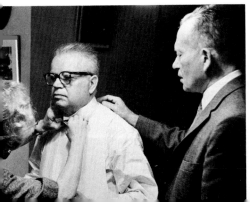

Being garbed for a formal dinner at White House in November 1961. Hannah Haskel, D.D.'s secretary, does the tying and Louis Stulberg the straightening. PHOTO–BURTON BERINSKY

In cap and gown after receiving honorary degree at Temple University, 1964.

With Martin Luther King, Jr., after civil rights leader had received Nobel Peace Prize, 1964.

D.D. prepares to demonstrate skill as a cutter to Vice President Johnson on visit to Seventh Avenue dress factory in 1962.

Busy straightening out the chairs before arrival of J.F.K. to dedicate I.L.G.W.U. housing development near New York's Garment Center on May 19, 1962. PHOTO—BURTON BERINSKY

Requiem. At fiftieth-anniversary observation of Triangle Shirtwaist fire where more than 200 women perished in 1911. PHOTO—BURTON BERINSKY

Tearful farewell.
D.D. and his suc
cessor, Louis Stu
berg, embrace at
D.D.'s retiremen
in 1966.

Mayor John V. Lindsay presents D.D. with New York
City's Diamond Jubilee Medal in City Hall ceremony
November 15, 1973.

When it came to the voting for vice-president, they decided I was the one to defeat. They were going to give us four seats and they went along with three of our choices—Hyman, Joseph Boruchowitz and Julius Portnoy—but they defeated me and instead picked David Gingold, the least committed of the left-wingers, a man almost on the borderline. They considered me the party whip and therefore they didn't want me on the board. They were right in considering me the strategist inside our faction, but I think they made a mistake in not electing me.

I had joined the Communist Party in 1920 when it was formed here after the Russian revolution. Until then I had been a left-winger inside the Socialist Party but never too active. By 1925 there were three main factions in the party. I was with Lewis Corey, who under his real name, Louis Fraina, had been one of the founders of American Communism. The needle trades were generally with him. Then there were the Fosterites and those with Jim Cannon, the Trotskyites. In 1927 after the death of Charles Ruttenberg there was a realignment. Lovestone became the general secretary, and we who were with Corey joined Lovestone, because the Fosterites were going in what I felt was a wrong direction. In 1928 I went to Moscow as a delegate to the Profintern. That was the beginning of the change in party line from working within the unions to splitting these unions. For us in the International the issue was not whether we should build *a* union, but rather that we should build *the* union. We had no sympathy with the idea that our policy should be to break this union and build an opposition union. That was what the fight would later be between the Lovestoneites and the Fosterites.

The 1925 convention ended with our electing four delegates—or, more correctly, three and a half delegates—to the General Executive Board. Back in New York we all plunged into the negotiation of a contract for 60,000 members in the cloak and suit industry. When it became plain that there might be a strike, Sigman went to Governor Smith, who appointed a distinguished committee headed by George Gordon Battle and including Herbert H. Lehman.

Sigman had come out with a fourteen-point program, the most important of which was a guaranteed period of employment, the first guaranteed annual wage. I don't have to remind you it was a seasonal industry and so the union demand was not for fifty-two weeks of guaranteed pay but for thirty-six weeks. We expected that some shops would operate forty or even forty-four weeks, but we knew some would operate less. The commission recommended twenty-eight weeks along with some other concessions that the union gave great priority to. Sigman and the International recommended acceptance. But the Communist leaders of the Joint Board found it much harder to make up their mind.

We went to a hotel away from New York to discuss the pros and cons, for there was division in our own ranks. A number of us favored the employment guarantee and other major provisions, but some thought that parts of the Battle report were bad. The worst was the one which gave the employer the right once a year to "reorganize" his shop in the interest of efficiency. That meant that the boss would be free unilaterally to fire 10 percent of the people. Now, in fairness, that was a period when the cloakmakers were on week work—they got paid by the week, no matter how much or how little they produced, instead of on the old piece-work basis. The commission accepted the employer argument that reorganization was necessary to maintain shop discipline and get productivity from the workers. Otherwise, they said, there was no way to get the right kind of productivity. The Communists as a party found that clause objectionable—class collaboration at its worst.

After protracted debate we rejected the report and prepared for a strike July 1. As usual, there was no negotiation in the early weeks of the strike but we were aiming for a settlement after about two months. All kinds of people intervened. One whom we especially respected was A. E. Rothstein, the father of the gambler and racketeer. He was as different from his son as day from night. He was a Talmudic scholar and respectable and respected citizen, a public-spirited man who had served often as conciliator and arbitrator.

Thanks to his contacts in the industry and to the help Dubinsky has talked about from Rothstein's son, I got in touch with Sadowsky, who was the largest manufacturer, employing about a thousand people. By the eighth week of the strike I had worked out with him a settlement that I was satisfied with. It called for a 30- instead of a 28-week guarantee, and it also modified the reorganization clause somewhat in our favor. We urged acceptance, and the top party leadership, the New York State Politburo, went along. They approved the settlement, but it still needed clearance inside the party from the secondary leadership. There were the chairmen in the strike halls—in effect, the shop delegates—about 150 or 200 of them, who were in contact with the masses of the people. So, we of the strike leadership and the Politburo members went together to meet with this larger group. I made a report that the top officials of the party—and they were all sitting right there—joined us in approving the settlement and recommending acceptance by the full body.

So far, fine. Then Boruchowitz spoke. He had a Yiddish way of expressing himself, like a rabbi or a judge weighing all the issues. And he said, "Maybe we could have gotten more, but we think on balance this is the best package." His intention, of course, was to help get the pact approved, but it worked out just the opposite. There was a bitter factional fight raging inside the top party leadership, and each one was looking for a way to show that he was more revolutionary than anybody else. The minute Boruchowitz got through saying, "Maybe we could have gotten more," William W. Weinstone, a member of the Politburo, was on his feet shouting, "They didn't get more. If there is a possibility of getting more, go and get more." Ben Gitlow couldn't afford to let Weinstone get ahead of him in militancy so he jumped up and echoed: "Sure, get going. Try and get more if there is a possibility."

Well, by this time, the Talmudic doubt that Boruchowitz had expressed had become a certainty. There was more to be gotten, everybody began to think, even though it wasn't true. At that stage, of course, Charles Krumbein, the party's state director, could not sit back and let himself be out-classed in militancy. So he took up the cry, and the whole thing kept escalating. Right then the original decision was reversed, the settlement was rejected, and we were in-structed to go and get more. I had to start negotiating all over again, but I couldn't get another thing. Furthermore, Sadowsky felt he had been double-crossed and didn't trust our good faith any more. It was hopeless.

Finally, Sigman stepped in and negotiated a settlement with the jobbers and the inside shops, the stable elements in the industry, in the nineteenth week of the strike. But it took another six or seven weeks to settle with the contractors and let the industry resume production. The strike had lasted exactly half a year. It was disaster. The tradition was that strikes lasted about eight weeks. That was the maximum. We had never even contemplated that a strike might drag on for twenty-six weeks. The entire industry was exhausted and the union was bankrupt. Sigman suspended the strike leadership and took over the Joint Board. If the original settlement had prevailed, we would have taken over the whole International, just as sure as we're sitting here.

INTERPOLATION BY D.D.: *That's right. What makes it all crazier is that the whole issue of people being paid by the week rather than on a piece-work basis, one of the issues on which they had been prolonging the strike, was a fake. Week work existed only on paper. It was actually all piece work in the shops that were most likely to abuse or exploit the people. The better shops, the more legitimate employers who lived up to the agreement, were the victims. They had people who were paid by the week and abused it by soldier-*

*ing on the job. We had an editor at that time, Saul Yanovsky,
of Gerechtiskeit, the Yiddish version of Justice. In line with
instructions from Schlesinger, he went to a meeting of
cloakmakers to advocate the original change from piece
work to week work. He had a tough job of convincing them.
They knew that under piece work they could work fast and
make money. They said, "What is the difference between
week work and piece work?"*

*"I'll tell you," he says, "it's very plain. Piece work, you've
got to work in your shirtsleeves, without a jacket, and rush.
Week work, you'll be able to work with your jacket on, with
your collar and tie, you'll look respectable." And he sold
them the idea. They would sit and the money would roll in,
irrespective of the number of garments they'd produce. The
whole demand of the employers for reorganization rights
came because they could not survive on that kind of non-
production.*

*There is another thing Zimmerman didn't mention.
Those in the strike were part of the International, but the
International had nothing to do with calling the strike. The
International recommended settlement; the Communists rejected it. Sigman's position was, "Take it or leave it." They
could have come to the settlement committee if they had
something better. But I was chairman of the settlement committee, and they had sent me to Siberia. They had to give me
a post, because I was manager of Cutters Local 10 and they
needed Local 10. But I was naturally a right-winger, so
I was not consulted; they did all the negotiating on the main
contract. The settlement committee was limited to dealing
with individual employers who wanted to break away from
the main association. They would come to my office in the
old Claridge Hotel to post security to be allowed to operate.
More than a million dollars in security had accumulated that
way, and the Communists had used it all for the strike.
Afterward that was a debt the International had to take
over.*

Paying the employers back took us years. And that was

after Roosevelt, after the New Deal, when the union was reestablished on a sound basis. The Cloakmakers Branch alone had 60,000 members at the time of the strike, and the International as a whole had 190,000 members throughout the country. In 1929, when Sigman reorganized the union after we expelled the Communists, we had a national total of only 60,000. And when I became president, three years later, we were down to 24,000. That's what happened to the union as a result of this strike.

ZIMMERMAN: During the strike, we of the leading Communist faction inside the union used to meet frequently with Foster and some of the others at the top level of the party. In that period Foster advocated amalgamation of the craft unions, of all smaller unions, to form powerful industrial unions. In the middle of the strike he told us we had to come before the strike committee and propose amalgamation of the garment workers with the other needle-trades unions—the Furriers, the Amalgamated Clothing Workers, the Millinery Workers and the rest. I told Foster, "It's crazy to propose such a thing when all our energies are tied up in the strike," and I refused to do it.

So, without any notice, at the next meeting of our strike committee Ben Gold of the Furriers, who was a member of the national board of the party, walked in and announced that he had been sent by the party to speak in support of amalgamation. He made a fiery speech, saying that amalgamation would help us win the strike, but he got nowhere with it.

INTERPOLATION BY D.D.: *Even though I was nominally chairman of the settlement committee, they never trusted me as manager of the Cutters Union. Traditionally, the Cutters Union always had a separate strike hall, but the Joint Board was divided over whether they would let us have a separate hall. In the end they had to give it, because they didn't dare start up with the Cutters, but I had to have Zimmerman sitting on the platform every time I delivered a speech to my own members.*

ZIMMERMAN: In 1928 the policy of the Profintern began changing, the general idea being to split unions and form new unions. It was different from the policy of amalgamation the party had advocated during the big strike. Now the idea was to form a big industrial union in the needle trades through a breakaway of all the party sympathizers from the established unions, except the Furriers where they controlled everything. And, of course, the Furriers would be in the new group.

I was a delegate to the 1928 Profintern Congress in Moscow, and I disagreed with this policy. But right afterward in 1929 the Trade Union Unity League was formed, and our directions were to start agitating for a Needle Trades Industrial Union. Arnold Lozovsky, the head of the Profintern, laid down the new line in the magazine of the Communist International in an article that said we would not shout from the housetops our aim to break these unions, but it would be without question our purpose to disrupt and demoralize them from within. The theory behind it was that we were entering a new economic situation and a new political situation on a worldwide basis—the so-called third period, where capitalism was breaking down. And since unions are traditionally conservative and right-wing they would stand in the way of revolution. Therefore, it was our duty to break the reactionary unions and build new, revolutionary ones that would help overthrow a dying capitalism.

Up until this time we were still calling ourselves the Joint Board. We refused to recognize our expulsion by the International, insisting we were the only legitimate Joint Board, and so there were two Joint Boards side by side fighting it out. But with the change in the party line we came under intense pressure to form a separate union. The I.L.G., by Moscow's standards, was a conservative union and it had to become a laboratory for testing Communist philosophy and strategy. The matter came up a second time at a Comintern Congress in Moscow in 1929. Jay Lovestone and I were there, and the whole internal fight in the American party was under discussion. We met with Stalin and the executive of the Comintern, but we also had a side conference, and Lozovsky, the Commissar on union matters, took an unqualified position that we had to build new unions. That was when the formal decision to form the Trade Union Unity League (T.U.U.L.) was made. Jay and I both opposed this position. I was still trying to fight from inside the party but I was on my way out.

When the Needle Trades Industrial Union was formed at a convention in the New Star Casino in New York I submitted a minority report. That made me an outcast, even though I was manager of the dress division and a key leader of the union. Everyone privately agreed with my position—the entire needle-trades faction: Ben Gold, Boruchowitz, Rose Wortis, and all the others—but because of the 1929 visit to Moscow they all fought me as a pariah. I remember walking with Gold a few nights after we received the order to break. He said, "We'll be able to accomplish more from within the party. We must submit." My reply was, "By submitting, you're not going to accomplish a damn thing."

I was expelled from the official Communist Party in October 1929. At the very end, when I was called before the control committee on charges, the chairman of the committee asked whether I would accept all the decisions of the party without question. My answer was that I would, provided that I had an opportunity before any decision was reached to set forth my own opinion and to fight for it. If I was defeated after such a discussion, then I would consider myself bound by the decision, but not otherwise. The chairman said, "No, this cannot be." I knew I was finished, but I told him, "If you want people to accept decisions without fighting for what they believe, you'll have a party of robots, and robots don't make revolutions." We didn't proceed any further. They had all the evidence they needed to convict me.

Even before that, though, the sycophants in the industrial union knew I was doomed, and I was isolated. The first one to call me a traitor was not a party member but a hanger-on, Julius Portnoy, the secretary-treasurer of Local 22, the left-wing Local 22. When I was the recognized party leader in clear control, he used to run to open the door for me—something I hated very much. But the moment he sensed that I was on the way out, he was the first to turn on me and brand me a renegade. As soon as I was out of the party, they began shoving me aside in the Joint Board. I couldn't function in the union leadership any more and I was compelled to look for a job in the shops. But the shops made it hard for me too. I got some temporary work in a knit-goods factory but that didn't last long: they wouldn't let me work in the left-wing shops, and the right-wing shops still suspected me. I was considered an enemy by both sides. Because of the depression I was out of work for quite some time. When the city organized the first emergency relief committee under Hugh Gibson I got a job at twenty-five dollars a week making children's dresses for the families of the unemployed. It was make-work employment before the W.P.A.

In 1930 I continued to fight inside the industrial union against the Moscow policy. On May 15, 1931, I and a number in the Lovestone group rejoined the International. We negotiated with Max Bluestein, an Anarchist and strong Sigmanite and then the manager of what was left of Dressmakers Local 22. We agreed to form a Committee of Twenty-five to conduct an active program of rebuilding the International's membership in New York. I was elected chairman, and Murray Gross, a member of the Young People's Socialist League, was elected secretary. The new group included not only Lovestoneites but also Socialists and Anarchists.

When the Committee of Twenty-five began to organize shops and picket in the market, the Communists issued leaflets telling everybody to stay away from us, but at the same time they extended peace offers trying to get us to unite with them again. In that connection they called a conference of shop chairmen in Irving Plaza on Irving Place and Fifteenth Street to discuss the question of a single union and peace within the union. I organized our people and went there to explore the possibility of getting together. The meeting opened with a speech by Ben Gold denouncing us and everybody connected with us, calling us traitors. It was a declaration of more war, not of peace. I took the floor and castigated them for prolonging the division. My whole emphasis was on the need for reunion. A fight broke out and they beat us with their fists.

The 1932 elections in Local 22 were in April, a little less than a year after I came back. I was nominated as a member of the local executive board. Bluestein and the other leaders apparently had talked to Dubinsky, who was now running things in the International, even though Schlesinger was still nominally president, and they got a green light to go ahead with restoring me to the official family. However, a right-wing group in the local objected strenuously. They pointed out that under the constitution no one could run for office unless he had been a member in good standing for at least a year. I was back only ten months. Their objections were overruled by the local executive board, but they took an appeal to the General Executive Board, which met in New Haven and sustained my right to take office. Then the right-wingers filed another appeal, this time to the 1932 convention in Philadelphia. I attended, though not as a delegate, and demanded the floor. Dubinsky also spoke in my support, and I was allowed to serve.

INTERPOLATION BY D.D.: *We had two cases to consider that involved the same problem of not paying dues for a full year. Israel Feinberg, who had been forced out by the Communists as manager of the Joint Board, had been elected as a delegate to the convention, but during his period in purgatory he had neglected to pay his dues. It was the depression, and nobody had money to spare. So I came to the convention with two important problems on my mind, to establish the election rights of both Feinberg and Zimmerman. I didn't want to lose Feinberg; he was a victim. I didn't want to lose Zimmerman; he was a returned prodigal son.*

At the convention we of the administration had a slim majority. My idea was to proceed to take Zimmerman's case first, but the convention committee felt this was a mistake. They thought it would be easier to get Feinberg, a right-winger, approved. My way we might lose both. But I insisted that they let me handle it with Zimmerman voted on first. Schlesinger did not understand what I was trying to do, but he was a sick man and he left all the fighting to me. The idea I had was to put up the strongest defense I could make for letting Zimmerman take the office to which he had been elected. And, with me as spokesman for him, the right-wing critics would be afraid to challenge and the left-wing opposition would be afraid to challenge. It worked; very few voted against the proposition.

When Feinberg's case came up, there was immediate dissent by delegates from the three Joint Board locals which had been reconstituted, but still contained strong left-wing elements. Anarchists, Lovestoneites, Socialists and, above all, the Sigmanites, who still had no use for Schlesinger, got up to object. I taunted them that when it came to Zimmerman all three locals had been for waiving the rule. But when it came to Feinberg, whose politics were different from theirs, then the constitution had to be followed to the last comma. And I threw it in their face. "For you who play partners in games, one is—in Russian, I say this—one is allowed to write his own rules, and the other is hung by the neck. Because it's Zimmerman it's kosher, but it's trafe when Feinberg does the same thing." That left them very much embarrassed and they had to vote for it.

We also had one other ticklish question at that convention. The union, as you know, was broke. So the General Executive Board decided to vote an assessment to replenish *the treasury. Schlesinger, being a publicity man, came up with the gimmick of asking for $3.75 from each member. That was because dresses sold at $3.75 and $4.75. They were never $4 or $5 or any even figure. So he thought $3.75 would be attractive. I was against it, not because of the fancy number, but because I knew we couldn't collect it. I knew I would have to be the salesman, going around to the locals and trying to get their members to pay. Not only did they have very few members, they had even less work. But my objections didn't stop the General Executive Board from voting the assessment and then leaving it up to me as secretary-treasurer to figure out how to get the money.*

I went to the tough customers first, the three Joint Board locals, what was left of them. They had a meeting in Bryant Hall and I delivered an impassioned speech, but I never had a chance. When I sat down I noticed that one of my closest friends in these locals, a business agent named Fannie Jokel, voted against me along with the rest. "You, too?" I said. And her response was, "Yes, we got instructions. You made a good speech, but I got to carry out instructions and vote against the assessment."

Well, when the three locals decided not to collect the assessment, there was great excitement on the General Executive Board, all those heroes a long way from the battlefield. My friend Isidore Nagler said it was essential to establish discipline in the union once and for all. So they came up with a resolution to expel the three locals, the remnants of the three locals that had gone over to the Communists. And everybody was for it, including Schlesinger, everybody except me. I said, "I had enough fights and I don't want any more fights. If you'll decide, you'll enforce the decision. I will refuse to enforce it."

So this problem was still hanging over when we got to the convention. I knew the assessment could not be collected. To a bankrupt union, a $3.75 assessment looked like a fortune. But the problem took care of itself. The cloakmakers were on strike at the time of the convention, and they *needed a strike fund. So we recommended a $10 tax, instead of the $3.75 assessment, and both sides voted for it.*

ZIMMERMAN: At the end of 1932, after the convention had cleared my election to the Local 22 executive board, Bluestein decided to step down as manager, and he proposed that I succeed him. At that time there were three principal groups in the union: the Dressmakers Circle, made up primarily of the Anarchists, the Sigmanites; the Progressive group, which we the Lovestoneites organized; and finally what was left of the Communists, standing aloof from both groups, with one leg in the Needle Trades Industrial Union and the other in the International. Both of the first two groups supported my nomination; the Communists put up an opposition slate.

At that time the local had altogether about 2,500 members, with 1,800 in good standing. A little less than 800 took part in the election and I won over the Communist candidate, Morris Stempler. In the meantime, two other elections had taken place which were very important to our union. F.D.R. was elected President of the United States, and David Dubinsky was elected to succeed Schlesinger as president of the International. Schlesinger had died a month or two after the convention, and it became Dubinsky's task to lay down policies to revive the union. These went into high gear after Roosevelt's Inauguration in March and the famous Hundred Days that started the New Deal. The very first strike Dubinsky authorized was in the Philadelphia dress industry in May.

INTERPOLATION BY D.D.: *The girls were supposed to start the Philadelphia strike when Roosevelt closed the banks, right at the very beginning of his term. They had had an enthusiastic meeting and authorized the strike, and were eager to go out. But I told them not to call the strike, to call it off. Some of them came to me in great anger. "Dubinsky, what are you doing to us?" they demanded. "We had a meet-*

ing and we decided to walk out. If we go back to the shop and say stay, they'll tear our hair out." I said, "Yes, that will happen. But if you call a strike now when the banks are closed, you'll be out of a job for good. What will they do to you then? They wouldn't stop with tearing your hair out and spitting in your face. They'd blame you as the cause of all their misery and beat you up."

These were good girls, dedicated girls, and they held off. A few weeks later when the New Deal was beginning to take hold and business was reviving, I called our manager in Philadelphia and asked, "What's doing in the trade?" When he said, "It's busy," my instructions were, "Get ready, call a strike."

"But you told us not to."

"At that time I told you no, now I'm telling you the time is right. I'll come there myself to help you negotiate."

I got there before the strike, and the employers told me the whole thing was a mistake. They said the union was too weak. If we insisted on going out, all we'd get would be a few girls in a few shops. We'd wind up being destroyed. If we waited a year, they said, then they'd be willing to talk. I told them all I wanted was a token increase of 5 percent, plus union recognition. The union was ready to settle for that. I couldn't get it. They were so sure we had no strength that they wanted to see us break our neck.

It turned out they were wrong. We did call the strike and it was a huge success. Ninety percent of the workers left the shops, far more than we ever expected. When settlement negotiations began a few days later, I told the manufacturers, "Now it can't be 5 percent. The price went up. Now it's got to be 10 percent. And it's got to be thirty-five hours, no more forty hours." When we had the ratification meeting in a big hall filled to overflowing, a girl in the balcony got up and said: "Mr. President, I want to ask a question."

"All right, ask your question."

"I work now for twenty dollars a week. With a 10 percent

raise, I'll get two dollars more. Can I make a living on twenty-two dollars a week?"

"No, what I brought you is not wages but a union. Your strike has opened the door for a union the bosses will have to respect. Why did you earn only twenty dollars when in New York the girls earn thirty dollars and forty dollars? It is because they had a union. In Philadelphia until now you had only a record of lost strikes, not a union. Now you have a union."

The agreement was overwhelmingly approved. Two years later when we negotiated a renewal, conditions had improved tremendously. I come to the same hall and I deliver again a speech. And I ask, "Is the girl who asked me a question two years ago here in the hall?" The girl stood up.

"What are you earning now?"

"Forty-five dollars."

"What did I tell you after we won recognition? It's the union."

Today that may sound like a pittance. But remember, this was before Congress passed the first Wage-Hour Law. And even when they did, the minimum was fixed at only twenty-five cents an hour.

ZIMMERMAN: Anyway, at about the time when Philadelphia went out the first time, we took up the question of a New York dress strike. And after long discussion in the Joint Board it was decided that we should go out. But this was 1933, and the treasury was still empty from the 1926 strike and all the turmoil that followed. We couldn't pay the rent, we couldn't pay the telephone bill. We had a one-way telephone—you could get incoming calls, but you couldn't make any calls yourself. There was no money at all in the Joint Board, and the International wasn't much richer.

When we voted to strike, we went to Dubinsky and he approved it. We began scurrying around for money, and so we found a guy by the name of Weinberg who worked for the Morris Plan. It was the forerunner of all those easy-credit loan outfits we have today, except that the standards in those depression days were much tougher than they are now. He said he'd take a chance on the union provided all the top officials, Dubinsky for the International, and Luigi Antonini, Julius Hochman and myself for the locals, sign a note to secure the $5,000 loan. We all met with Weinberg in Dubinsky's office and we got the loan, with us acting as guarantors.

The Communists were still carrying forward the industrial union. And when we announced our plans for a strike they issued leaflets and conducted a strong campaign to dissuade people from responding to our call. The theme was that we were a company union and that workers should have nothing to do with us but should go to the real union. And on August 16, 1933, the day our strike began, they had loud-speakers in the streets shouting appeals to the workers not to listen to the company union. But the response was so overwhelming that we were astonished ourselves. We had estimated that 30,000 workers might go out, or at most 35,000. The actual outpouring was in the neighborhood of 70,000, shops we had never been near, shops that did not have a single union member. We did not have halls enough to hold them, so we had to take an armory. It was enormous, just enormous.

We issued a special manifesto telling workers they could join the union at bargain rates—$3.75 or $5, I don't remember exactly. And we began negotiating right away with a few weak employer associations. Settlement headquarters were established in Washington Irving High School on Irving Place. Grover Whalen was the New York City administrator of the N.R.A., and I began negotiating with him for a dress-industry code. He went to Washington and conferred with General Hugh S. Johnson, the national administrator. We got a go-ahead to hammer out an agreement with the manufacturers on terms of a code, and it was something really startling.

No one of us would ever have dreamt it possible, but we got a 35-hour week. This at a time when many of the people in our industry were working until nine or ten o'clock in the evening without overtime. If they earned $25 a week, that was a lot. We got 75 to 90 cents an hour for operators as the minimum, with piece work on top of that. We had one of the best agreements, and we began rebuilding the union.

INTERPOLATION BY D.D.: *Grover Whalen announced that President Roosevelt authorized the strike, which was untrue. The newspapers ran it. And that helped. We were able to start stabilizing the industry and the union, both at the same time.*

ZIMMERMAN: The Needle Trades Industrial Union was finally dissolved in 1935, again on instruction from Moscow. The policy shifted back to working inside the established unions. Suddenly they stopped denouncing us for not enforcing conditions, for betraying the membership, and they began coming back—first in driblets, then all of them. It was a humiliation to see them forced to come back, especially because they didn't all learn about the new orders at the same time. When I went to Toronto to speak to a mass meeting of garment workers, the party people were in the hall heckling and creating all kinds of disruptions. I said, "It's clear you don't know what's going on. Let me enlighten you. It's not the style to create commotions any more, because very soon you'll get your instructions to go back. They just didn't reach you yet." And very soon they did get their orders and they did just what the Communists did everywhere else. But, of course, as soon as they got back in, they organized a left-wing opposition in the name of the rank and file, although the only voice that still counted with them was Moscow's.

INTERPOLATION BY D.D.: *It was partly for that reason that the union adopted a rule against clubs. We had had enough of dual unions functioning inside the I.L.G. Under the new rule, slates were given ninety days before elections in which to carry on organized political activity in union affairs. They couldn't function on a year-round basis, whether they were the Anarchists, the trade-union circles, the Communists or anybody else.*

ZIMMERMAN: From the time I came back in May of 1931, I found that I could count on full support for any worthwhile organizing project not only from the officers of Local 22 but also from Dubinsky, first as secretary-treasurer and then as president of the International. Any program that we decided needed action was immediately approved. And that convinced me I could work with the leaders of the International whom I had previously denounced. And when it came to the most important question of all, in 1933, of deciding on an industry-wide strike by this bankrupt union, again there was no question. Just the opposite. All the machinery of the union throughout the country was mobilized in our support. None of these was a matter of abstract philosophy or theory; they were matters of practical trade-union action.

So this naturally made it possible for me to adjust myself to working cooperatively on reconstruction of the union although politically we were still in total disagreement. I remained a convinced member of the Lovestone group in the Communist opposition movement and joined with it in activities that Dubinsky did not approve of. The local became a base for the distribution of literature and for other activities. We had the biggest educational department, a vastly expanded department, with Will Herberg as director, and we did whatever we wanted. When we disagreed with the International on political policy, we published pamphlets setting forth our position. The most notable was on the N.R.A., which we considered a Fascist idea, despite the great assistance our union had derived from it. We felt that way about most of Roosevelt's New Deal.

Dubinsky called a meeting of the local executive board in New York to give his reasons for endorsing the N.R.A. and the dress-industry code. I made a speech against it. At the 1934 convention of the International we had the same debate all over again. Dubinsky's view was reflected in the majority report of the Resolutions Committee. I presented the minority report denouncing the N.R.A. I didn't make any converts, but there was no interference with my right to dissent or to publicize my views. We distributed the minority report afterward as a pamphlet. Nothing happened. And again nothing happened when I exchanged letters with William Green, the president of the American Federation of Labor, criticizing him for not supporting the 1934 waterfront strike in San Francisco. This freedom of action without any interference from Dubinsky and without his taking any action against me showed us that the International did subscribe to independence of expression and of political position.

In fact, I was elected a vice-president in 1934 at that first convention after the N.R.A. Despite my disagreement on this fundamental issue, I was elected with the support of the administration.

INTERPOLATION BY D.D.: *I never expected that speech at the convention, because at that time the union was saved, and we owed it to the N.R.A. and the New Deal. When he made that speech, unexpected as it was, I made notes and I replied. I think my speech is probably more important than Zimmerman's speech, but what happens? The convention majority supports the N.R.A. He comes back; he doesn't print the decision of the convention. Instead, he prints pamphlets on the minority, a majority which does not exist.*

I never told Zimmerman anything then, but I resented it, especially because here is a Communist where they learn discipline and when the majority makes a decision they comply. But in this case Communist discipline is to disobey

*to the letter just because I say, "Here you're free to do any-
thing."*

ZIMMERMAN: You forget one thing: you forget that I was
in a process of transition. To me the Socialists and our right-
wing trade-unionists were still agents of the devil, you know,
not to be trusted. To me it would be the height of treachery
to have rejoined the Socialist Party at that time. It was so
hammered in, so imbued, you know, the treacherous role of
the Socialists and the right-wing trade-unionists, that you
just don't jump in at once. It takes a period of adjusting.

INTERPOLATION BY D.D.: *It is this here, you printing your
ideas.*

ZIMMERMAN: I know, I know, propaganda.

INTERPOLATION BY D.D.: *Propaganda against the union.*

ZIMMERMAN: We in the Lovestone group were still in a
stage of feeling that we were the injured party—injured both
by the official Communist Party and by the union bureaucracy. And the transition, you know, into giving adequate
consideration to the viewpoint of the other side was not so
simple. But the adjustment did take place; on the basis of
programs and activities within the union we came to work
more closely together. It wasn't that I ever came to Dubinsky
or that Dubinsky called me in to make a deal on something
or other. It was strictly on the basis of activity within the
union and for the union.

Another big help was our general activity in the community. Take, for instance, all the educational activities
which we expanded. You see, that too was encouraged. One
important example was my involvement very early in the
civil-rights movement. As soon as I became manager of
Local 22 in 1933, I sent letters to the Urban League and to
the Y.W.C.A. asking them to assist me in organizing Negro

workers and developing black leadership. That was not a popular approach in most unions at that time, but I was encouraged, not discouraged, by the International. These practical aspects of working with Dubinsky brought us closer together, and we even began to work with him in the political field. In 1936 we helped organize the American Labor Party in connection with Roosevelt's second term, and when I disagreed with Dubinsky on specific aspects of the party I did not hesitate to express myself. It was not until 1937, after our working relationship had been firmly established on union affairs, the A.L.P. and the formation of the C.I.O., that Dubinsky sent me a personal letter on the need for preserving unity within the organization and not always going off on separate roads. But by that time the transition had been made.

FIVE

Away from Strikes

AT THE START we were a union of strikes. It was rare that we didn't have at least one strike every six months. And the employers locked us out as often as we struck them. It took a long time for the bosses to make peace with the idea that they have to have a union—that a union could be constructive for them and not just a coat of iron for the workers.

The fight with the Communists in the 1920s was a big educator for the employers as well as for us. The union was practically dismembered, and only a limited number of shops were still organized. If you accept all the classic ideas of who wins under such circumstances, the owners should have had everything their own way. They didn't. The employers in the stable shops with employees whom they were anxious to keep suffered as much as we did because the union was weak. They had to pay decent wages and maintain decent conditions, but they also had to compete with the fly-by-nights and chiselers. They began to recognize that the union was a necessary stabilizing force. They could not meet conditions if their competitors were free to ignore them. Everything would be back to dog eat dog.

And gradually they moved to being pro-union instead of antiunion. And we, with our Socialist background, injected our own thinking. We were sick and tired of these perpetual strikes, so we gradually moved to long-term agreements. We used to make them for five years, but that didn't prove to be practical. Conditions change, and the workers get restless.

The union's own internal discipline breaks down when it cannot do anything to get at the roots of this restlessness, especially when the workers' discontents are justified. The employers point to the contract and resist any adjustments. The result is that the workers take things in their own hands and resort to illegal stoppages. That is no good for the union, but it is just as bad, maybe worse, for the boss.

I had to argue with the dress manufacturers when I suggested that a five-year agreement was too long, that they ought to settle for three. Their representatives were against it, and they had good reasons. They wanted five years of peace. My argument was that they wouldn't get peace. That might have been possible when the workers felt powerless and could not press for additional demands. But now there would have to be demands, and if you couldn't have a strike legally, you would have it illegally and you would be forced to give under-the-table increases. So the practice was changed and we made three-year agreements. By the time I retired in 1966 I recognized that even three years might be too long. So we in the General Office recommended that our locals and joint boards make two years the basic contract period, with provision that it could be extended for a third year if there was a wage reopener. These wage reopeners were a pressure valve to keep the shops from exploding. They proved very important when inflation was robbing the workers.

The basic agreement continued to prevail, but when consumer prices jumped more than 2 percent, an adjustment had to be made—not only in earnings for those already on the job but in the minimum wage for those coming in. Our floor help, the most unskilled people in our union, always had a very low wage. That was one reason why the I.L.G.W.U. always fought hard for federal legislation to put a floor under wages, but we fought equally hard to make sure that workers under our contracts would always get something above the federal minimum.

We were championing a federal wage-hour law when the

American Federation of Labor still felt anything of that nature was a socialistic interference with free collective bargaining. I remember in pre-New Deal days appearing before a Congressional committee to argue for a minimum-wage law when William Green was appearing to argue against. In every case, when Congress did act—whether it was the original 25 cents an hour under F.D.R., or 40 cents, or 60 cents, or 75 cents, or later the dollar, or eventually the $2.30 it is now—our union was always in the vanguard of those urging a higher minimum for all low-paid workers. But we could not be satisfied with what we got from Congress. In the first place, no matter how much better it got, it was never enough for people to live on. And obviously workers would not have much incentive to join the union if all they got was what their employers had to pay them under the law.

We adopted a formula that the lowest minimum of our contracts had to be ten or fifteen cents an hour above the federal floor. That way the worker could get the feeling that he was getting not only the benefit of the minimum wage, but also the benefit of the union. And that proved a *mitzvah* to nonunion people and not just those in the union. In the South, where the employers stayed awake nights thinking up ways to keep us out, they recognized that they would have a hard time if they did not match the payments in union shops. So a lot of these nonunion companies copied our method and gave their people ten or fifteen cents on top of the minimum. The result was that they did not have a competitive edge in terms of labor cost over our unionized employers. The workers in the nonunion shops came out better off. So did our members because their jobs were made more secure.

That is a real problem in our industry, much more than in most others. Nearly 200,000 workers—half of our total union membership—leave the industry in the three years from one I.L.G.W.U. convention to the next. Only about 5,000 retire each year. More than ten times that many leave, sometimes because their shops go broke or their employers quit business, sometimes because they marry or become mothers and decide to devote themselves to bringing up a family. Roughly as many new members come in as leave. No union has so monumental a task of reorganizing the organized.

When I retired, the I.L.G.W.U. had contractual relations with ninety-five employer associations. They embraced 2,000 individual firms with 12,200 factories. But the composition of the industry had begun to change drastically from the tiny shops that were the pattern when I became president. The trend was away from such shaky, here-today, gone-tomorrow units to large publicly owned corporations, some of them parts of giant conglomerates. At my retirement there were seventy-six such companies, yet they accounted for 20 percent of the industry's sales. Recognizing the special problems these companies presented, especially with their great concentration in dresses and sportswear, the I.L.G. began in 1966 to negotiate master contracts covering them. But none, even now, approaches the status of a General Motors or a United States Steel. The two biggest, Jonathan Logan and Bobbie Brooks, are so decentralized that 120 separate factories contribute to their output. The total personnel of these lions of the "rag jungle" does not come anywhere near the number of workers at a single auto or steel plant of the River Rouge or Gary type.

The small size that still characterizes most of the units in the industry makes it easier for them to adjust to the strange twists of the style market—skirts six inches below the navel one year and scraping the sidewalk the next. But it means great insecurity for the union and its members. Eighty percent of those members are women. They and their sisters all over the country indulge the designers in the ups and downs of the hemline. That makes the jobs. It also makes them sudden-death jobs. The chaos this creates for everybody connected with satisfying women's fickle taste in clothes brought the union into being as a cry of anguish against the injustices inflicted on workers by vicious industrial competition. But in the end we found we couldn't do our job for our members if we didn't become chief guardian of the employers as well as the workers.

The result is that many people, experts in traditional labor-management relations, accuse us of having become too strong as against our employers. They say the employer associations are really puppets of the union. Sometimes employers themselves join in saying that. I don't believe the statement is true, but I have to admit the relationship is unusual. It would be terrible if it weren't the way it is—for our members, for the employers and for our customers. The reality is that our industry is very different from most, and therefore our structure is different, too.

The employers have a decided interest in having the union function as a stabilizing force. It was miserable enough in the earliest days, when most of the manufacturing of coats and dresses was done in one place, except for the bundles some workers took home to sew at night. But when the manufacturer running his own shop became a jobber farming out his work to contractors, the difference was like night from day. We went from just being miserable to being in hell. The jobber was the important figure, but he had no direct responsibility where labor was involved. He employed designers; he employed cutters. But the actual work of making the garments he gave to contractors, and they had to cut one another's throats—and the workers' throats—to get the assignment. The contractor didn't need much investment. All he needed was some machines, usually bought on credit, and enough money to pay rent, usually late. The material was supplied to him, already cut, by the jobber. And when it came time to meet the week's payroll, the jobber would advance money to the contractor, who had no funds of his own for that.

Most of the contractors were former workers in the industry—cutters or pressers who scrounged together a few dollars to start in business for themselves. They were exploited, and they exploited the workers. The union was in trouble because the contractor was not the actual boss. The jobber was the man who counted, but the man you could not reach to enforce labor standards. He used his control to grind down the contractors and they then had to grind down the workers. It became a chain of exploitation, so naturally we developed an interest in organizing the contractors and getting them to join us in fixing responsibility on the jobber. That way he would have to guarantee meeting the union wage scales and also take care of the contractors' overhead and other costs.

The whole contracting business mushroomed. It became the dominant factor in the employment of our people. We depended on the contractors, but just as much they depended on us. When the jobbers had the whip hand, they would take the work away from one contractor and give it to another if the first wanted a dime more. They would look for nonunion contractors to hack away at the wages and conditions of the workers. You had to be an idiot not to see that the union would be neglecting its duty to its members if it did not see that the contractors had a strong organization of their own to make sure that they got from the jobbers what was needed for the workers and also what was needed for themselves. Actually, the contractors were closer to the union in economic interests than they were to the jobbers. Left to their own devices, the jobbers would always chisel on them.

But we had plenty of fights with the contractors, even after the basic principle of jobber responsibility was established. A group of Italian contractors organized in Brooklyn to break away from the regular contractors' organization in the New York market. They wanted to have a separate contract, but we could see the damage that separate dealing would do to the whole structure of industrial stability. It would be once again dog eat dog. We fought them in the courts and out of the courts. They had confidence that our Italian members would side with them and so split our ranks. They failed, because our Italian locals recognized as clearly as all the rest of us that the contractors had no legitimate claim. And we had many similar tests from other associations, especially in the runaway areas outside New York, where underworld elements were strong. But we beat them all.

Of course, there will always be a segment of the industry demanding full freedom of the seas to sail under the pirate flag. Many of the contractors now have substantial resources and would like to exact conditions for themeslves without worrying about how it affects the rest of the industry. And many jobbers would prefer it if there were no organization representing the contractors and no relationship between the contractors and the union. But the more decent employers recognize as well as we do how chaotic things would be without that relationship. The fact that one contractor can't be played against another, all at the expense of the worker, is as constructive as it is socially sound.

Unfortunately, a lot of chiseling still goes on. My own philosophy was always that a little bit of chiseling is legitimate. But they abused the privilege in many cases by chiseling too much. You can't stop it all in an industry that is so competitive and that involves so many risks. Jobbers invest a lot of money in buying material and creating styles. Then if things get bad—or even if they're not bad—their impulse is to exploit those who work for them and get an edge that way. And they had outlets for garments they made when they did not live up to the union agreement. That is why we became the only union in the country with a contractual right to examine the books of the employer. That way we could discover whether they were sending out work to non-union shops. And when they sent it out, the work wasn't done on the basis of the standard 35-hour week, but on that of a 40-hour week. And they didn't pay health and welfare contributions that amounted to 10 or 12 percent of payroll. Those were tremendous advantages for the chiselers in an industry where profit margins are figured in pennies.

Fortunately, our audit of employer books enabled us to recover millions of dollars for restoration to the health and welfare funds—money that had been stolen from the workers. And I wouldn't pretend that we recovered fully. Some employers maintained double sets of books to hide their chiseling, and they listed their contractors under fictitious names. And so we had to build up an elaborate staff of accountants, far beyond any other union, not just to police our own locals and make sure that their union finances were in order, but to keep tabs on the employers. It was a joke for us when Walter Reuther, in the first auto negotiation after VJ Day in 1945, called for a look at the books of the Big Three companies to see whether they could give a raise in wages without raising car prices. It was a gimmick for him, and he never did get it. But for us it was a life-or-death matter, not an ornament. The health and welfare of both the union and the members depended on it, and still do. And so do the health and welfare of the industry.

Over the years the I.L.G. became the principal—indeed, the only—force working consistently not just to uphold its own contract standards but to advance the interests of the manufacturers through stabilization, productive efficiency and even bigger sales of dresses and other female garments. The things that in other industries were the exclusive concern of employers and employer associations became preoccupations of the union, because there could be no safety for its members without such attention. The union's role went far beyond that of a cop enforcing wages and other protective standards.

As Professor Joel Seidman of the University of Chicago, a perceptive student of the needle trades, has noted, this concern started from the union's earliest days when it was still trying to get its head a little out of the muddy tide of sweatshop oppression. One of the missions of the famous Protocol of Peace, negotiated with the help of Louis D. Brandeis after the needle trades strikes of 1909–10, was to curb homework and subcontracting. The N.R.A. codes of the early New Deal were designed to control some of the most destructive aspects of competition in our industry. When the

Supreme Court struck down the N.R.A. in 1935 in the "sick chicken" case, the union persuaded the cloak manufacturers to join in establishing the National Coat and Suit Industry Recovery Board to carry forward on a nonlegislative basis the same essential function of regulating destructive commercial practices and maintaining decent labor standards. Because that kind of self-policing was so plainly in the best interest of the economy, attempts to smash this civilized regulatory machinery as collusion in violation of the antitrust laws never got anywhere in the courts.

But we went much further than just keeping the employers from committing suicide by cutting one another up into little pieces. The New York dress agreement of 1941 imposed a contractual obligation on employers to operate their shops efficiently. Imagine, a union telling the boss he had to be efficient or he would be hauled up before the impartial chairman and made to pay damages for not running his plant right. That was certainly a new twist in industrial relations, a big switch from the idea that unions are enemies of efficiency, always plotting to help their members goof off or to keep people in jobs that long ago became superfluous, if they ever were needed at all.

In July 1941 we established a Management Engineering Department in the international office under the direction of William Gomberg, a young City College student who had come out of the Yipsel (Young People's Socialist League) movement to work as an organizer of the shipping clerks in the New Deal period. Today he is a professor of industry at the Wharton School of Finance of the University of Pennsylvania. In those days he was an outstanding example of the dedicated young people who gravitated to our union as a center of practical idealism. Gomberg was extremely bright, resentful of a system that had forced millions into joblessness and eager to help the most deprived. Along with his fire and talent went a sense of humor as salty as it was refreshing. It was not strange that he concentrated at first on the boys who push carts loaded with dresses through Seventh

Avenue, dodging trucks and hijackers, a group gypped by everybody.

Gomberg had the right combination of good sense and *chutzpah*, and I didn't worry about the employers putting anything over on him. Also, he had learned in college many aspects of industrial engineering, including time study. That made him a logical choice to head a union department assigned to help the bosses be better bosses. The idea was to assist the employers in improving their operating methods, on the theory that the more efficient they were, the more likely they were to prosper and the higher the standards we could ask for our members. The department also served as a central clearing house for the exchange of information on fair piece rates and on fair methods for determining what the rates should be and making sure that they were paid. This was necessary not only for the protection of our people; it was just as necessary to keep the ethical employer from being undercut by a chiseler. Still a third function was to train union shop committees in time-study practices. That way they could be mainstays of a self-policing endeavor that further contributed to stabilizing the industry as well as protecting the workers themselves.

The problem from the beginning was to be sure that the union did not carry its proper concern in all these fields to lengths that would put it in the position of taking over the employers' managerial responsibilities. We were not telling them how to run their business. We were not compelling them to pioneer in new techniques; much less were we trying to block progress in favor of ancient featherbedding practices. I think the record will show that we maintained a balance in which they gained and we gained, and American women could be well-dressed without having to pay so much for their changing styles that they had to go naked three days out of seven.

Part of the explanation for the union relationship lies unquestionably in the fact that ours was such an homogeneous industry. The same kind of people sat on both sides of the bargaining table. Most of the employers were Jewish; most came from Eastern Europe or were the sons of immigrants from Eastern Europe; most started as union members working in the shops or inherited their businesses from men who started that way. The union, for its part, moved steadily away from its early radical view that each agreement was merely a truce for a regrouping of forces preliminary to the next round in a ceaseless class struggle. The lessons we learned in the very earliest days of the destructive sectarianism of Daniel De Leon were reinforced when Communist finagling carried the union to the brink of annihilation in the 1920s, a period in which general prosperity should have insured our members a golden thimble. The notion that workers had nothing to lose but their chains was replaced by a recognition that if we didn't learn to live together on the basis of mutual respect we would always stay in chains. I started by saying, "Down with the bosses." Now I'm a little smarter. If they go down, our people go down with them.

I have to admit, though, that the chopped-up nature of our industry with so many small employers made it hard to keep up with the wage parade, even when we used the union's money to help the employers promote the market for women's clothing. That was especially true after World War II when the share of the consumer dollar for buying apparel went down. We had benefited enormously from the fact that the demands of the wartime economy for metal had forced a suspension of production on such durable goods for civilian use as automobiles, washing machines, refrigerators and other household appliances. That brought a boom in our industry, some of it in shops making parachutes and other military paraphernalia but also in those making garments. Rosie the Riveter might be calling for overalls and slacks, but she still bought dresses too. One result was that, even with the corset of the Little Steel formula, which limited wartime wages, some of our crafts at the end of the war enjoyed pay rates above those in steel and other pace-setting basic industries.

In the postwar period other wages surged upward much faster than ours. A study by Professor Seidman, based on the General Executive Board report to the 1965 convention a year before my retirement, showed that in the preceding decade workers in the coat-and-suit branch of our industry had had an 18 percent increase in wages. Their average went from $2 an hour in 1954 to $2.36 ten years later. But in the same period the average wage for all manufacturing rose by 42 percent. It rose from $1.78 to $2.53. Put in its most painful terms, that means cloakmakers started 22 cents above the national factory average and wound up 17 cents behind. The auto workers, whom our union helped to organize, moved up 46 percent in that decade, from $2.20 to $3.21. Their average pay went up nearly three times as fast as ours. The comparison was less unfavorable in other branches of our industry, partly because they started with lower scales than the cloakmakers and also because the shift in styles caused a faster expansion in sales and in work opportunities in dresses, sportswear and other fields.

Part of the explanation for the faster postwar wage progress in the mass-production industries—but by no means the biggest part—lies in the fact that we began more than three decades earlier to use the collective strength of the workers to advance standards. The unions that grew out of the New Deal had a longer wait before these gains showed up in their pay envelopes, especially since wartime wage restraints impeded their growth at almost the very moment they got out of swaddling clothes. Once these restraints were removed, they could run while we were forced to walk. In fact, they started running so fast that wages became an engine of inflation and it was hard to tell how much of any increase was causing more grief than gain.

Far more fundamental than union pressure, however, was the extent to which a few monster companies in steel and autos dominated the market and could function in defiance of the laws of a free economy on the Adam Smith model. They operated on much higher—and much more predictable—profit ratios than the garment industry. And industrial mortalities were not the obsessive problem they were for us. The smaller fish in the mass-production industries had been gobbled up through mergers and competitive squeeze in an earlier era. Whatever these corporate oligarchs decided to give the union, with or without a strike, they passed on—with an edge to cover their own hefty profit margin. Union leverage was even greater, of course, in such fields as building construction, where monopoly control over the skilled-labor supply in an essential local service puts consumers at the mercy of the unions and the contractors, usually operating in collusion. Costs could be pushed up without effective check, because a person who wanted to put up a skyscraper in midtown Manhattan could not be tempted away by the knowledge that he could do it for less in Big Swamp, Missouri. It was not until the 1970s that the construction-industry unions learned that even they could price themselves out of the market. Their rates got so high that nonunion contractors took over half the business.

For us in the garment field the situation was always unique. The industry's labor costs represent a third to a half of the total cost of the product, machinery is inexpensive and easily shifted from one locality to another, and access to markets is little influenced by where a garment is made. A nonunion segment based on cheap labor offers constant competition in price for comparable style and workmanship. If union wages are pushed too high under such circumstances, the result may be impressive union pay scales in comparison with other industries but no union jobs. In one New York negotiation the employers in the dress industry offered too much for their own good. "If I take it," I told Louis Rubin of the Popular-Priced Dress Group, the industry's spokesman, "you'll have no money to give me next time because there will be no jobs left in New York." We worked out a more reasonable deal in return for a three-year contract.

It was not domestic factors alone that put the union in that kind of bind. There was the even worse pinch created by the zoom of sweatshop imports, first from Japan and then from Hong Kong, Taiwan, the Philippines and other low-wage areas. In the decade before my retirement, imports increased by more than 500 percent in dollar volume, while exports of American garments showed almost no gain. On a visit to Hong Kong shortly before the 1965 convention, I went through efficient garment factories where workers put in a 70-hour week for total earnings of only $7. Our hourly rates were twenty times as high as theirs. In fact, if fringe benefits were taken into account, the difference would more likely be thirty to one.

The place where our ingenuity was most severely tested was in devising methods for assuring the highest possible degree of job security to workers in so volatile an industry. When the employers were sitting on a volcano, how could we keep the worker's job from being blown out from under her? From one convention to another we would lose one fifth of the firms in some branches of the industry. Manufacturers would go out of business altogether or reorganize under two or three names in a single season. That gave us two special kinds of problems that did not exist in the trustified industries, where workers didn't have to be afraid that their boss would fade away overnight—and their job with him. The first need was to keep jobs from disappearing; the other was to build up centralized responsibility for severance pay, health and hospital insurance and especially retirement income in the many cases where workers were left stranded without a pay check.

I look back with special pride on what we did to face these challenges. We pioneered by making our employers accept the idea that protecting the workers against the hazards of industrial life was a legitimate charge that producers had to pay as part of the cost of doing business. Even before steel, autos and the other mammoth industries reluctantly agreed to finance a comprehensive program of social security under the union label, we had convinced our manufacturers that they had to pick up the bill for welfare benefits to cushion the insecurities that were a special mark of our industry and a common affliction of workers in all industries. By the time I left office, assets in the funds covering such forms of protection as pensions for our members, severance pay and hospital, disability and medical benefits were approaching the half-billion-dollar level. Annual contributions, all from employers, exceeded one hundred million dollars.

From the start we realized that none of these funds would mean much if it rested on the solvency of a single employer. So we put all the money from all employers in each branch of the industry in each market into a pooled fund. That guaranteed that there would be no loss of protection for workers when they moved from one shop to another. It also kept their protection intact if their particular employer went out of business. But even that degree of pooling was too little, because it meant sealing the worker into a watertight compartment limited to a particular branch of the industry in a particular market. If a New York dressmaker switched into sportswear, even in New York, or if she moved to Los Angeles and went into a dress shop there, she lost the pension equity that she had built up in her original job. To correct that injustice, we carried through, in December 1964, what had always been my dream: a merger of forty-one separate retirement funds into a single national fund.

In its first year of operation this fund paid out twenty-four million dollars in benefits to 37,000 retired workers. For the first time workers could move anywhere within the unionized industry without having to sacrifice the protection they had built up in earlier years. The amalgamation was far from a simple matter. Employer contributions were not uniform in the various branches of the industry. The age composition of the union membership differed markedly in each branch. So did the turnover. But we had already licked that kind of complexity in 1960, when we set up a national fund financed by the employers to provide lump-sum payments, plus weekly unemployment benefits, to workers made jobless by the closing of the companies they worked for. We had had since 1937 a death-benefit fund, which gave a worker's family up to a thousand dollars when the worker died. Now we had a death-benefit fund for the worker's job as well.

Few men have contributed more to solidifying the pattern of peaceful relations in our once hectic industry than did Harry Uviller, who served for many years as impartial chairman of the New York dress industry. He was a man of great intensity, very serious, a fantastic worker, thin as straw, so much so that he looked like a walking corpse, but strong and always resourceful.

We first met in 1919, when he was general manager of the American Cloak and Suit Manufacturers Association and I was a cutter working for a contractor who belonged to that group. Under the contract, disputes that could not be settled inside a shop could be appealed for joint consideration by the head of the association and the manager of the union's joint board. If they disagreed, the case went to arbitration. My employer had filed a complaint that he gave me cutting tickets that included large sizes but I only made the smaller sizes. The size range in those days ran from 14 to 48, but I cut only up to size 40 and left unfilled the orders for sizes 42 to 48. It is true that in an order for several hundred coats not more than two dozen at the outside would be for the bigger sizes. Nevertheless, when the contractor made his deliveries, the jobber would dock him for failing to send everything he had asked for. The contractor said he had repeatedly told me that I had to follow the ticket but I kept refusing to cut above size 40. The result was that he fired me.

My answer to Uviller at the hearing was that every day while I was at the cutting table the contractor would tell me how the jobber kept squeezing down his prices to such a point that my employer didn't see how he could stay in business. Since all I heard was how much money my boss was losing, I felt I had to try to help him survive. My skill as a cutter was in the precision with which I could figure out a "lay" that would get the most garments out of a certain number of yards of cloth. It was something I had learned in my father's shop as a baker many years before. There I made the older bakers marvel by figuring out how to get more loaves of bread in the oven at one time than anyone else and still getting them all out unburned. Call it a jigsaw-puzzle knack, if you like, but it was most useful for a cutter.

So when my employer told me of his troubles, I decided I could get two garments of a smaller size out of the yardage that would be needed for one of the extra-large sizes. It wasn't that I had anything against putting tents around fat ladies. It was just that, if I did it my way, my contractor could get paid for forty or fifty coats in place of the couple of dozen he was supposed to make in the jumbo sizes. When I gave that explanation to Uviller, the contractor came back: "Yes, but I need at least a few of the larger garments so the jobber doesn't feel I am putting him on the spot with store owners who need the full range of sizes for their customers."

At that I began looking around the walls of Uviller's office, where the hearing was being held. He asked what I was looking for. "Well," I answered, "in my factory there are 'No Smoking' signs. I don't see any here." He looked at me as if I had lost my mind. "What's that got to do with the matter we're here about?" he inquired.

"Well, in the hallways of the building where our factory is, the signs say, 'No Smoking Permitted,' but the people do smoke. Inside the factory I see signs, 'Positively No Smoking,' and nobody smokes. I wish to say here and now that if my employer will write out the cutting ticket, 'Positively I want the large sizes,' I will cut the large sizes. But if he just writes down large sizes along with all the others, I will use my discretion and continue to help him get more garments out of the lay." My employer was delighted. "Dave, if you mean that, I will accept happily. I never wanted to discharge you in the first place." Then he turned to Uviller: "I didn't want to lose Dubinsky as a cutter, but I do want him to pay attention and do what I ask."

After I became manager of the Cutters Union, Local 10,

my relationship with Uviller ripened. In his capacity as head of the contractors' association, we used to have many intimate chats outside the framework of the regular grievance structure or of contract negotiations. One day I called Uviller at the association offices and said I had to see him on a very important matter. When we met I told him I had been very upset when I reviewed the wage reports for the industry. They showed that the cutters, the most skilled craft in the industry, were averaging only a dollar or two more than the weekly minimum fixed in the contract. I said I didn't feel it was fair or proper for them to be hugging the minimum so closely when sewing-machine operators and others paid on a piece-rate basis were averaging well above the minimum. It is true that cutters were paid on a weekly basis, with no special recognition for how fast they worked, where the rest of the workers were on an hourly rate geared to how much they actually produced. Still it seemed nonsensical to me that cutters who were fast and productive got little or nothing in increases above the minimum.

I might have felt less strongly on this point if I had not remembered my own experience as a cutter. I was often called on to work Saturdays when rush jobs were brought in. "If it's a rush job, give it to Dubinsky. He's a fast worker," was my employer's motto. Even without overtime for working on Saturdays, I used to earn seventy dollars a week when the contract minimum was fifty dollars. It was plain to me that fast workers were no longer getting any kind of special reward.

Uviller agreed that it could be a source of irritation to cutters, especially those who really made an effort for their employers, but he said the right time to correct the situation would be at the next contract negotiations. I insisted that would be too late, that there was too much discontent among the cutters. My idea was that Uviller should urge the members of his association to raise the average wage by five dollars a week. The cutter with minimum skill and productivity could stay at the minimum, which was then forty-five dollars a week, but the cutter who did a better-than-average job would get more money. Uviller doubted that anything could be done in the middle of a contract. My reply to him was: "Well, you think it over, and in the meantime I'll see what I can do by way of persuasion."

In the next day or two the cutters failed to report in several of the biggest shops, and complaints were filed by the employers with the impartial chairman. He took the matter up with Uviller and the executive board of the contractors' association, using the same argument I had—that unquestionably an adjustment for paying wages higher than the minimum to good cutters would have to be included in the next agreement, and it would be a good thing for harmony and high productivity if they granted the five dollars right away. Once the contractors said yes, I went to the Protective Association of Coat and Suit Manufacturers, representing the large inside shops. They did not wait for me to turn on the persuasion. Within twenty-four hours they agreed to raise the average wage for cutters five dollars above the contract floor.

In the middle 1920s there was opposition within the union to the introduction of a new pressing machine that could cut the amount of labor needed by as much as 50 percent. The union's first position was that the new machine would be allowed only in shops that had at least six or eight pressers. The employers, through Uviller, objected that this was unfair to small shops. It appeared to me, as a member of the union committee appointed by the General Executive Board to negotiate with the industry on the question, that two problems had to be met. The first was to get more money for the pressers who worked on the new machines. They were paid on a weekly basis, like cutters, so the boss was getting many more pressed garments from each man than he expected when the agreement was signed. The second problem was to build up a fund to take care of pressers who weren't needed because the machine was so efficient. This was long before Social Security was enacted by Congress. There was no government unemployment insurance, much less any supplemental benefit funds of the type now common in many industries. So setting up a fund was a very important consideration for us.

Uviller and I talked the matter over confidentially, and out of our discussions came what I believe was the first program in any industry to tax a machine to take care of the workers it displaced. Under the plan every employer who installed one of the new machines would have to pay ten dollars a week into an unemployment fund that provided payments for pressers who applied to the union for work but could not get it. As for the pressers who did work, they got ten dollars a week extra as their share of the increased production the employer was getting by substituting the machine for hand pressing. In the next contract the pressers went off weekly wages and began getting paid on a piecework basis. That way the boss got an even better return on his investment in efficiency and our people got more money if they worked harder.

The first position the employers took in the negotiations was that there ought to be two piece rates—a lower one for pressers on the new machine than for those working by hand. The union insisted that it could not have two rates for pressers, and the employers did not fight too hard on that issue. But they took the view that a single piece rate would give the machine pressers such a big advantage in earnings over the hand pressers that they ought to assume responsibility for paying the ten-dollar tax instead of making the employer pay it. When Uviller said the manufacturers would not sign an agreement without having the tax shifted, I persuaded the union committee to put the question in arbitration before George W. Alger, a distinguished lawyer, who was then the impartial chairman. He agreed with the industry that the tax should come out of the joint payroll of all the pressers and not be paid by the employer. Alger's argument was that because the piece rate was the same for everybody the employer no longer was receiving the benefit of the extra production from the machine. That argument made no sense to me—then or now.

I was never one to conceal my feelings. As soon as the award was announced, I rushed over to Uviller and screamed, "You'll pay for this." Then I stormed out of the hearing room, with Uviller right behind me. He knew that Alger kept a bottle of whiskey in a desk drawer in his office next door. The first thing Uviller did was to pull out the bottle, but before he could raise it to his lips I grabbed it away from him. Alger walked in just at that moment. "I'm delighted to see that you are friends again," he said.

"Yes," I replied, "we're drinking to the fact that not only will there be a proper unemployment fund for pressers but there will be an enlightened welfare fund to meet all the needs of the workers in this industry. I'll see to that. Uviller won this round, but after this the employers will do all the paying."

It took quite a few years before that boast became a fact, but I never doubted that we'd do it. And I don't think Uviller doubted it either.

He was a marvelous man, with extremely sound judgment, a vast knowledge of the industry and, above all, the ability to see both sides of every issue. In 1936, when we needed a new impartial chairman for the dress industry, the biggest of all our branches, I went to Uviller for the post, even though his experience up to then had been as chief representative of the employers in the coat-and-suit trade. It was a tribute to his fairness, because the job of impartial chairman was a most powerful one. His decisions had the force of law, and they often covered matters that went beyond the four corners of the contract. Brandeis had been our first impartial chairman, from 1910 until his appointment to the Supreme Court in 1916. Most of the other occupants of the post in both cloak and dress industries had been men of distinction—people like Newton D. Baker, who was Secretary of War in Woodrow Wilson's Cabinet, and Raymond V. Ingersoll, an outstanding Fusion reformer in the La Guardia period. Later on in the cloak industry we had Harry L. Hopkins, former Mayor James J. Walker, Arthur J. Goldberg, fresh from his service as United Nations ambassador, and David A. Morse, winner of the Nobel Peace Prize at the International Labor Organization. But, impressive as were all of these impartial chairmen, none compared in contribution to Uviller.

Under his chairmanship the tempestuous dress industry in New York went from 1936 to 1958 without a marketwide strike. And in that period the various welfare and pension funds were instituted, all financed by the employers. Uviller's duties included presiding over these funds, which meant he had to decide disputes over who was eligible. It was always our purpose to have the rules applied liberally, and frankly that was the way they were applied. Still there would always be heartbreaking cases of people who had left the industry for one reason or another at various times and then found they didn't have enough service to their credit when it came time to retire. One rule, for instance, was that workers needed at least ten years of consecutive service. They also needed a minimum of twenty years of total service. If they had one without the other, they were out of luck.

Usually, people who were caught in that kind of technical web would write to me as international president, or telephone, or come to the office to plead for my help. In a strict sense, of course, I was supposed to stay out of things. None of the agreements gave me any unilateral right to suspend the rules of funds that were under joint labor-management trusteeship. But my eyes would always fill with tears when I read or listened to the stories of these poor workers deprived of protection in their old age because of some fine print in the pension regulations. So I would tell them to request a hearing from Uviller and I made myself a one-man nuisance squad to lobby in their behalf. Finally, Uviller got so sick and tired of my butting into cases with pleas for special consideration that he called me and said: "Dubinsky, I always knew that you were interested in the general labor movement and so you saw the forest. But I never expected that you would also see each and every individual tree. The trouble with you is that the members have such easy access to you and you feel so much sympathy for every separate case that you try to establish an equity position for each person who comes to you. Please be interested in the forest, and don't be so much interested in the individual trees." That was advice I never could take.

Then, in 1958, after nearly a quarter century of strikeless relations, 80,000 dressmakers struck. There were a lot of issues, all important, but the one that caused the strike was not specifically on the table at all. It was an intangible without which nothing in the contract mattered. We were striking because the foundation of stability on which contract enforcement rested was crumbling, and there would be no value to any agreement we made on money or other issues unless we rebuilt that foundation.

It was not a situation that we could blame entirely on the employers. It was just as much our fault, maybe more, and a strike seemed the only way to make everybody on each side face the facts before the whole structure of mutually beneficial relationships collapsed. What had brought the matter to a head was our discovery in the middle of the pre-strike negotiation that the executive directors of the associations representing the dress manufacturers had lost their influence with their members. They admitted that they did not dare go to the employers with proposals concerning things that the I.L.G. considered absolutely essential for a settlement, even though the association leaders recognized that these proposals were justified. The reluctant employers had something on their side, not because our demands were unreasonable, but because the union had slipped quite a bit in its responsibility to be an effective stabilizing force. The manufacturers inside the city complained that they were being killed by out-of-town competition from areas near New York. This was an old story, but it had got worse, and for reasons that did the union no credit. The fact was that nearly as much of a problem came from shops operating with union contracts as it did from racket-protected non-union shops.

Pennsylvania, where the union's membership had grown substantially, was in many respects providing tougher competition for the shops employing our members in New York than were the runaway manufacturers in the South. After all, Pennsylvania is closer, and trucking garments into the New York market is cheaper. Our union officials out of town had tended to become empire builders. They worried more about getting additional members than they did about getting decent standards. They had raised wages, but not as much as was needed. When I made a survey I learned that the pay scale in northeast Pennsylvania was only two cents an hour above Dallas, Texas, where everything was non-union. So I rang the firebell and told our people that such a situation could not be tolerated any longer. What we had to do was to get much better-balanced protection for everybody. Pennsylvania and the other out-of-town districts would still get authority to negotiate a lower wage than New York—a differential that was within reason—but it could not be so great that it would hurt union members elsewhere by putting their bosses out of business.

Under the new policy the out-of-town workers would get a break in that their standards would be improved. At the same time the workers in New York, where more than half of our members still are, would not be undercut by unfair competition from within the union. The interesting thing is that, once we put that philosophy into effect, it did not stop Pennsylvania from growing. The truth is that New York has been finding it harder and harder for a long time to get new workers. The wages are not high by comparison with those in most other industries, and it is still seasonal work. Employment in the garment shops is affected by style changes and by every slump in the economy; jobs are up and down—usually down, it seems to most workers in the industry. On top of that, young people want to be white-collar workers. Our own members, blacks and Puerto Ricans as well as Jews and Italians, want their children to go into other fields—lawyers, doctors, accountants, teachers, secretaries, anything but working at a sewing machine or a pressing machine or a cutting table. Designers maybe, but that's about the extent of it.

But that gets us away from the 1958 strike. The old contract expired in February, when I was attending the midwinter meeting of the A.F.L–C.I.O. Executive Council in Miami Beach. A call came from Julius Hochman, manager of the Dress Joint Board: "We can't get anything from the executive directors, not even an answer. The agreement is running out and we'll have to call a strike. I want you to come to New York. Maybe you can make them move." My first question was, "What's going on in the trade? Is there work?" Hochman's answer was that nobody was working in most shops. If he says, "No trade," what's the sense of my coming? We'll strike and no one will know we're gone. "Let's wait till there's work in the trade," I advised. "Then I'll come." About a week later Hochman called again. "It's getting busy," he reported. "All right," I promised, "now I'll come and arrange a conference."

Before the first meeting in New York I looked over the demands Hochman had submitted. One demand that was cardinal for our union was not there. That was the union label. Our conventions had called over and over for a union label in every garment and I told Hochman this was the year we had to get it. I felt it would help our manufacturers as well as our members if we built up genuine consumer support for the I.L.G.W.U. label. What's more, I had a plan for how we could do it in an effective way. So I told Hochman, "You invited me to the conference. Now there must be an additional demand—the union label." To prepare the ground, I met in advance of the first session with Louis Rubin, head of the Popular-Priced Dress Group, who was the key man on the industry side of the bargaining table. My private talks with him convinced me that we would have to have a strike. We would get nowhere otherwise. Suddenly our union, which had gone since the first flush of the New Deal without a strike, would have to be a striking union again.

But I didn't want a strike that would last till the needles and the cutting knives rusted away. Even before we posted the first pickets, I took steps to make sure that the strike would end as quickly as possible. I went to Mayor Wagner and explained that the main point of the strike was to make the New York industry more secure against out-of-town competition. I told him I believed the walkout would be a short one if the Mayor would give it plenty of oomph at the start by showing how important dress manufacture was to the New York economy and building up public clamor to get the strike over in a hurry. The jack to give that necessary lift, I suggested, was for Wagner to appoint a special mediation panel consisting of former Governor Herbert H. Lehman and Uviller. Lehman, who was then serving in the United States Senate, had a history of concern for our industry. Uviller would complement Lehman's prestige by bringing to the panel the necessary expert knowledge of the competitive situation, plus great resourcefulness as a peacemaker. The Mayor welcomed the suggestion and the panel was named.

As soon as we began negotiating, the employers objected to the union label, but I bribed them. I promised them that the union would spend a million dollars a year to promote the label. All of that money would be a contribution to the prosperity of the employers by encouraging women to buy union-made dresses containing the label. The only cost to the manufacturers would be the cost of the label, but the union would tax its own members to pay for the promotion. My idea was that we would go to the next convention and explain that we had carried out the mandate to insist on the label, then ask the delegates to assess everybody a quarter each month to pay for the advertising. With 400,000 members, that authorization not only would give us the million dollars I had guaranteed the employers that the union would spend, but would even give us a little profit. And we did get it through, first by getting the employers to agree to the label and second by getting the next convention to approve the tax. The ads for the label were valuable insights into union history of benefit to all labor as well as to our own members and manufacturers. Up to the time of our break-through, no union ever established a label that aroused genuine consumer enthusiasm and support.

So far as the purely industrial issues were concerned, the employers did not hesitate long in giving the union what it was after, once we had satisfied them that we were as determined as they were to see the last of unfair competition between shops operating with union contracts inside and outside the city. George Meany claimed that I had called it only to advertise that we had gone a quarter century without a strike.

SIX

Mammon's Mobsters

RACKETEERING IS THE CANCER that almost destroyed the American trade-union movement. When you were selling labor, there was always the temptation to sell your soul, and there were plenty of people ready to buy, especially in an industry like ours, where a few pennies' difference in the labor cost of a garment may represent the difference between a successful business and bankruptcy. With thousands of small employers and with trucking a vital chain between jobber and contractor, particularly to out-of-town shops, we were vulnerable to the bloodsucking activities of hoodlums eager to cash in on the chaos in the trade. These harpies made themselves merchants of illegal protection, controllers of a faucet that could turn crime on or off. And they tried always to infiltrate the union itself, so that it could become an instrument of robbery and special privilege rather than the one stable force in the industry fighting for decency and enforcement of contract standards.

Our tradition that a union was a cause, not a business, kept us from falling prey to the leeches. But even at the very beginning, when the employers had brought in strong-arm men to try to kill the establishment of the union, our own record was sullied by the corrupt payoffs we made to the police to match the payoffs by the employers. Then, when the Communists were playing their destructive brand of power politics, the racketeers had a field day working for the leftists and the employers. Still, we always found a strong shield in our tradition. Corruption could never become a way of life for us. I remember in the 1920s, when Morris Sigman was president, a business agent gave him an unitemized bill for $1,200 to cover strike expenses.

"Can't you make it cheaper?" Sigman asked.

"All right, let's make it a thousand," said the business agent.

"Oh, come on, make it cheaper."

"Eight hundred," came the reply.

With that, Sigman picked up a heavy metal inkstand on his desk and brought it down on the man's head so hard that he required five stitches. "You lousy son of a bitch," Sigman shouted, "how can you afford to lose $400 out of your own pocket?"

I was in Sigman's office once just before Christmas when a deliveryman arrived with a case of wine that had been sent to him by Jacob Sperber, the largest manufacturer in the cloak industry. At that time the cost would probably have been fifteen or twenty dollars for the whole case. But without hesitation Sigman ordered the wine returned. I objected. "Sigman, I think you're making a mistake," I said. "This is not graft. You can't corrupt the president of the I.L.G. with fifteen dollars. He's the outstanding employer. I think it will be an insult."

"If I take this," Sigman answered, "the others will take this and more. I have to set the example." I couldn't argue with that. As a result we have a rule in our union: Because we are a charitable organization, we participate in all legitimate charities, and we make generous gifts running over the years into many millions of dollars; but no union officer may collect from an employer for charity, no matter how worthy the cause or how tight the accounting procedure. And we have a rule in the constitution that forbids taking any gifts. At a meeting of the staff I interpreted this as meaning that the maximum you could take for Christmas was either a box of cigars or a bottle of whiskey. This would not be considered graft. Anything beyond that is graft. And with this we had a standard.

I don't think anyone can cure graft completely, but we made a strong effort to. I am proud of what we did. It was a clean union, even if some of those who listened to me when I made the rule later on had to be forced out. I had in my desk all the time the undated resignation of every officer just to protect the union if we had trouble of that kind. In the thirty-four years I was president and the two years before that as secretary-treasurer, a total of ninety-three people had to be dismissed from office for taking money from employers. When you consider that thousands of people were on our staff, perhaps that is not a large number; but these were people who came to office after years of dedication, not believing they could ever take graft. But they did, and for that they had to go.

One was an outstanding revolutionary in our early days, a low-salaried man. And when five thousand dollars was put into his hands, it was like five million to him. He had a taste of it, he wanted more, and I called him in and began asking him questions. When was he there? How did he settle the prices? What happened? Then I said, "You took money from the employer." You should have seen the way he laughed, his eyes down and his nose on the side. And I said, "You'll have to resign." So he said, "As of when?" I said, "As of right now. Go ahead and sign this."

But after he resigned some of his friends told him, "You were a goddamn fool. Why didn't you ask for a committee, for a trial?" Three or four weeks later he came in to ask for a trial. I refused. "Your resignation is in effect," I told him. That man was a leader in the revolutionary movement, an idealist, not the average type of leader. I felt like doing what Sigman had done, splitting his head.

During the 1950 I.L.G. convention the manager of Dress Pressers Local 60 died, and its local executive board met quickly to elect a successor. I knew they favored Jack Spitzer, a business agent, but I was against him because there were already rumors of unsavory friendships and of too-close relations with employers. I wanted another man, an old-timer who had had anarchistic ideas in his young days and who was a dedicated man, with a good reputation. He got only one vote, so Spitzer was elected.

After his election I called him in and said, "You know I was against you, but now that you are elected you have a chance to be a credit to yourself and to this organization. You are young; you have ability; you could go far in this union, provided you are clean and stay away from unhealthy influences." He shook my hand and promised I would have reason to be proud of him. Some time later I learned that he had been subpoenaed to appear before a grand jury by District Attorney Frank S. Hogan. Emil Schlesinger, the son of my predecessor as president, who had become an outstanding lawyer for the union, asked Spitzer if he had been involved in any discreditable activities. Spitzer insisted that he had done nothing to be ashamed of, so Schlesinger advised him to go before the grand jury, waive immunity and clear his name by answering all questions forthrightly. Spitzer said that was just what he wanted to do, but first he'd like a conference with the Assistant D.A. to see what their line of questioning was going to be. One of the questions that came out in that conference was whether he had accepted a twenty-five-hundred-dollar fur stole as a gift from a certain employer. Spitzer became flustered and ducked the question. When he came out, Schlesinger told him, "Look, you'd better get yourself another lawyer." And he did. He got himself a lawyer who had represented all the underworld characters for many years.

The case never came to trial, not because there was any doubt of the facts, but because all the incriminating evidence came from a wiretap that could not be introduced in evidence under a sudden change in Supreme Court rulings. However, we did not wait to find out whether the D.A. would or would not prosecute. As soon as I heard of the subpoena, I called in Spitzer and told him to take a leave of absence until the whole matter was cleared up. I reminded him that I had an undated resignation from him and I could expel him on the spot. I still preferred to give him every chance to clear himself. I spent hours with him impressing him with the need to answer all questions about gifts from employers, and he always had the same answer: "I'm ready to do it; my lawyer won't let me." And I said, "You're the officer of the union, not your lawyer. Your responsibility is to the union and yourself, not to the lawyer." He was unswayed. When it became plain that he would not give us the facts, I called the General Executive Board into special meeting and his resignation was enforced.

Our main problems, however, were not with internal renegades; they were with crooks from outside who wanted to take over our union and our industry. In the early years we had to contend with professional strikebreaking goons like "Dopey Benny" Fine and "Curley" Holtz. My own direct experience with Curley was mild, a poor preparation for what happened to others who crossed him. When I was manager of the Cutters Union, we were extremely strict about enforcing the rules against illegal hours; that was a key to abolishing the sweatshop. We had one case of a third offender, and the executive board imposed a one-hundred-dollar fine. Not long after, as I was about to enter a night meeting, I found Curley waiting outside. It was the first time we had ever met.

"Mr. Dubinsky?"

"Yes."

"You fined so-and-so a hundred dollars?"

"Yes, I remember. We did it a couple of weeks ago."

"I want you to lift that fine."

I decided to play dumb. "How can I do it?" I asked. "The executive board has decided. If I should go and tell them I'm reversing their decision, they'd suspect monkey business and I'd have to quit. Do you want me to lose my job?"

"I don't want you to lose your job, but I want you to do me a favor."

Again I was the artless dummy. "A favor I could do you if you need a few dollars," I volunteered. "That I could let you have. But I can't rescind the board's decision."

He went away and there was no rough stuff, no threats, no more pressure. But Sasha Zimmerman had a very different get-acquainted session with Curley in the early period of the fight with the Communists. In November 1925, just before Zimmerman became manager of the dress division of the New York Joint Board for the left-wing faction, Curley came to his office. He announced himself, but his name meant nothing to Zimmerman. Curley explained he was protecting a shop against which the union was striking, the Roth Costume Company at 498 Seventh Avenue, and he wanted Zimmerman to call off the pickets for two or three days. "You'll get fifteen thousand dollars from the firm," Curley said. "You'll get paid off, then you can resume the strike if you want to." Of course, Zimmerman refused. He felt it was arrogance on Curley's part even to come up with such a proposition. Also he knew that once he started anything like that he would be a captive of the underworld.

Curley showed no anger and went away without a word. A few days later, however, Zimmerman left his office at about 6:30 P.M. with his wife, Rose. They were walking along Twenty-fifth Street and stopped for a moment to look in a store window. As they turned around, three men appeared from nowhere and started beating up Zimmerman. His wife began screaming but that didn't discourage them. He had an overcoat over his arm, which he used to cover his face, but he was so beaten that he was laid up for weeks. The strike was not called off until the firm settled with the union. Later on, however, the gangsters became open allies of the Communists, with Arnold Rothstein acting as supreme commander of the expeditionary forces representing the underworld.

The systematic penetration of the industry by big-time mobsters came in the early 1930s, with the emergence of organized crime as the ugly child of the Volstead Act. Not long after I became president, one of our business agents had his face cut up by hoodlums from a protected shop. One eye was blinded and he was so scared that he quit the union and opened a candy store. I went to the District Attorney, Thomas C. T. Crain, to complain about the gangster reign of terror. Almost as soon as I got back to my own office on West Sixteenth Street, not more than fifteen minutes away, I got a telephone call. "You went to the D.A.," said a voice. "He can't help you." He repeated some of the information I had given in confidence to the District Attorney. Under Tammany rule, the underworld's connections with the D.A.'s office were extraordinary. They had a fix in all over.

One of their go-betweens was a promoter who always carried around a photograph of himself with President Roosevelt. He would make it a practice to drift into the offices of the Dress Joint Board when Julius Hochman was manager "just to *schmooze*," but always he would call one manufacturer or another from Hochman's outer office. The conversation would always start, "I'm in Julius's office, Julius Hochman's office." That was his way of establishing that he had an "in" at union headquarters and could perform God knows what miracles for people who bought his services. One day that man took a suitcase from his home and disappeared. The police searched for him for years, but no trace of him was ever discovered. Evidently he was one of those underworld types who didn't share properly with the boys.

Our biggest problem came after World War II, when organized crime was moving more and more openly into ownership of so-called legitimate business. We thought we had seen overwhelming abuse of power in the prewar period, when Lepke and Gurrah were operating in partnership with Murder, Inc. But all that became petty larceny with the entry of such figures as "Three Finger" Brown and Johnny Dio as front men for the Mafia. Whenever we conducted an organizing drive to get at these new elements in the industry, the goons would come out in force and beat up our pickets. In 1947, after one of our people had his jaw broken and others had been mauled outside one racket-owned shop, Zimmerman went with his counsel, Emil Schlesinger, to see Mayor O'Dwyer. When the union complained that the police were not enforcing the law against the hoodlums, O'Dwyer recalled how he had played a major role in breaking up Murder, Inc. "Under my administration," he promised, "gangsterism will not be tolerated." The next day the police were out in large numbers, flooding the market. The only trouble was that they arrested all our pickets. They did a better job of stopping our organizing drive than the hoodlums. When that kind of police "assistance" in keeping the peace continued, Zimmerman called on Paul Hall of the Seafarers International Union. He sent out fifty of his white-capped sailors to join our picket line and make sure that no one molested our people. They could not be pushed around as easily as the girls from the sewing machines and for the rest of that season we made a little headway.

When the next season rolled around we decided to do the job on our own without sending out an S.O.S. to the Seafarers. This time the underworld fought back with murder as well as mayhem. William Lurye, one of our most dedicated organizers, was trapped in a phone booth outside a struck building on Seventh Avenue. He was stabbed to death. Mayor O'Dwyer called me to express the city's grief. He asked me to come to City Hall to discuss what the city could do, but I was so furious that I refused to go. I sent Zimmerman instead. You can imagine how he felt at that meeting. He told O'Dwyer: "Mr. Mayor, we came down here time after time to warn you. We told you the kind of scum we were dealing with. We begged you for help in enforcing the law. You sent out the cops and arrested our people. Why do you ask me now how this horrible thing happened? You knew the situation and you didn't do anything. Why not? Who reached you?" Zimmerman asked the same question from a public platform on the streets of the garment center, when we stopped the whole industry and 60,000 persons turned out for a mass funeral of Lurye. The Mayor never answered.

District Attorney Frank S. Hogan and the police were diligent in tracking down Lurye's killer. I am convinced they finally did find him—a partner in an underworld trucking firm—but when he was brought to trial the mob leaned on the key witness against him, who changed his testimony, so that the case collapsed. Today the gangsters play the respectable game. The syndicate is a big element in ownership. If you strike against a jobber, they'll always have a shop somewhere to do scab work. This is an industry, you know, where you can take the bundles to Massachusetts or Virginia or Florida or the Carolinas or Mississippi to be made up. It doesn't make any difference. It's not like a construction project that you can't build somewhere else or a hospital you can't move to the middle of nowhere. Strike against a jobber in New York and he'll take the bundles out. They'll find a shop for him, get the work done and find a trucker to deliver the goods both ways.

Ours is an industry on wheels, so trucking was always the easy point for penetration by organized crime. Our trucking local, Local 102, did not follow the principles and ethics of our union, because its members were teamsters. And they were dealing with trucking employers associated with the underworld. It was, on a smaller scale, the same situation that made the International Brotherhood of Teamsters such a sewer of corruption in the labor movement. That is why, despite all our banging on their heads, the officers of Local 102 could never be as strict in enforcing the rules of our union as we wanted them to be or as we insisted all other locals be. We always had our quarrels with them. We always demanded that they live by the rules, but all we ever got was alibis. Everyone made promises that things would improve, but they didn't. The simple thing would have been to throw them all out and let them wind up in the Teamsters Union, where they belonged in morality as well as function. The reason we had them in our union was that we wanted a control over nonunion work. We had an idea that having our own I.L.G. truckmen who knew where shipments go and where production is made would help us police the industry. It didn't.

But there never was any complacency on our part about that situation. If we could not depend on the truckers, we simply had to fight harder to prevent the chiselers from destroying the legitimate forces in the industry. In the old days we had to slug it out with the strong-arm men on the picket line. Our people would stand in front of the shop with bloody noses and black eyes, refusing to let scabs pass. Now the assailants have widened the battleground. They can operate anywhere, and they can beat up our people anywhere. In the late 1950s we had a strike against a big New York jobber who was connected with the gangsters who had attended the underworld convention at Apalachin, New York. The Dress Joint Board learned that this jobber had several thousand garments farmed out to contracting shops in Virginia and Pennsylvania. Zimmerman was able to stop most of these shops just before he went to Miami Beach to attend an I.L.G. convention. While he was there, he walked out of the Empire Hotel on Collins Avenue and a thug leaped at him from between two parked cars. He banged Zimmerman with a blackjack, but it was a glancing blow. Sasha was able to knock the blackjack from the man's hand as he was bringing it down a second time. While the goon reached down to pick it up, Zimmerman ran back into the hotel lobby. The Miami police didn't catch the thug, but we have no doubt where he came from.

Today you don't see the enemy. First, the National Labor Relations Board offers the scab employer protection with an injunction against secondary boycotts and long-drawn-out legal proceedings. Then, he can take his work and put it on a truck. And the thing that angers me most is these big retailers, all these sanctimonious community leaders who make syrupy speeches about the need for being pure and honest and decent. Let the racketeers give them a nickel less on a garment and they don't give a hang whom they deal with, whether it's the Mafia or any other underworld. The large retailers, chain stores and giant distributors all deal with them; they couldn't exist if the retailers refused to support them. The stores know which manufacturers deal with the underworld, but they don't care, if it makes their profit margins a little fatter.

Every now and then some legitimate manufacturer who falls into the mob's clutches does try to break away, but he has a hell of a time. Liquidation may be his fate—liquidation not of his business but of him personally. However, in at least one important case an employer did succeed in freeing himself from the underworld. One of the largest and most successful firms in our industry operated for years on a non-union basis with gangster protection. The owner paid and paid, until he got tired of paying. Finally he retained A. A. Berle, Jr., as his attorney and he approached us about unionization. It took time to negotiate a contract, and we made a number of concessions because it was important for us to have this company as a union shop. The contract enabled the manufacturer to get the mob off his back, to end his unofficial partnership with them. Gradually his became a truly outstanding firm with hundreds of millions of dollars in volume and millions in profit. The owner told me afterward: "The union saved me. My life had become a hell. Now I don't have to pay any more and, more important, I am my own boss, not their slave."

Because our experience made us conscious of how readily a union could be converted into an instrument for extortion, especially in a fragmented industry, we felt a special responsibility to demand that the labor movement as a whole be vigilant in preventing corruption from thriving in its affiliated units. This was not just a matter of idealism. The good name of all labor was endangered by the extent to which racketeers held power in the teamsters, the building trades and many of the service unions. The integrity of contractual commitments was always a bedrock of labor-management relations. And the foundation was cut out from under all of us every time collusion or crookedness was part of negotiating any contract. We could never sympathize with the view that each union was a law unto itself, immune from disciplinary action by the central federation, no matter how completely it allowed its inner processes to be taken over by men concerned solely with self-profit, betrayers of the interests of the union's members.

Our attitude was totally at odds with the traditional posture of the American Federation of Labor, which had been founded by Samuel Gompers on the concept that each international union had absolute sovereignty over its own internal affairs. Autonomy was so sacred that the worst crooks could wrap themselves into a union charter and use it as a license for industrial piracy. The situation became scandalous in the 1930s, partly because the repeal of Prohibition made so many of the superchiefs of the bootlegging rings turn to organized labor to guarantee full employment and lush profits for their legions in organized crime. Another reason for their swift rise to dominance of important unions was that the forces of industrial unionism withdrew in 1935 to form the C.I.O., leaving the A.F.L. much more open to access by the underworld. I'm not pretending that those of us who joined with John L. Lewis in establishing the C.I.O. were saints, but it was certainly true that corruption never had any important foothold in our unions. It was entrenched in the craft unions, which were left in sole possession of the A.F.L. Leaders like William Green, Matthew Woll and George Meany, though themselves untainted, preferred to look the other way. "Live and let live," was their philosophy. That was just the way hoodlums George Scalise of the Building Service Employees International Union and Willie Bioff of the International Alliance of Theatrical Stage Employees, along with all their fellow graduates of the Capone mob and Murder, Inc., preferred to have it. They wanted no one looking over their shoulder as they shook down employers through sweetheart contracts and victimized the workers they were supposed to protect. Their thievery and thuggery became so brazen that it eventually threw a heavy blanket of filth over the whole A.F.L.

When Lewis's empire building and the machinations of Communist elements caused the I.L.G.W.U. to leave the C.I.O., we refused to move right back into the Federation, principally because we could not stomach the idea of identification—even by association—with these despicable thugs who operated with total abandon under the label of the A.F.L. However, private talks with Green in the year and a half after we decided to remain independent of both the C.I.O. and A.F.L., made me believe there was a chance to move the Federation away from its hands-off position. That position, I told Green, had allowed "individuals who should have no place in the labor movement" to use the shield of autonomy to misrepresent workers and bring discredit on all labor. Green sent to our 1940 convention in New York a letter which conspicuously avoided commitment on whether the Federation would modify this shameful head-in-the-sand policy. But my own talks with Green had left me so optimistic on this point that we decided to reaffiliate anyhow. We announced that the first act of the I.L.G. delegation at the Federation's next annual convention would be to push for adoption of a constitutional change giving the parent organization "summary power" to order the ouster by any affiliated union of officers involved in racketeering or graft. If the union failed to act on its own, the Federation would be authorized to "use its full moral force" to compel the filing of charges and the holding of ouster proceedings.

Our resolution on racketeering had been drawn up at my request by Emil Schlesinger, one of our ablest lawyers. I gave him the assignment on the opening day of the convention, with instructions to bring it back the next morning. So many other obligations crowded in on Schlesinger that he didn't give it another thought till he woke up in his hotel room the next day. He had a pencil but no pad or paper. Finally, he pulled a dozen sheets of tissue off a roll of toilet paper and wrote out the text of the resolution. It was exactly what we wanted. Not a word was changed, and it became the official position of the I.L.G.W.U. for presentation to the Federation.

When I arrived in New Orleans in November for our formal "welcome home" at the A.F.L. convention, the weather was warm, but the convention atmosphere was ice cold. It was plain that, so far as the gangster elements in the Federation were concerned, such things as the onrush of Hitler and Mussolini in Europe and the re-election of F.D.R. for a third term over the opposition of John L. Lewis were inconsequential. The one thing that was important to them was to demolish our resolution on racketeering so completely that no one would ever again have the presumption even to suggest such an encroachment on their right to steal under the banner of unionism. What's more, it was plain that this gangster element was so powerful, thanks to their allies in the building trades and the teamsters, that Green and all the rest of the respectable leaders in the Federation were in panicky retreat before them. We were the villains, not they.

The whole A.F.L. establishment would have been much happier if we had just faded away quietly, taking our resolution with us. Forgotten were all the warm sentiments that Green had expressed when he came to our convention in Carnegie Hall six months earlier, bringing with him our original charter of 1900 signed by Samuel Gompers. "Here is the symbol that binds us for all the years to come," Green had said as we embraced in front of the I.L.G. delegates. The antiracketeering resolution was all it took to rip that bond. The crooks had served private notice that they were in no mood to be answerable to the Federation, any more than they were to the law. Inside the resolutions committee all the sanctimonious front men read us moral lessons about that greatest crime, socialism, which would be advanced if we began trifling with the sacred autonomy of the international unions. But the hoodlums themselves were not satisfied to beat us with words. They wanted blood.

On Thanksgiving Eve, the third day of the convention, I walked out of a frustrating meeting at which we were still butting against a stone wall in trying to convince the resolutions committee that some minimal step toward control had to be taken, if only to show the American people that the A.F.L. was not intimidated by the mob. I walked into the bar to get a nightcap before going to bed, and I spotted my daughter, Jean, sitting with Fred Umhey, the executive secretary of our union, and Abe Raskin, then covering his first important labor story for *The New York Times*.

Almost before I sat down, a big, beefy man whom I didn't know came over from a table in the back of the room. As he started to introduce himself, it was quickly apparent that he was very drunk and also very nasty. He was Joe Fay, a vice-president of the Operating Engineers Union and the kingpin of all the building-trades leaders in New York and New Jersey. His reputation was as bad as his power was great. Not long before the convention he had been suspected of being responsible for the murder of the head of the Sandhogs Union, Norman Redwood, a clean, decent unionist who had been marked for death because he objected to sellout contracts negotiated by Fay and his lieutenants on the Holland Tunnel. No one was ever able to pin the killing on Fay, whose political connections were as strong as his ties to the mob. But it was an open secret that he was exacting tribute on a wholesale scale on every big construction job in the metropolitan area, public or private. Fay symbolized everything we felt the A.F.L. should be able to act against in the interest of labor's good name.

Without waiting for an invitation, he pushed himself into a chair and began denouncing me for my demand that the Federation have the power to crack down on crooked union officials where their own unions were too afraid or too completely racket-controlled to move on their own. Every minute or two he would repeat the same sentence: "How do you have the nerve to come here and offer such a dirty, lousy, sonuvabitch resolution?" It got to be a kind of theme song. In between he rambled on about Lepke and Gurrah and other hoodlums in the garment industry and about what noble organizations the building trades were and about how the American system was built on freedom, and on and on. I hoped I could discourage him by politeness instead of argument. Whenever he stopped for a second, I would say, "Mr. Fay, you are entitled to your position and I am entitled to mine," hoping that would end it. It didn't. His language got more and more obscene until finally Umhey reminded him that we had a young lady at the table who was not used to such profanity. Jean, who had been listening with great interest, hadn't realized until then that she should be insulted.

Fay reacted with outrage at the suggestion that he might be something less than a perfect gentleman. He jumped to his feet in fury, and we all jumped up with him. Unfortunately, the tables in the bar were all crowded so close together that the sudden pushing back of our chairs upset glasses all around us and there was general yelling and confusion. Fay flailed around with his fists, but he was too drunk to know where he was hitting. One wild blow flattened my cigar against my face but that was the only damage. Within a few seconds the men Fay had been sitting with before we came in formed a flying wedge and rushed across the bar to pull him back to his old seat. That set more glasses and tables flying until they got him quieted down by putting another drink in front of him. We sat down at our table, finished our drinks and paid our check, then the four of us went out into the marble corridor leading to the elegant Roosevelt lobby and started toward the elevators.

Suddenly, we heard behind us a noise like elephants crashing through a jungle. We looked around and saw two men stumbling down the hall, heads lowered and arms swinging, with angry bellows coming from their throats. One was Fay and the other was Tom Foley, head of one of his New York locals, who had been his drinking companion on a day-and-night binge since they both got to New Orleans more than a week earlier. We decided to stand and take their charge. The next thing I knew Umhey and Foley were rolling around the tile floor, first one on top and then the other. Raskin and Fay were waltzing around the lobby, each trying to get a hammerlock on the other until it occurred to Raskin that he was supposed to be there covering the story, not making it, and he rushed off to the Western Union telegraph office in the lobby (those were the days when there was still competition between Western Union and Postal Telegraph and it was possible to send messages from hotel lobbies even at midnight). That ended the fight, but I knew enough about Fay's reputation to feel that I had better arrange for a detective to keep guard over the Dubinsky suite that night. About 3 A.M. I got a call from Fay. He had shifted his headquarters to an all-night bar across the street, and he wanted me to come over for some more talk. I hung up.

The next day was Thanksgiving, but not for Fay. Raskin's story had created a sensation, even though it had come in so late that it had missed most of the Thursday edition and it was so short that most of the detail had to wait for the next day's paper. There was still enough there to make everybody at the convention recognize that the antiracketeering resolution was not going to be as easy to smother as they had originally believed. Fay's mistake in physically attacking me had dramatized the corruption issue in a way that made it impossible to bury under the old autonomy shroud. Even at that, the first impulse of the Federation's old guard was to try to brazen it out. When Bill Green came down to breakfast in the morning, the reporters were waiting in the lobby to question him about the fight, but he scuttled away from them like a scared rabbit. Inside the hotel restaurant Mrs. Dubinsky and Jean were sitting at a table after a sleepless night, but Green was careful not to see them. He walked right past them without even a "Good morning," much less a word of concern.

When he finished breakfast and couldn't escape the press any more, Green tried to pass off the whole incident as "a personal matter"—something that would have no effect on the work of the convention. Fay had his own version to give to the press when Raskin and another reporter knocked on his door in midafternoon and found him with a mouse under his eye. He insisted that he had merely been telling me as "an old friend" that I had made a terrible mistake in ever taking the I.L.G. into the C.I.O. That made me so sore, according to him, that I had begun punching. He didn't even realize while he was making up that fairy tale that Raskin had been sitting at the table from beginning to end of the conversation.

From the standpoint of the A.F.L. hierarchy, the brawl was doubly embarrassing because it came just at a time when they felt the tide was beginning to run strongly in their favor in their war with the C.I.O. The Communists, who exercised so much power inside the C.I.O., were in particularly bad odor because of the Stalin-Hitler pact. From a trade-union viewpoint, their refusal to denounce that cynical deal branded them as Moscow stooges much more clearly than anything that had gone before. John L. Lewis had got himself out on a long limb with his endorsement of Wendell Willkie and his call on all workers to line up with Lewis in denying F.D.R. a third term. In the election only three weeks before the convention, union members—C.I.O. and A.F.L. alike—had overwhelmingly rejected Lewis's advice and strung along with the father of the New Deal.

In Atlantic City, where the C.I.O. was holding its annual convention at the same time the A.F.L. was meeting in New Orleans, Lewis had to swallow the bitter pill of making good his pre-election promise to resign as C.I.O. president if Roosevelt won. The Communists begged him not to do it, but he knew he had to. There was no grace, however, in the way he stepped down. He made a sneering speech in which he denounced "the Dubinskys, the Zaritskys and the Hillmans" as the agents of disruption and division in progressive labor—a vulgar relapse into the crude anti-Semitism of his early days. It was as unfair to Sidney Hillman of the Amalgamated and Max Zaritsky of the United Hatters as it was to me—so unfair that it boomeranged against Lewis and in the process hurt the C.I.O. as well.

Against the background of C.I.O. disruption it was extremely galling to the A.F.L. to have its hour of gloating spoiled by the reminder of how powerful racketeers were in the Federation and how powerless it was to discipline them. To make matters worse, Hillman and some of the other C.I.O. leaders twisted the knife by sending personal telegrams to me from Atlantic City expressing sympathy about the Fay attack. They took pains to add that it was an outrage that goons could operate so shamelessly at a labor convention. All this while Green, Matt Woll and George Meany were busy looking the other way and pretending they did not see me whenever we passed in public. None of the Federation big shots wanted to appear to be taking sides against Fay. To all of them, it was what Green had said, "a personal matter," nothing at all to do with the work of the convention.

Well, of course, they couldn't get away with that. In the next days a flood of editorial criticism descended on the Federation from every corner of the country. The resolutions committee decided that it couldn't just bury our proposal in the old "autonomy" casket. Under the lash of national attention, a compromise version was worked out and ratified by the full convention. I have to admit it was a pitifully watered-down version of what we wanted, but at least it got away from the earlier official position of the A.F.L. Executive Council. The resolution suggested that every international adopt rules or constitutional amendments empowering it to take necessary action against officers or members who had been found guilty of betraying their union trust or of using their union position for illegal personal gain. That represented no great advance, but the next provision did: "Whenever the Executive Council has valid reason to believe that a trade-union official is guilty of any such offense, and the national or international union in question seem-

ingly evades its responsibility, the Executive Council shal
be authorized to apply all its influence to secure such actior
as will correct the situation."

We had to be satisfied with that, and it quickly became
plain that the Federation had no intention of making anything at all of this new grant of power. In fact, the same
convention re-elected George E. Browne of the International
Alliance of Theatrical Stage Employees, a stand-in for the
Capone mob, as twelfth vice-president. Our delegation refused to vote for him, and he was later sent to jail for extortion. The same fate eventually also befell Fay, but he remained boss of the New York–New Jersey building trades
even while he was in prison. In fact, so many deals were
arranged from his cell that Governor Thomas E. Dewey
finally transferred him to the most remote jail he could find.

For all practical purposes, our resolution on racketeering
remained a dead letter until 1952, when the New York State
Crime Commission, headed by former Judge Joseph M.
Proskauer, conducted a series of hearings which made it
plain that the International Longshoremen's Association had
become a nest for waterfront pirates—a racket, not a union.
George Meany had just become president of the A.F.L., and
his views had changed profoundly since 1940. Meany had
grown up as a close friend of Joseph P. Ryan, the I.L.A.
president, but I was sure that this old association would not
make him wink at the outrageous abuses the Crime Commission was exposing. So I wrote Meany a letter reminding him
that our resolution was still on the books and that the problem of criminal penetration inside labor had become more
acute than it ever was.

Meany replied that he agreed entirely that the Executive
Council should use all its influence to correct the situation in
the I.L.A. and that the 1940 resolution gave it the needed
authority. He put the subject before the council meeting in
February 1953 and was empowered to tell the I.L.A. it had
to clean house. When the dock union tried to hide under the
tarpaulin of "autonomy," Meany stressed that protecting

ll labor against being dragged into the slime had a higher
priority in his scale of values. He felt so strongly on the
ubject that he did not want to stop with suspending the
.L.A. when it refused to go all the way on reform. Meany
ecommended that the 1953 A.F.L. convention in St. Louis
expel the longshore union and charter a brand-new organiza-
ion, the International Brotherhood of Longshoremen, to
ake over its jurisdiction. I admired his spirit, but I thought
suspension was as far as we should go. Expelling unions re-
moves whatever influence you have over them; the only ones
who benefit from that are the crooks. When Meany proposed
o the Executive Council that the Federation kick out the
.L.A., instead of just putting it under suspension, I decided
to abstain from voting. If I voted against expulsion, it might
seem that I was opposed to disciplinary action against the
.L.A., which was definitely not the case; it was simply that I
thought what we were doing was self-defeating.

Unhappily, the practical results were about what I expected. The Federation put a lot of money and effort into a
campaign to break the power of the I.L.A. in the Port of
New York, where the crooks were strongest; but the longshoremen stayed with the old gang. In the end, the rival
union just faded away and the I.L.A. did a good enough job
of putting on a clean face to get reinstated in the Federation.
Most of what it did in the way of reform was because New
York and New Jersey adopted a bistate compact outlawing
the shape-up—the corrupt system of hiring that had given
the I.L.A. make-or-break control over the lives of the men on
the docks—and establishing a Waterfont Commission to
keep out hoodlums. Even with that, the I.L.A. was still far
from the purest union in America when it came back. But
the important thing was that Meany was willing to break
with tradition and the Federation followed him in recognizing that it could not be an ostrich about corruption. To
me that was one of the longest forward steps the Federation
had ever taken, and I was proud that it was our thirteen-year-
old resolution that provided the door opener.

From then on Meany was a tiger fighting the racketeers all over, so much so that Walter Reuther, Jim Carey and the other holier-than-thou types in the C.I.O. lost one of their big excuses for keeping labor separated—namely, that the A.F.L. was too tolerant of scum. When the merger was concluded in 1955, the constitution of the united body gave the central organization specific responsibility for keeping labor free of "any and all corrupt influences." A permanent Ethical Practices Committee was created to police all the affiliates and make recommendations for disciplining any that did not stay clean. Meany wanted me to be the committee's chairman, but I knew that was no place for a Jew. I settled for being one of the five members.

Our first big test came in 1957, when the United States Senate's McClellan Committee, with Robert F. Kennedy as chief counsel, was conducting its televised hearings on union racketeering. It was a story to turn the strongest stomach: every variety of crookedness and betrayal and brutality, carried on in the name of organized labor. And there could be no doubt that the black heart of it lay in the biggest and strongest of all the affiliates of the A.F.L.–C.I.O., the International Brotherhood of Teamsters. Dave Beck, who was then the president of the Teamsters and also a vice-president of the Federation, was among the worst offenders. Whenever the Senators asked him anything about his own conduct he would hide behind the Fifth Amendment, and that became as much of a liability to labor as all the things the committee was bringing out about strong-arm tactics and shakedowns and high living by union officials.

My own feeling was that, even though any union officer had a right—even a duty—to use his constitutional immunity against self-incrimination to protect his union, a person in a position of union trust did not have the right to use it to refuse to answer questions under oath on matters affecting his faithfulness to that union trust. One afternoon I was sitting in the cabana area of the Monte Carlo Hotel in Miami Beach playing gin rummy with George Meany, when Emil

Schlesinger came over from another hotel to say good-bye. He was leaving the next day after having sat in on some I.L.G.W.U. executive board sessions. I asked him to stay, because Arthur Goldberg, the Ethical Practices Committee counsel, was coming down in a few days and I wanted the two of them to collaborate in drawing up a statement for the A.F.L.–C.I.O. on the Fifth Amendment.

Schlesinger and I had many talks before Goldberg arrived, and finally Emil prepared a rough draft on some hotel stationery he picked up in the lobby. When Goldberg came, he had his own draft. It dealt in general terms with the McClellan hearings, but it did not say anything about Beck or any other labor leader taking the Fifth Amendment. It was a long *magilla* that didn't seem to me to answer our problem. I suggested that we keep the first half of it and make the statement Schlesinger and I had drawn up the second half. We argued for quite a while, but in the end that was the way it came out. Meany looked it over for three minutes and said, "That's it." And the Executive Council accepted it just that way, even though Dave Beck objected violently to the whole idea. And so we moved another long step in making the Federation the guardian of the good name of all labor.

The end of that process was the Federation's expulsion of the Teamsters and other tainted unions which refused to rid themselves of racket domination. I had a prominent part in all of it as a member of the Ethical Practices Committee, and I voted for all the disciplinary actions, including the expulsions. But I have to admit that I never felt that was the right remedy, any more than I had when we in the A.F.L. voted to expel the longshoremen. My own preference would have been for a disciplinary procedure similar to the one the old A.F.L. used for Communists. There was a constitutional provision under which no Communist could sit as a delegate to the A.F.L. convention. I wanted to deal with racketeers the same way. The Russians used to say when they wanted to restrict Jews, "Everybody can be a citizen *kromye Hebrayev* (except Jews)." For the A.F.L. I wanted it to be—"Everybody in the labor movement can be a delegate except crooks, thieves and racketeers."

In my opinion, that kind of rule would have had a greater effect on the rank and file of the unions than we ever had by suspending or expelling the whole union. To let the members know that their president is considered a fifth-class citizen inside labor, not third-class even, would have been the ultimate instrument for encouraging reform. What we did just left the whole organization—more than a million members—floating around as exiles. But I voted along with my colleagues in the Executive Council and with the majority in the convention because I did not want to seem to be championing the cause of Dave Beck or Jimmy Hoffa or any other labor renegade.

My reservations about the course of action are not about the rightness of labor's determination to draw a clear line between it and the people who were degrading it. The labor movement had an obligation to its traditions, to its membership and to the community. It discharged it more courageously and responsibly than did the banks, business or any other institution in our society when confronted with large-scale corruption.

Quite a few people who had no place in labor were eliminated, and the country as well as the labor movement was better for their elimination. I think the effect would have been greater still if President Eisenhower and Congress had not decided in 1959 to pass the Landrum-Griffin Labor Reform Bill, which had the effect of making government the monitor of union morality instead of leaving that job to the responsible elements in the House of Labor. Even though I feel labor handled itself foolishly in the whole fight over Landrum-Griffin, the reality is that the passage of the law gave all the people in the A.F.L.–C.I.O. who never had much appetite for the clean-up campaign an excuse for saying, "Let Uncle Sam do it." The Ethical Practices Committee just folded its tent after the law came into being. It never did another thing.

Its death was a tragedy, because its record served as proof that unionism was not a business but a cause. People say the committee failed, because the Teamsters got stronger, not weaker, after they were kicked out, thus justifying Hoffa's taunt, "The Federation needs us more than we need them." But that misses the real point. The purpose of the Ethical Practices Committee was not to make the labor movement stronger in per capita dues or even in economic muscle. It was to make the movement deserving of respect, an honorable custodian of the interests of its members. The vigor with which we acted—and for this I give Meany all the credit in the world—had an effect on the workers of this country. It had an effect on public opinion. It restored faith that idealism was not dead in the labor movement. People knew that we were not asleep or indifferent to corruption. Did we cure the evils? No. Has Landrum-Griffin cured them? No. Perhaps in a capitalist system built on profits and money, it is impossible to eliminate graft. But we tried, and we were true to our trust.

SEVEN

Waltzing with Little Nell

AMONG THE BITTEREST organizational battles the I.L.G.W.U. ever had was the fight to unionize the Kansas City dress plant of the Donnelly Garment Company. It took us forty years of struggle—a struggle we did not win until after I left the union presidency. In the early New Deal period, no company gave us greater trouble or proved a harder nut to crack. That was because we had two formidable adversaries at the head of the firm. One was the owner, Nell Donnelly; the other was her second husband and counsel, former Senator James A. Reed of Missouri.

Nell Donnelly had started out as a maker of aprons. She made a great success of that, and turned to manufacturing housedresses. She sold them to retailers, and again she was highly successful. That led her to manufacturing regular dresses, but to hold down labor costs and avoid confrontation with the union she insisted that she was still making housedresses exclusively.

This became very much of an issue in 1933, when General Hugh S. Johnson, the National Recovery Administrator, approved two separate N.R.A. codes—one for the dress industry, and one with much lower standards, for the cotton-garment industry, which included housedresses. The minimum wages and maximum hours in the dress code were in line with those prevailing in our union contracts. The minimum wage under the cotton-garment code was only thirteen dollars a week, far below our scale. General Johnson called a joint hearing of industry and labor representatives for November. His aim was to draw a proper line between dresses and housedresses, so there would be no unfair advantage for those who manufactured under the cotton-garment code.

That hearing was our first meeting with Senator Reed. At the end of World War I he had been one of the twelve Senators whom Woodrow Wilson denounced as a "little band of willful men" blocking United States entry into the League of Nations. Less well known, however, is the fact that this same Jim Reed cast the deciding vote inside the Judiciary Committee in favor of confirming the nomination of Louis D. Brandeis to the Supreme Court.

His marriage to Mrs. Donnelly came a few weeks after the hearing. Some years earlier she had been kidnapped from her home in Kansas City. Her first husband took the ransom note to Senator Reed, who lived close by and who had been a District Attorney before entering the Senate. The Senator promised Mr. Donnelly that he would have his wife back in three days—and without the payment of a dime in ransom. Reed packed his bag. Three days later he came back with Mrs. Donnelly, just as he had promised he would.

The Senator told the story with great relish to our lawyer, Emil Schlesinger, long after the initial N.R.A. hearing, when Emil was visiting at his country home in the Ozarks to discuss phases of our long litigation against Nell Donnelly. When Emil asked Reed how he had managed to get Mrs. Donnelly released, the Senator replied with a question of his own: "Did you ever read Lincoln Steffens' book *The Shame of the Cities?*" When Emil said yes, Reed went on: "Do you remember the stories Steffens told about how district attorneys make deals with the underworld? They agree that certain persons will not be prosecuted if other people the district attorney feels he must have are brought in for trial. Well, I traded in on some of the connections I made while I was District Attorney and I was able to track her down and bring her back." The result of all this was that the Senator and Mrs. Donnelly became much closer friends than either Mrs. Reed or Mr. Donnelly liked. In the end Donnelly drank himself to death and Mrs. Reed died of a broken heart. Not long after that, Mrs. Donnelly became the second Mrs. Reed.

At the time of the hearing, however, we were all unaware of the impending marriage or of any other special attachment between Reed and Mrs. Donnelly. The Senator did everything he could to disguise the intimacy of his interest. He was at pains to announce early in the proceedings before General Johnson that he did not appear as an attorney for any fee. The whole impression he tried to create was of a disinterested friend of the court eager to be of help to the code administrators. As part of that smokescreen he started off by professing great personal respect for me; but all pretense vanished when it became plain that we would not go along with his maneuvers. He wanted a definition of housedresses that would leave the Donnelly Garment Company free to chisel at the expense of manufacturers who made comparable dresses at the much higher wage rates required by the dress code. The amendment he proposed to the cotton-garment code was so artfully worded that it would have enabled Donnelly to undersell by a ruinous margin all of our unionized dress manufacturers. Had Reed been successful, the effect would have been murderous to the stability and order our union was trying to substitute for the wreckage left by the routed Communists.

In 1934 Kansas City was made a special concentration point in a nationwide drive undertaken by the I.L.G. to organize dress shops. It was picked not primarily because of our difficulties with Senator Reed and Mrs. Donnelly, but because a Department of Labor survey showed that the wage standards in that city were shockingly low. Half the workers in the needle trades there were earning less than ten dollars a week. One out of every five was under six dollars a week. Such terrible standards in any area were inevitably a threat to standards everywhere else.

Donnelly fought us with all the usual techniques of the

union buster, plus a few new ones of its own invention. Right after twelve workers met at the home of one of them and decided to join the I.L.G., orders came through transferring all but one from the main plant into a temporary building, which came to be known as the "isolation ward." Very soon all the transferred workers were fired. The sole survivor of the original dozen was plainly the stool pigeon who had betrayed the rest to the company.

The union filed charges with the N.R.A. in an attempt to get the workers reinstated, but the Blue Eagle was shot down by the Supreme Court before the case was completed. While it was still on, something called the "Nelly Don Loyalty League" suddenly blossomed forth in the plant. Its chief organizer was the manager of the company's outlet store, and its membership included all the management personnel except the president and the production manager. The league's business was conducted on company time and company property. Ostensibly, it was a social organization, but everything it did had the clear purpose of countering our efforts to unionize Donnelly employees.

As soon as the N.R.A. was declared unconstitutional and our organizational activity tapered off, the Loyalty League vanished from the scene. But in March 1937, right after the I.L.G. announced a new drive, lo and behold, it showed up again. A loyalty pledge under which workers committed themselves never to join any outside labor organization was put in circulation throughout the plant. It was sent around during working hours, and supervisors stood over the workers while they signed right at their machines.

On March 9, 1937, our union sent a letter to the company requesting a meeting to discuss matters affecting the industry as a whole and also the status of the workers fired during the N.R.A. Instead of replying, Mrs. Donnelly read the letter at a meeting of the Loyalty League. She told its members that neither Dubinsky nor any other "sky" could tell her how to run her business. She said flatly that there would never be a union in her plant, she would shut it down first. As for the closed shop, that was un-American and totally unacceptable. The only kind of organization she proposed to deal with, she said, was the Loyalty League.

But just a month later, after the Supreme Court upheld the constitutionality of the Wagner Labor Relations Act in a landmark case affecting the Jones & Laughlin Steel Corporation, a remarkable change of heart came over the Donnelly management and its stooges in the Loyalty League. Suddenly, their distaste for anything that smacked of unionism evaporated. Not that they were ready to embrace the I.L.G.—nothing that radical. But the Loyalty League retained lawyers to convert the league into the Donnelly Garment Workers Union. In the course of a single month, all the workers who had vowed they would never join a union and all the management people who had vowed they would never deal with a union flocked to the banner of the new union.

Never has anyone seen such a tidal wave of union consciousness. The workers rushed to join the union as if someone were shoving a red-hot poker under their skirts. And not only the workers, but also the supervisors, the instructors, and even the company representatives who fixed the piece rates that determined how much each worker would earn at the end of the week. All of them were cheerfully welcomed into the ranks of this broad-minded union.

As for the company, the transformation in its attitude was no less magical. It was not content to recognize the union, in contradiction of Mrs. Donnelly's earlier declaration of undying refusal ever to deal with any union; the concessions went far beyond that. The union was given a closed shop in its very first contract, along with the company's blessing. Indeed, the company could not do enough for this particular union. It gave space in its factory for union meetings. It permitted the meetings to be held on company time. The union officers were allowed to use the telephones on each floor of the plant to get out their meeting calls. Then, just to make sure that everyone would attend, the company turned off the electricity on the machine lines while the meetings were on.

This was union recognition with a vengeance—all the vengeance being directed against us. To make sure that the Donnelly workers were never in doubt about what management wanted them to think, all this coddling of the company union was accompanied by a drumfire of propaganda in newspaper advertisements, circulars and letters to malign me personally and to run down the I.L.G. When two women employees did show up at the plant one day wearing I.L.G. union buttons, workers from various floors swarmed around their machines and threatened to throw the workers bodily out the window if they did not leave under their own power. When the first group dispersed, a second group came around mouthing similar threats. The mood grew so ugly that the two girls finally had to go home. Neither ever got her job back, though we fought for seven years before the N.L.R.B. The company did nothing at all to reprimand or discipline those who intimidated them. That was Donnelly's idea of "noninterference" in union affairs.

Throughout all these events and the interminable litigation they spawned, there was never any act of violence on our part against the company. On the contrary, not only did we not call a strike against Donnelly, we never threatened to call one, nor did we ever post a picket line. All we did was invite the company to a conference to discuss our over-all objectives, plus our specific grievances. When the company failed to reply, except through its in-plant declaration of eternal warfare on the whole concept of unionism, we did what we had every legal right to do: publicized the facts in the dispute.

But that was not the way the facts emerged in the lurid case concocted by Senator Reed to support a petition he filed for an injunction to keep us out under the antitrust laws. He sought to muddy the legal waters by entering into the record before the courts, the National Labor Relations Board and a special Congressional committee every instance he could find of scuffles in I.L.G. strike situations anywhere, no matter how remote in time or place or circumstance—all with a view to establishing that ours was a violent union dedicated to destruction of the existing order. It was a turbulent period in labor relations, and it was easy enough to find instances of violence—especially if you didn't inquire too closely into the circumstances that brought them about. It wasn't until several years later that the investigation by the LaFollette Committee of the United States Senate spread on the record the whole miserable story of how many of the picket-line disorders that beset industry at the start of the New Deal were deliberately provoked by men and women planted inside unions by employers. One of the most notorious of these strikebreaking firms operated in Kansas City and supplied scabs and provocateurs for employers in the women's-garment industry.

All of this—and the fact that many of our own people did not exercise sound judgment in the heat of organizing battles—gave Reed plenty of material. In some places scabs had been chained to posts and water hydrants, in others they had been stripped of their clothing as they tried to go through picket lines. The fact that none of this had ever happened at Donnelly was no impediment to the Reed imagination in conjuring up a reign of terror directed at the plant. He made much of a speech made in Italian at a mass rally in Kansas City by Luigi Antonini, the first vice-president of our international. It wound up with an emotional call in English to "fight, fight, fight." Reed made even more of a letter written by Meyer Perlstein, our regional vice-president, accusing Donnelly of conducting a speed-up so inhuman that girls fell to the floor from exhaustion—a condition aggravated by the emaciation they suffered as a result of the company's starvation wages. It was an exaggerated letter, to say the least.

When we got word in New York that Reed was bringing his antitrust action, Emil Schlesinger and I went to a Turkish bath to talk over who should represent the union at the trial. I felt the steam would help us both think more clearly, because it was plain that this could be as crucial a case for labor law as the famous Danbury Hatters case, which caused Congress to change the antitrust laws so that human labor could no longer be considered a commodity.

We finally decided on Frank P. Walsh, the famous labor lawyer, who had an office in Kansas City as well as in New York. When Reed was District Attorney, Walsh had argued many cases against him and had often emerged the winner. Unfortunately, Walsh never seemed able to get the hang of the Donnelly case. The trial went on for five and one-half weeks, and the judge ruled for the company right from the bench. The morning after Walsh returned from Kansas City, he dropped dead while going up the steps of the Federal Court House in New York.

We needed another lawyer, so I turned to Washington for guidance. I talked to two of F.D.R.'s brightest young advisers, Tommy Corcoran and Ben Cohen, and they recommended Dean G. Acheson. When Schlesinger and I went to see him, he was startled. "Why should you want me to represent you?" he asked. "I am no labor lawyer; I represent the biggest of corporate interests. And besides I am not an orator on the style of Jim Reed." I assured him that we had confidence in him, that his lack of familiarity with labor might even be an asset, and he took the case.

By this time the dispute had taken on national political overtones, despite our constant insistence that we were not after Mr. Reed the politician, only Mr. Reed the dress manufacturer. The Senator had been a dark-horse contender for the Democratic Presidential nomination in 1928, when it was believed that Alfred E. Smith and William Gibbs McAdoo would end up by knocking each other out. Reed remained a powerful figure in Democratic politics, and when I was named as a Democratic Presidential elector for Roosevelt in 1936, he launched a vicious personal attack on me, one I knew was designed to undercut our organizers at Donnelly much more than to hurt me.

On the train from New York to Kansas City before Acheson's first appearance in our behalf, I met Erwin Feldman, a lawyer representing the New York manufacturers of housedresses. He was very secretive about the purposes of his trip, but it didn't take a genius to figure out that he would be called as a witness for Donnelly. I felt anything he had to say could only muddy the record. Moreover, I wanted to have a little fun at Reed's expense to pay him back for some of the dirty tricks he had pulled on us.

During the original N.L.R.B. case, Reed had arranged for an off-the-record meeting at his home with Cliff Langsdale, one of our local attorneys. They explored in a very frank and open way the possibility of settling the case without further litigation. Unbeknownst to Langsdale, Reed had arranged to have his personal secretary hide behind a portiere in the room where they were meeting. She took verbatim notes of their conversation, and these notes later became an important element in the case both in the Labor Board and in the federal courts. That same girl was given a strategic spot at the counsel table in the trial of the injunction case, and it quickly became apparent to me that she was keeping an eye on all the material our lawyers had before them, undoubtedly as a spy for Reed so he could get a line on what we were up to.

That gave me a great opportunity. One day I came into court with a huge folder under my arm and laid it down on the counsel table. The folder had a label on top of it, marked in bold letters "Feldman File." There was no way Reed's secretary could avoid spotting it right away. At lunchtime that very day, Feldman disappeared from the courtroom, never to return. They sent him home, apparently because they were afraid of God-knows-what dirt Dubinsky had got on Feldman.

Acheson presented his appeal argument brilliantly, though what stands out most sharply in my memory was not what he said in court but his appearance still dressed in frock coat and striped trousers at a dinner given in his honor at the home of our chief local counsel, Roy Rucker, a fabulous host, whose custom was to serve a gourmet repast, then follow it up with a crap game on his living-room floor. The place was full of judges and other dignitaries. Acheson managed to look more dignified than any of them as he got down on one knee and rolled the dice far into the morning.

For sheer drama in the courtroom, however, nothing could match Reed's attempt to defame our pickets in a fervent peroration to the appeals bench. "If all the cauldrons of hell boiled over," he told the judges, "you could find no more diabolical act in all American history"— and he waved a photograph at the court—"than the stripping of women in the streets of our fair city . . ." Again a pause, and he went on with trembling tone, ". . . in the presence of three Negroes." Happily, this appeal to Southern chivalry—based on an incident that occurred in another situation, in Memphis, more than 350 miles removed from Kansas City—did not make up for the weakness of his legal case. The appeals court directed that the original verdict be set aside, and later the case was ordered retried. Even before the ruling came down, Acheson had been called into the State Department and had to withdraw as our lawyer. At that point I decided we had had enough of big names, and I picked Emil Schlesinger to take over. He knew more about the case than anyone else, and he had much more of a head for this kind of litigation than Reed or anybody we could find in the fanciest law firm.

Most of the federal judges in the district owed their appointment to Reed. To avoid any suggestion of improper influence, a judge named Gunnar M. Nordbye was brought in from Minnesota to preside at the trial. But before the proceedings got under way Reed decided to make a big thing of subpoenaing the books of the international union as well as the minutes of the meetings of the General Executive Board. We felt it would be a terrible precedent to give any employer access to everything that went on inside the union. However, we did offer through Schlesinger to make all the records and minutes available to the judge. He could then pick out whatever information he deemed pertinent to the case and we would put that in the record. Our refusal to turn everything over to the company led to a motion by Donnelly to have me put in jail for contempt. That motion was heard in New York, where I had my headquarters. Judge Harold Medina listened to the rival presentations until nearly midnight. Then he pointed out to both counsel that Judge Nordbye was going to be in New York the next day to attend a judicial conference. Medina said he would leave it up to Nordbye to rule on the move to put me behind bars. Judge Nordbye accepted our view that the purposes of justice would be served by letting him cull from our records whatever had some relation to the case.

During the six weeks of the second trial I called Schlesinger from New York every day, and sometimes several times a day. While the witnesses for the company were on, things looked bad for us, but Emil kept assuring me, "Our day is coming." Reed had a very able trial lawyer, William Hogsett, associated with him, a master at asking double-edged questions. He went so far in that direction when I was on the stand in the first trial that the judge himself had felt obliged at one stage to volunteer the remark, "If there's an objection, I'll sustain it." In the second trial Hogsett was hoping for another crack at me. He had prepared a thousand questions, all intended to lead me into damaging admissions. Every day during our presentation, he would ask Schlesinger, "When is Mr. Dubinsky coming?" And always Emil would reply—even though we had decided I would not appear at all, because it would only serve to fog up the legal issues on which we were building our case—"I'll let you know in due course, Bill, in due course."

When Mrs. Reed was on the stand, Schlesinger tried to get into evidence a clipping from the St. Louis Post-Dispatch quoting her statement at the 1937 meeting of the Nelly Don Loyalty League to the effect that "no Dubinsky or any other 'sky' will ever organize my plant or have anything to do with my shop." She denied under oath that she had ever made the statement, and the judge refused to let the clipping go in the record. When Emil pressed Mrs. Reed to explain how such a quotation could have been attributed to her in a responsible newspaper if it had no basis in fact, she kept insisting that she had no way of knowing, that she had never said it. And the Senator sat at the counsel table, saying nothing.

When Emil telephoned to tell me of the impasse, we agreed that he should call up the *Post-Dispatch* and find out whether they had any corroboration we could use to sustain the accuracy of their story. He got one of the news editors on the phone and said, "I just don't understand this. On such-and-such date, you had this statement in your paper as a direct quote attributed to Mrs. Reed. Now she denies under oath that she ever made such a statement. You are a respected and responsible paper. Is there anything you have by way of substantiation of your report?"

The editor asked him to hold the wire while he checked the morgue. When the editor came back, he was incredulous. "What do you mean, she denies it? She sent us a statement in writing with her own signature on it. I have it right here." That was the best news we could get. All we needed was to get it to court. So Emil asked the editor if he could send someone to court with the signed statement and, of course, we would pay the expenses. At seven o'clock the next morning Emil met the woman in charge of the *Post-Dispatch* morgue at the railroad station. They had breakfast together and then went to court. But Emil's strategy was not to put her on until Mrs. Reed was in the courtroom. As soon as Hogsett saw a strange face on our side, he wanted to know who she was. And Emil gave him his usual answer, "I'll let you know in due course, Bill, in due course."

As soon as Mrs. Reed did come in, Emil abruptly stopped examining the witness we had on the stand and asked an associate from Washington, Charles Horsky, to put the *Post-*

Dispatch representative on the stand and get her story into evidence. The minute she produced the signed statement by Mrs. Reed, the Senator rose and said, "I object."

"On what grounds?" asked the judge.

"The fact is that Mrs. Reed never read that statement," her husband said. "She never wrote that statement. I wrote that statement, and she merely signed it."

"Well," said Schlesinger, "that's very cavalier of you, Senator. Where were you yesterday when all this was being asked of Mrs. Reed? Why didn't you tell us about this yesterday? You're too late. Your Honor, we again ask that this be marked and received in evidence."

The judge said, "It's received."

"Your Honor, I object," Reed said again.

The judge was very sharp. "Senator Reed, sit down. This clipping is marked in evidence."

This was one of the highlights of the case.

On Reed's side a major thrust of the company's case was to establish the notion that we were trying to organize by fear and terror. The speech by Antonini which wound up, "Fight, fight, fight," they kept throwing up at us all the time. When the manager of the Donnelly plant was on the stand and was asked whether there had been any violence against the firm, she fell back on this same statement. So Schlesinger decided he had better knock that whole argument on the head. We asked the manager, "Did you ever hear the expression 'The fight against higher electric rates'?" And when the manager said yes, Schlesinger asked, "Do you consider that an incitement to violence?" And the manager said, "It could be." Schlesinger kept leading her in deeper and deeper with questions about "the fight against cancer" and "the fight against the slums" and so on, and always the manager would say lamely it involved violence against whatever the subject was.

Then Schlesinger read a series of quotes about fights against various social ills, and each one wound up a list of accomplishments in these fields with the slogan repeated over and over, "And we've just begun to fight." And he asked, "Do you regard each of those statements as a call to arms?" The manager answered with a very positive "Yes." "Well, Your Honor," said Schlesinger, "I don't think I have to ask this witness any more questions about violence, merely to point out that what I have just quoted is all from a speech by President Franklin D. Roosevelt in Madison Square Garden in his [1936] re-election campaign." And that brought a roar of laughter all over the courtroom.

We did a lot of novel things in that case, including putting on a fashion show in the courtroom. We wanted to prove that the Donnelly dresses were too good to qualify as housedresses. So we bought some of Mrs. Reed's dresses in a Philadelphia store and then bought a dozen or so others from union manufacturers in New York. We got a bunch of pretty girls from the University of Kansas, and the judge let us parade the whole group past the bench while Mrs. Reed tried to pick out which had come from her shop and which from regular dress houses. She couldn't do it. There was no way to distinguish her "housedresses" from all the standard dresses.

In the end the court overturned the injunction against the I.L.G.W.U. It held that there was no federal jurisdiction for finding us guilty of violating the antitrust laws. That ruling did not end Donnelly's resistance to organization. The company continued to fight, but we never gave up our efforts. They were finally crowned with success long after I left the presidency. Both Senator Reed and his wife were out of the picture when the company finally signed its first contract in 1971.

The final phase of my active personal involvement in the case came on May 10, 1940, after Senator Reed had testified on the case as a witness before a House committee investigating the National Labor Relations Board and the operation of the Wagner Act. His whole effort was to discredit our union as one that had no members in the company and that relied on violence. That fitted in with the whole theme of the committee, which was committed to reviling organized labor and to excoriating the N.L.R.B. as its accomplice in crime. I asked for an opportunity to reply, and I went to Washington a day ahead of time with Schlesinger and my secretary, Hannah Haskel. We talked about what I wanted to say, and Emil dictated a draft to Hannah, then he polished it and we worked on it some more. And finally about 10 P.M. the statement was ready. Then Emil said, "Look, forget this statement, because no matter how good it is it won't be effective if you try to read it." And I knew he was right about that, because I never could read a statement in a way that would make any kind of impression. I was always best when I tried to put my thoughts in order as I talked, maybe with a few notes to remind me of certain things, certain points, I wanted especially to make.

So Emil and Elias Lieberman, another mainstay of our legal staff, put themselves in the role of devil's advocate. They pretended to be members of the committee—unfriendly members—throwing at me every nasty question they could think of about the Donnelly case. And we kept at it without a break until 2:30 A.M., when finally Elias said he was tired and had to go to bed. Emil and I continued for a few more hours to make sure there was no line of questioning they could catch us on. Then Emil said, "Dave, it's a quarter to five. We all have to meet for breakfast at eight so we can get to the hearing room on time. There's such a thing as preparing too well; and anyway you need a couple of hours sleep. And so do I."

I agreed with him and we parted to meet again at eight. When I saw him then at eight sharp, Emil said, "You look fresh as a daisy. You must have slept well."

"Who slept?" I said. "After I left you, I thought I'd take a little walk before turning in. On the way I found a Childs Restaurant. I went in and had some pancakes. Then I bought a paper and came back to the hotel. There were some interesting things in the paper so I never did get to bed. I took a cold shower and here I am."

At the hearing Representative Howard W. Smith of Virginia, the committee chairman, and Edmund M. Toland, its general counsel, tried to show that we had the Labor Board in our vest pocket.

They were delighted when Senator Reed brought up for the thousandth time reference to charges that in an organizing campaign in Memphis some of our pickets had stripped a woman naked on the street as she started into the struck plant. Testimony about that incident, plus a news photo, had been put into the court record in the first Donnelly injunction suit in Kansas City. Representative Smith asked me to explain how our union could stand for such tactics in view of my emphatic statement that we abhorred all violence. I tried to evade specific discussion of the episode by repeating that we did our best to keep such things from happening but that in the heat of a dispute it was not always possible to prevent some worker from doing something that ran counter to all our rules.

When Smith persisted that he did not care about my opinions but only about what happened, I came back with something that had happened just the day before in New York, something I had learned through my predawn reading of the morning paper. A union organizer had gone into a Seventh Avenue garment shop and been shot dead by an employer. "It happened," I told the Congressman, and I pounded the witness table for emphasis. "He is dead. He is buried today. Sure it happened that an employer pulled a gun and killed [our organizer] instantly when he came into the shop. Of course, it happened. There they stripped a girl; here they shot a man to death, murdered him."

And even that did not turn off Smith's questions about how I could expect the girls at Donnelly to join an organization whose members could commit such "atrocities" as stripping a girl on the street for trying to cross a picket line. I told him that to damn an organization because someone somewhere violated its rules was as unfair as it would be to consider all Congressmen crooks because one betrayed his trust.

I told the Smith Committee that, in terms of the dues that would come to the International if we succeeded in organizing all one thousand Donnelly workers, it would take seventy-five years to cover the International's investment in the original organizing drive. And that would not account for the legal and court costs, which all alone would have been enough to bankrupt most internationals. I made it plain that our sole motivation was a desire to preserve and protect the standards of our 150,000 members in the dress industry and the 7,000 employers with whom we bargained.

But that committee was a stacked deck, basically hostile to the Labor Board and to us. Representative Harry N. Routzohn of Ohio, a constant critic of organized labor, sought to demonstrate that I was automatically subject to classification as a subversive because I was born in Russia. So, when he turned the questioning to when and where I was born, I took cognizance of the altered lineage created by the Nazi occupation of Poland at the outset of World War II. I just dropped Russia out of the spectrum and said I was born in Lodz, Poland, possession of Germany. Later under more sympathetic interrogation by Representative Abe Murdock of Utah, I stressed my pride that I had become an American by choice and not by the accident of birth. That was always my proudest choice, one the Reeds and the Routzohns could not respect.

EIGHT

Union Firsts

To ME, WAGES AND HOURS are only the beginning of a union's duty to its members. A union is a way of life: it improves economic standards so that workers and their families can live better. It establishes principles of justice within the shop so that the worker can feel a sense of dignity and independence. But the worker does not live exclusively in the shop. He is part of the larger community, and so the union must be part of that larger community, making its own contribution to the welfare of the community and also broadening opportunities for effective participation and enjoyment by its members.

I am proud that the International Ladies Garment Workers Union blazed many new trails for all of labor in service to its membership and in community involvement. We pioneered in pension and welfare funds, in union health centers, in adult-education programs, in the organization of management engineering and research departments and in the systematic distribution over a period of a little more than a quarter century of $42,304,000 in gifts to philanthropic and labor causes—gifts from a union with a heart, with a soul, with a spirit, with ideals. No suffering anywhere in the world was foreign to our interest and our sense of responsibility. The human wreckage of war, the victims of Nazi persecution, the fighters for freedom in every land—all these were our brothers and sisters. We could not refuse them, nor did we try.

None of this was my invention. From the earliest days of our union, when having a roof over their heads and food for their bellies was a worry for all our members, our slogan always was, "Not by Bread Alone." Education in its broadest sense was a prime expression of this philosophy. At first the great task was to bring into the full stream of metropolitan culture the immigrants pouring in through Ellis Island and finding jobs at the sewing machine. They enrolled for every type of course not only at the city's own night schools but in classes organized by their locals. These ranged far beyond learning English or the history of trade-unionism into the whole cultural life of New York—its fabulous museums, opera, concerts. Our people were hungry for education. They were hungry for books, for lectures, for learning— everything from the classics to Karl Marx.

An education department that became a standard-setter for the rest of labor was established in the General Office before World War I. One of its pioneer accomplishments was the organization of a Workers' University that operated in Washington Irving High School near Union Square. It opened its doors in January 1918. The whole educational effort fell victim to the destructive internal struggle of the 1920s, but its restoration became a priority item as soon as I took office. With the New Deal helping us to enroll tens of thousands of new members overnight, I took personal command of revitalizing our program and pushing it in new directions. The budget and personnel of the educational department were greatly expanded, even though my field directors were telling me that we needed every dollar and every organizer to bring in new members. "It is not enough they should pay us dues," I told the complainers. "They should know what we stand for." By mid-1936 I was able to assure a world congress of the International Federation of Trade Unions in London that the revitalized I.L.G.W.U. educational program had become a model for many other unions, including those that were springing up in the mass-production industries. It was no exaggeration.

But, for me, education without some salesmanship was not education. In my book, that meant showmanship. In 1931 I made a visit to Europe and while there attended an international Socialist congress in Vienna.* Its highlight was a mass spectacle, a pageant in which thousands upon thousands of Austrian trade-unionists took part. It was staged in a huge stadium, with at least a quarter million people watching. The whole thing was most impressive. I could not get it out of my mind—the mood it created of unity and hope, the friendship it built. The next year when two new presidents were elected in the United States—Franklin D. Roosevelt and me; only, I beat him by a few months—I kept wondering how we could do something like that pageant, for the I.L.G.'s great influx of new members, raw, green, inexperienced.

I turned to a good friend with considerable experience in theatrical matters—Louis Schaffer, then on the staff of the *Jewish Daily Forward*—and described what I had seen in Vienna. "We got to establish a department of recreational activities," I told him. "Will you take the job?" He started by arranging programs of dancing, acting, painting and lectures. By 1936 the project had developed to a point where the I.L.G. bought a small, vacant theater on West Thirty-ninth Street, in the heart of the garment district, and rechistened it "Labor Stage." The new group's first major production was an intensely serious drama about a steel strike

* I almost did not get into the congress. When I presented myself at the door seeking admission as an observer, I was stopped by Clarence Senior, secretary of the American Socialist Party, who was checking credentials. He told me I could not get in because I did not have a membership card showing good standing in the party. I asked him to call Morris Hillquit, our lawyer, who was one of the party's leading lights. He vouched for me, but after we got on the other side of the entrance he asked, "Dave, are you still a member?" I had to reply, "I consider myself a member—a half member. When we had the fight with the Communists, I raised the issue 'No politics in the union. You have a right to be a Communist in your party; you have a right to be a Socialist in your party, but here it's trade-unionism.' And I had to show the example. I stopped paying Socialist Party dues, although I still considered myself a Socialist."

called *Steel* by the playwright John Wexley. The actors were men and women from the shops, and they gave a splendid account of themselves at fifty performances held on weekends in the first half of 1937. But we didn't set the world afire.

The next production was a total change of pace—and a sensation. It was a revue of a type never seen before or since on Broadway. Its title was *Pins and Needles*, and it was a zany commentary on the politics of world, nation, city and labor movement and on depression life in general, all as seen through the rollicking imagination of Harold Rome. Every member of the cast was recruited from behind a sewing machine, a shipping cart, or a cutting table. Before the first showing, in November 1937, Schaffer came to me and urged me to invite a lot of celebrities to the opening. My reply was: "No. First I want to see it. Our name and reputation are too important, and unless we have something worthwhile, I wouldn't do it. When you had the other show, *Steel*, it was good—good for us and our workers. But for the outside it didn't mean anything. Now I'm going to invite strangers only when I'm sure."

So *Pins and Needles* slipped in very quietly on a cold, rainy night. But within a week or two its fame began to spread. I had myself done everything I could to promote it once I saw how good it was. The wit of the script was made more enchanting by the excitement and freshness of the actors. It was topical; it was also irresistible. The critics praised it lavishly, and the original plan of showing it only on weekends soon had to be abandoned in favor of nightly performances. The acclaim was so great and the enthusiasm of the audiences so overwhelming that Secretary of Labor Frances Perkins got in touch with me to arrange a command performance for President Roosevelt at the White House. We had to dispense with the scenery and even the orchestra. The President sat only a few feet away from the improvised stage in the East Room. I took a seat with the rest of the small group he had invited, but Mrs. Roosevelt came over and said, "You have to sit near the President." That gave me a good chance to see how much he enjoyed the show, especially the skits that lampooned the Fascist dictators who were bringing war to the world. There was one called "Three Angels of Peace," a takeoff on Hitler, Mussolini and Neville Chamberlain apropos of Munich. "You ought to take out that S.O.B.," Roosevelt said when he caught his first glimpse of Chamberlain. But there was no question that the evening was a delight for him. And he took everything, including the domestic political digs, with great good humor.

I can't say the same for Fanny Perkins, who asked us to give another special performance in Washington that same week in connection with the twenty-fifth anniversary of the Department of Labor. Some worrywarts on her staff got her panicky about some of the juicier lines dealing with American bigwigs. So she set herself up as a board of censorship and insisted that we knock out references to Mayor Frank Hague of Jersey City, who was described as Führer Hague, and to J. P. Morgan in a number called "Doing the Reactionary." Once she got started cutting, she apparently couldn't stop. Even the numbers about the dictators had to go, because the United States was theoretically at peace with them. I was glad to discover that F.D.R. had more tolerance than his Secretary of Labor.

Not too long after the White House gala, the original company went on a national tour, and another group of talented seamstresses and men from the shops took over in New York. The road company packed them in all over the country. Its tour stretched out over ten months. Meanwhile Harold Rome was rewriting many of the numbers to keep up with fast-breaking developments at home and abroad. A wholly new 1939 edition moved into a much larger theater on Broadway, and it too was an overwhelming success. We kept the admission price low to encourage workers and low-income people to see it as well as those who were accustomed to regular Great White Way ticket standards. At the end of the summer, however, we had to do a basic re-

structuring of the entire revue to adjust to the formal out-
break of World War II in Europe. By Thanksgiving Day, a
third edition was launched. Many of the numbers needed
constant change, but the *New Pins and Needles* kept playing
to appreciative audiences until May 1941, six months before
Pearl Harbor.

I was probably its best customer. I saw it at least forty
times. Whenever I had an evening free, I was there. So much
so that they drafted me once to ride across the stage on my
bicycle in the "Sunday in the Park" number. The crowd gave
a great roar when they recognized me pedaling away, but all
I was doing was what I did maybe a thousand times on
Sundays in Central Park. Labor Stage did not have the
heaviness of many productions put on by the W.P.A. Federal
Theater Project, but it left a lasting mark as an indication
that a union could deliver an important social message with
a light touch. We laughed at everybody, including ourselves,
and the world learned while it laughed.

When the time for our Golden Jubilee convention rolled
around in 1950, it seemed to me that we needed a movie that
would record with dignity and drama the story of this im-
migrant-built union and the climb of the garment workers
out of the industrial jungle. The International and its locals
had made a number of films over the years, but I wanted
something truly memorable. Once again, as with Harold
Rome, we were blessed in our choice of a writer. I asked
Morton Wishengrad, who had been education director of the
New York Dress Joint Board in the New Deal period and
who had a great sensitivity to the suffering and aspirations
of those who struggled up from the slums, to prepare a
script. He was a playwright, with a solid record of accomplishment on Broadway and in television. More important,
he was a poet, with a feel for our traditions that was almost
spiritual. The hour-long film that was made out of his script
exceeded all our hopes, and the hopes were high. It was all
done professionally. We did not feel we could get on film the
same kind of spontaneity and charm we had had by using

amateurs from the shops in *Pins and Needles*. The three main parts were done by Sam Levene, Joseph Wiseman and Arlene Francis, all of whom performed superbly.

The movie, entitled *With These Hands*, had its debut in the Convention Hall in Atlantic City in June before a thousand delegates to the fiftieth-anniversary convention, plus several hundred invited guests. It excited the same kind of admiration that had greeted *Pins and Needles* more than a decade earlier. Right after the convention we leased the Gotham Theater on Broadway, where the film ran for several weeks. Our locals throughout the United States and Canada showed it over and over for years. Other trade-union members and the general public flocked to see it. Universities, high schools and community groups clamored for prints. Indeed, the demand was worldwide. The United States Information Service found it an invaluable aid in building appreciation overseas of the openness of American society. The sound track was translated into twelve languages. That was a help not only in countries as remote as Japan and Israel, but in showings for our own growing number of Spanish-speaking garment workers. The durability of the film's appeal was underscored by the sudden decision of the Indian government in June 1956—more than five years after the first showing of *With These Hands* in that country—to insist on cutting out twenty-eight lines of script dealing with our successful fight against the Communists in the twenties.

Nikita Khrushchev had made an ostentatious visit to India not long before the crackdown, and it was obvious that the regime in New Delhi wanted to emphasize its cordiality toward Moscow. Up to then our film had been hugely popular when shown under the auspices of the U.S.I.S. in cities and villages in every section of India. When I learned of the crude attempt at censorship, I issued a public statement noting that the only place the film was banned was behind the Iron Curtain. The A.F.L.–C.I.O. joined me in demanding a formal State Department protest. But, angry as

I was, I was still pleased that anybody halfway across the world remembered there was a *With These Hands* and felt its educational impact a half decade after its issuance was strong enough to make what it said worth arguing about.

Another expression of our pioneering spirit was Unity House, the magnificent vacation resort maintained by the union in Pennsylvania's Pocono Mountains. This was an innovation that in the fullest sense started with the members. After the great strike of the waistmakers in 1909, some of the women from the shops decided to form a cooperative in a village in the Catskills so they would have a place to go to and enjoy themselves in the summer. The venture took hold, and the dress locals got involved along with the original sponsors. In 1919 they learned that they could get a bargain on a tract of almost one thousand acres of superb land in the Poconos. A group of bankers and businessmen, most of them German, had been coming to a resort called the Forest Park Hotel. It had a luxurious main house, a couple of dozen cottages, a mile-long lake full of fish, and lovely wooded hills. Anti-German spirit arising out of World War I had made the wealthy Germans unpopular in the area, and they decided to get rid of the property.

The women from the New York locals pitched in to make the project a success. They waited on table and did much of the housecleaning. Only the chef was hired from outside. Everybody with a union card was welcome, at a rate of only thirteen dollars a week. But after two or three years the cooperators found the job was too much for them. The cost of living was skyrocketing, and it was no picnic—and certainly no vacation—for them. The International came to the rescue and put the place on a professional basis without destroying its trade-union character. In 1934, two years after I became president, a kitchen fire wrecked the main house and several of the bungalows. We enlisted an outstanding architect, William Lescaze, to design a beautiful, rambling replacement for the main building, one that combined modernism and rusticity. We got one unexpectedly good break.

John D. Rockefeller, Jr., had commissioned Diego Rivera, the great Mexican artist, to do a series of murals for the lobby of the R.C.A. Building, which was in the process of construction as part of Radio City (now Rockefeller Center), the massive antidepression project that the family had undertaken partly to provide jobs for thousands of idle construction workers and partly to show its faith in the revival of the American economy. But the Rivera frescoes proved much too radical for the conservative head of Standard Oil. They were anti-Fascist in tone and decidedly revolutionary. Most involved scenes from the Spanish civil war, powerful indictments of Franco and his Fascist allies from Italy and Germany.

After Rockefeller rejected them, we got duplicates free from Rivera, thanks to some help from Jay Lovestone. These breathtaking murals became the proudest adornment of Unity House after its restoration. We could not display two of them at Unity House, however. They lampooned Mussolini, and we were afraid of antagonizing our Italian members, many of whom still had faith in him. I am not happy to confess our cowardice on that score, but it was 1934 and many lapses were still being made by people who should have been outspoken in their hostility to the Italian dictator. In that year, for example, the national A.F.L. convention, to its credit, adopted a resolution condemning Hitler and Mussolini. Yet George Meany, then president of the New York State Federation of Labor, was so insensitive that he sailed to Europe on an Italian liner a few months later.

The fact that a garment worker could live like a millionaire on vacation at Unity House did not make us forget that health was a perpetual concern to our members. The first great strikes in 1909 and 1910 were as much a product of that concern as they were a revolt against sweatshop wages. Tuberculosis spun the wheel of every sewing machine in the "lung blocks" on the Lower East Side. The Protocol of Peace that ended the epic strike of the cloakmakers recognized that tie between work and death by creating a Board of

Sanitary Control to inspect shops for unsanitary conditions. Among the board's early actions was a call for health examinations. The first series in 1912 resulted in a finding that more than 800 cloakmakers were suffering from lung disease, a finding that prompted one local union to tax its 9,000 members one dollar a year for a tuberculosis fund. Payments of one hundred to two hundred dollars a year were allowed for treatment of members who had tuberculosis. The other New York locals soon followed this example.

A logical extension of the health examinations, though one without precedent at the time, was the establishment of a Union Health Center to give tests to members and certify those eligible for membership. Set up originally in a two-room office, with one doctor on duty for a few hours a day, the center grew by 1919 into a comprehensive diagnostic and dental clinic occupying four well-equipped floors in its own building and operated on a cooperative basis by a group of New York locals.

Like so many other worthy activities, the center ran into hard times in the 1920s. It opened its doors to members of other labor organizations to help meet its deficit, but the depression added to the difficulties and it was facing bankruptcy when I assumed the presidency. At the 1934 convention I successfully sponsored a one-time one-dollar-per-member assessment to rescue Unity House and the Union Health Center. That turned the tide back toward fiscal health. The center moved to a skyscraper building on the southern fringe of the garment center, which it now owns.

The services of the Union Health Center are by no means a total answer to the health needs of garment workers and their families, but it has performed one above all the many invaluable services it provides. It broke down the workers' resistance to going to doctors regularly for preventive medicine. Check-ups were almost unknown to our people; they called the doctor usually when it was too late. The New York model was followed in many other women's-apparel markets, including Boston, Philadelphia, Chicago and Monreal. Healthmobiles have brought needed service to many who could not come to established centers, not only in semirural areas on the mainland but in Puerto Rico as well. In floods and other emergencies these mobile units have aided whole communities.

The fiftieth anniversary of the original Union Health Center was marked by Congressional authorization of a special commemorative medal. It was the last bill signed by John F. Kennedy, two days before his assassination.

We never deluded ourselves, however, that health centers were a substitute for universal protection against the hazards of illness, old age or disability. Long before the rest of the labor movement, the I.L.G. crusaded for federal social-security legislation of the most all-embracing kind. Indeed, at the outset of my presidency, I was in the embarrassing position of going before a Congressional committee to testify in favor of unemployment insurance when William Green was testifying just the opposite for the American Federation of Labor. But we educated them. The A.F.L. turned around early in the New Deal and joined us in support of the government paying the unemployed. Up to then they felt that would be unfair competition by government in a field that unions ought to take care of on their own. But that meant that the unions didn't do the job and the government didn't do it either, until the New Deal.

Our concept, again starting very early, was that you couldn't tax workers out of their slender earnings for all these social responsibilities. So, to the extent that government wasn't taking care of the problems, we felt it was the obligation of employers. In the early twenties the cloak-makers in Cleveland got their employers to establish a guaranteed annual wage in exchange for union cooperation in a plan for scientific production standards. At first the plan called for forty-one weeks of assured employment a year, with each worker to get two thirds of his normal pay out of an employer-financed fund in any week when he had no work. That proved too steep a guarantee for the industry to carry and in 1923 it was cut back to forty weeks, with half pay when there weren't enough jobs to go around. The plan covered only about two thousand workers, but it would have got a big extension if the struggle with the Communists had not upset a modified version instituted in New York on the basis of a 1924 recommendation by a commission appointed by Governor Alfred E. Smith. It called for a jointly administered fund made up of a 1 percent weekly contribution by the workers and a 2 percent contribution by the employers. The fund would provide idle workers with ten dollars a week in unemployment insurance for up to twelve weeks. It was not much even in those days of low wages, and the lefties objected to the whole idea on principle. So did a good many old-style Gompersites. Some denounced it as class collaboration; some insisted only employers should contribute. One left-winger at the 1924 convention grumbled: "Now we are in the life-insurance business and later we are going to build houses and railroads. Our problem is organizing the shops."

That was a problem all right, but it was not the only problem. Even after passage of the Social Security Act, it was clear to me that we had to revive the concept underlying the "Cleveland experiment" in a whole array of fields vital to our members. The insecurity of our industry made that essential. And employer payments, not taxes on workers, had to be the main reliance. In 1938 our big children's-dress local in New York pointed one useful way toward pooled funds to protect I.L.G. members. It persuaded its employers to put a regular percentage of payroll into a union-administered fund to provide paid vacations for workers. That way a worker who worked a few weeks in one shop, then a few weeks in another and a few more weeks in still another could acquire eligibility for vacation money, which otherwise the worker would never get. Other locals recognized that they could benefit from the same concept. We had already done something of the same sort by establishing a centralized death-benefit fund in the inter-

national office, but its resources came out of an allocation
of one dollar a year per member from union dues.

The real breakthrough came in World War II, when the
manufacturers were enjoying considerable prosperity as a
result of the large-scale entrance of women into defense industries. Part of their profits came from war orders for
parachutes, uniforms and other military software; part from
the fact that women workers didn't spend all their time in
overalls. With labor at a premium, the employers welcomed
ways around the straitjacket that wartime economic controls
had put on wage increases. The union was happy to oblige.
It suggested that rather than defy the anti-inflationary ceiling on pay raises, extra cash could be placed in funds paid for
by the employers and run by the union to provide workers
with health and hospital protection, life insurance and even
pensions. The War Labor Board found this an agreeable
detour. Its members had been taking a lot of punishment
from other unions for being too rigid about the board's own
anti-inflation guideline, and there was little justice in allowing employers to enjoy bloated profits without sharing a
portion of them with their employees.

In 1942 and 1943 several of our biggest locals and joint
boards in New York and Philadelphia set up funds to receive
contributions from all the employers. In the New York
Cloak Joint Board, with a particularly high percentage of
elderly members, the emphasis was on a retirement fund.
Most of the others concentrated first on health and other
insurance coverage. It provided a good one-two punch.
Within a few years those who didn't have pensions convinced their employers they had to have them to keep up
with the cloakmakers. The cloakmakers, in turn, had to have
health and life insurance. The employers went along with
the plan. The negotiations were always local, but I saw there
could be trouble if the International did not set up some
checks in the running of these funds, which were quickly
accumulating huge sums of money to be held in trust for
benefits to members.

There were two dangers, both of which could kill the funds as true contributors to the welfare of our members and our unions. One was to promise too much, to overload the funds with benefits they could not deliver without going broke or imposing such a heavy burden on our employers that they would go broke. The other was the temptation to steal, whether through direct larceny by officers in charge of the funds, or by bringing in an expensive apparatus of insurance companies and other outsiders to manage our money and seduce our officers with kickbacks or patronage. We acted immediately to protect the union on both fronts.

We carefully segregated money paid into welfare and retirement funds from all normal union assets; the union acted as a self-insurer, with auditors from the international office policing the locals and joint boards; and a constitutional ceiling of 5 percent was put on administrative expenses, as against the 25 to 50 percent that later came to prevail in the funds of some other unions. The limit was even tighter for retirement funds, a top of 3 percent on overhead. We began publishing detailed reports of the expenditures and reserves of all our funds long before federal law required such disclosure. We felt that ventilation had to be healthy. Indeed, in July 1954 I startled my colleagues in the A.F.L. Executive Council by writing in the *American Federationist* a call for labor to modify its traditional hostility to any form of governmental intervention in the internal affairs of unions. The scandals that surrounded the funds of unions in which welfare had become a license to steal were discrediting all labor, and I urged labor to cooperate in drafting constructive legal restraints against such larceny. It was the same philosophy that had made us fight so hard within the Federation itself against the concept that autonomy could become a shield for racketeers in unions that would not police themselves. If a union wouldn't act decently on its own, it was up to the Federation or the government to provide the essential protection for the interests of members and community.

So far as we were concerned, however, it was not enough to keep dishonesty away from our funds. We had to be sure that they were sound, which meant a constant balance between what our members needed and what our industry could give. The artificial prosperity that our manufacturers had in World War II gave way in the postwar years to the old dog-eat-dog scramble. Even the strongest employer could suddenly move away or simply go out of business. No amount of ingenuity on our part could erase that hard reality of life in the rag jungle. We tried to build a fence around union jobs through strict contractual prohibitions against runaway shops in low-wage areas. One of my first "victories" in 1936, when welfare funds were only a vague dream, involved a decision by New York State Supreme Court Justice Philip J. McCook upholding a clause in our contract with the dress industry that barred companies from moving out of the five-cent-fare zone (oh, blessed memory). Two firms that had locked out their two hundred workers on West Thirty-fifth Street and opened a cut-rate shop in the hard-coal region of Pennsylvania, ten miles north of Scranton, were ordered to return to New York and live up to their original agreement.

Even before that, at the start of my career as an executive-board member, the I.L.G. had established the principle that unions could use the law in their own defense, not always be the targets of manufacturers using the courts against labor. This was back in 1922, my first year as an international vice-president, when the New York employers sought to capitalize on the general antilabor feeling that followed World War I. It was the period of "the American way" and the open shop. Many of our manufacturers began to resent the arbitration procedures that had originated under the Protocol of Peace of 1910. Too often, in their estimation, the impartial people making the decisions would sustain the union on the facts of a particular complaint. This was not bias; it was a recognition that our grievances were valid, that the bosses were oppressing our members in disregard of contract. But that did not stop those who wanted to chisel from locking out thousands of our members in an effort to escape from the whole agreement. We took the rare step of going to court to force the shops to reopen. And we obtained the first labor injunction against an employer. It was issued, interestingly, by Robert F. Wagner, Sr., then sitting as a justice of the New York State Supreme Court. His decision was a forerunner of the social legislation that made him one of the master architects of the New Deal.

Both of those court rulings were landmarks for labor, proof that the courts could be used in defense of unions and not solely as instruments of employer coercion in strikes and other conflicts. We continued over the years to write protective language into our major contracts, and judges and arbitrators awarded us monetary damages and other indemnity for violations by employers. But in a real sense, it was a losing battle. Even when we built a plant of our own in the South as a reprisal against a notorious chiseler, we could not stem the tide of fugitives from Seventh Avenue, ready to go to the farthest corners of the earth to cut a nickel from the established labor standards.

That was one reason we preceded the A.F.L. in being strong champions of a federal minimum-wage law. That at least established a floor for pay throughout the United States, though it could do nothing to help us in Taiwan, or Indonesia, or Spain. I remember when I went to Puerto Rico in 1940 as a member of the first minimum-wage board for the island, we found the prevailing wage to be around 5 cents an hour, and in undergarment shops it was 2 or 2½ cents. And most of the shops were owned by New Yorkers. One of the employers testified that if we raised the rate to a nickel in the brassiere industry, grass would grow in the streets of San Juan.

When it came to the recommendation of our panel, I decided we should go for a minimum of 12½ cents an hour for homeworkers and a rate a few cents higher for those working in factories. Monsignor Francis J. Haas, a public member of the commission, said to me privately, "Dave, will you be able to come back to New York if you vote for a rate so much lower than the mainland?" I said, "Father, you and I took an oath. We swore we'll defend the interest of the island as well as the interest of the mainland. If you make it higher, you're cutting out the possibility for the island to earn anything. And if you make it the way I'm suggesting, it won't be what I want but I'll be able to explain to our members that we raised the Puerto Rican standard by 300, 400, and even 500 percent. So, as a starting point, I'm satisfied."

And that had to be our approach on wages in the cities where we were powerful, especially New York, and it became our approach on welfare funds as well. We had to accommodate to the fact that ours was an industry on wheels. You could not go to Jersey or Pennsylvania or the South, much less to Japan or Taiwan, if you wanted to build the Empire State Building. But you could go to any of those places to make garments. So we, the pioneers, tailored our welfare benefits to recognize that we had to give our members maximum protection, no matter where they moved in search of employment. The locals did not like to lose sole control, but in 1952 we standardized eligibility requirements and consolidated all the pension funds in the Eastern region. By 1964 a single merged fund covered 400,000 members throughout the country.

Our rule always was that no one retired unless the fund had enough reserves to guarantee full payment for life on an actuarial basis. We knew that would leave us behind in competition with steel and auto and other industries, where unions had secure, multibillion-dollar employers to deal with. But we also knew it was no service to promise our members pensions that the pooled fund could not support. Thus, when I told the heads of the associations representing cloakmakers in the early 1950s that we needed an increase in the fifty-dollar monthly payment to retired workers, one of them said: "We're ready to give you seventy-five dollars." I told him, "No, the fund can't afford it. I'll be satisfied with sixty-five." I did it because I knew we would have to disappoint many of our people if the seventy-five-dollar standard went in. As it was, there were many years in which hundreds of members qualified for retirement but had to wait because the fund was not big enough to let them in right away. With the sixty-five-dollar standard, they didn't have to wait too long. With seventy-five dollars it would have been much worse. Now, with the funds from the various branches of the industry merged into one, and the ages more graduated, it is easier; most of the locals do not have the same number of old-timers that the cloak-makers had at the beginning.

There was one inadequacy that bothered me: neither the pension program nor regular state unemployment insurance dealt with the problems of workers left stranded when their employers went out of business. This became clear when in the late 1940s one of the best-established cloak manufacturers in New York, Morris W. Haft, decided suddenly to close shop. It was the biggest single shop we had in the entire industry, with three thousand employees, and overnight not one of them had a job. A man who made millions and millions of dollars, who became one of the richest in the industry, walks out with no responsibility, no obligation, to the workers who helped him make all those millions.

I had had previous experiences with Haft that had soured me on him, even though they did not prepare me for his callousness in this instance. Once I got a call from John W. Davis, the onetime Democratic candidate for President, who was active in the American Red Cross. He said Morris W. Haft had assured him that if he called me personally I would arrange for a union contribution of $50,000 to the Red Cross. I replied: "Fifty thousand is a lot of money and I have no authority to make such a commitment on my own. Still I'm ready to take it up, but first I want to know what Haft does himself, because I know he's a millionaire many times over. Then I'll be able to give you an answer."

When I called Haft and told him we would have to give

$50,000 if he recommended it, and asked him what he was giving, he said, "Dave, don't you know? I'm giving a lot of money." I said, "A lot of money is all right, but I want to know what is a lot of money." He gulped. "I'm giving him a hundred dollars," Haft said. I hung up on him and called back Davis. "You stick to Morris W. Haft," I told him. "He'll collect money from others, not from himself." After that Haft and I weren't on speaking terms.

Even earlier I had had trouble with Haft's selfish idea of "philanthropy." At the very start of the New Deal I got a telephone call from Mrs. Roosevelt asking me to come to the White House to discuss a very important project. It developed that Morris W. Haft had convinced Rexford G. Tugwell, the brain-truster, who was then head of the Rural Resettlement Administration, that it would be a good idea to open a cooperative garment factory in Hightstown, New Jersey, very close to New York, where Jewish workers from New York could come and make coats and suits while also running little family farms. Mrs. Roosevelt was very enthusiastic. She told me the government was ready to invest several million dollars in the project. Haft had promised to provide jobs for several hundred workers and to take their product. She was sure the experiment could be expanded. It would be good for the workers. Having farms as well as factory work would make them independent, and that would be good for them. She didn't try to tell me that it wouldn't also be good for Morris W. Haft, because I think she was a little bit too smart for that. I told her right away I thought it was all a dream. Garment workers couldn't be farmers at the same time. Morris W. Haft wanted to dismiss a lot of his workers in New York and get cheaper labor in Hightstown; that was really what was behind the plan.

I argued with Mrs. Roosevelt for half an hour, and I thought I convinced her. But no sooner did I get back to New York than Ed McGrady, the former general organizer of the A.F.L., who was Assistant Secretary of Labor, was sent to see me. I had to take a lot more time going over all the same argument. I told him I couldn't see it. Not only would the workers not become farmers, but the union could not under any circumstances become a party to letting Morris W. Haft throw out several hundred workers in New York and open a runaway shop in New Jersey. That still didn't end it. A parade of other high government officials came to our headquarters to try to persuade me to change my mind. I couldn't tell who was the driving force, whether Tugwell or Haft, but I didn't budge.

Suddenly there was a call from Albert Einstein, who was living in Princeton, a few miles from Hightstown. He arrived at my office surrounded by reporters and photographers. We spent three quarters of an hour arguing about the project. He couldn't understand why I should oppose it as long as these workers would belong to the union and pay dues. If I wouldn't lose any members, why should I be against the cooperative? I explained that I would have no objection if this was a brand-new plant hiring additional workers. That would be my position, despite my feeling that the plan would never work. If the government wanted to do it, that was its responsibility, not mine. But here was a different proposition. Here was a question of several hundred people who were making a living from Morris W. Haft in New York and would lose their jobs. And Haft wants to get an advantage. Because of government subsidies, they'll work for lower wages. They'll only work part time, and part time they'll be farming. I told Einstein I was not willing to let Haft have that kind of advantage over other unionized manufacturers. I wouldn't help him out and victimize several hundred people.

The discussion dragged on and on so long that I got a little bit excited. When I saw I was having no effect on him, I finally said, "If there was a loaf of bread and that loaf of bread belongs to me, there's two ways we can proceed. We can share the loaf; you get half of it and I get half. But if you take it away, you'll satisfy your needs but I'll be hungry. Do you think under these circumstances I'd give you my loaf of bread, or vice versa? Would you give your loaf to me? That's what we're dealing with here. My members in New York would be hungry; other people would be eating instead of them. And I am their international president. How can I tell them, 'Be satisfied; the other ones will pay dues and therefore they'll eat what you should eat instead.'"

But, for all his brilliance, Einstein was a simple man in matters of this kind. He couldn't understand my point. So finally I had to break the conversation off by saying, "Professor, when it comes to the theory of relativity, you are the professor, but when it comes to the garment industry I am the professor."

In the end Haft had to drop out of the project, but the government went ahead. A group of cooperators got together. The town was renamed Roosevelt, and there was a big celebration when the plant was opened, with Mrs. Roosevelt and Tugwell there. And the workers were jubilant. They were going to sew and sow at the same time. But within two years the plant failed, even with all the money the government had put in.

When Haft, our biggest manufacturer, closed down his own operations without a crumb for the workers who had helped make him so wealthy, I went into our 1950 convention bloody mad. I told the delegates it was time to stop our members from being treated like dogs. They voted unanimously to insist that all future contracts contain a provision for employer contributions to a severance fund to protect workers when businesses shut their doors. One big Philadelphia manufacturer, Handmacher & Vogel, signed right there at the convention. But somehow our locals never followed up aggressively on the 1950 resolution. It was not until I was called into an impasse in the New York dress industry in 1958 and we had our first strike since the Great Depression that we really got off the ground on this cardinal issue.

In 1958, the agreement by the employers to contribute a regular percentage of payroll to the severance-pay fund spurred all our other units to do what they had failed to do in the eight years since our convention resolution—get similar provisions in their contracts. By 1960 we were able to establish a pooled nationwide fund to guarantee that none of our other members would ever find themselves totally without protection as our people at Morris W. Haft did when he locked his door forever.

One other innovative fund deserves mention, because it also developed out of the special insecurities that exist for workers in an industry on wheels. Our jobbers, especially in the popular-priced field, were always looking for an edge by farming out their work to nonunion contractors. That gave them a double advantage. First, the nonunion shops operated on a forty-hour week, not thirty-five hours. When a union contractor worked forty hours, he had to pay time and a half for the extra five hours. So there was a big saving there, if the jobber could get away with it. The other saving was that the nonunion contractor did not contribute to the union health, welfare and vacation funds. That was an even bigger item. We couldn't touch the nonunion contractors, but could reach the jobbers because their contracts obliged them to do all their work in union shops. And we did have a policing mechanism through our unique auditing system, by which we could audit the books of all the employers who signed up with us, as well as the books and records of our locals and joint boards. In this way we made sure that they were making all the payments they were supposed to be making, to their workers and to the various union funds.

When we audited the books of those jobbers who were trafficking with nonunion contractors, our union agreement gave us the authority to compel the jobbers to pay whatever they had chiseled. Some of the money was in the form of liquidated damages to workers who had been defrauded out of overtime. We knew whom that belonged to. But the money that we collected because it had not been paid into health and welfare funds gave us something of a problem. We could force the jobbers to pay it, but we could not credit it to the individual workers, because they were outside our contract. So we held this money in a separate account which I called a "*knippel*." It's a term that comes from the old country. When a peasant woman had saved a few pennies out of her allowance and didn't want her husband to know about it, she would hide it by tying a knot in a corner of her kerchief. That knot where she kept her money was called a *knippel*. We accumulated the money for unpaid health and welfare contributions in a *knippel* of our own to hide it from the local managers.

When it became quite substantial I realized that we could be in trouble if we did not report it to the government as part of our required filings under the Landrum-Griffin Act and other federal laws. This money was invested and we could account for it all. So we classified it as "Special Fund" and included it in our filings with the Labor Department. By the time I retired in 1966, this fund had mounted to six million dollars, and I felt I had to make some recommendation on how to use it before I left. Suddenly the answer seemed obvious. Why not use the *knippel* to take care of hundreds of borderline cases of people who had been in the industry a long time but did not technically qualify for pensions under our rules?

I'm sure this idea was inspired by one particular story, which had long stuck in my mind. It involved an eighty-two-year-old woman who was a survivor of the Triangle Shirtwaist Company fire in 1911. She had been a dedicated member of the union, first in New York and then in Chicago, a shop chairlady who worked hard to build the I.L.G. Then she got married and left the industry. After her husband's death, she sent me a letter saying she would never go on relief, but she did not qualify for a union pension and it was hard to survive on her Social Security of only fifty-five dollars a month. It was a desperate plea, but our rules did not permit any special exceptions. I took the case up with our Finance Committee and twice we decided to give her one hundred dollars, but that obviously was small help and no real solution.

Our *knippel* could be a source of revenue for such people as that old lady. I suggested that we establish a Retiree Service Department that would not only provide financial aid in hardship cases but also plan cultural activities and make it clear to our retired members that they were still very much part of the union. The General Executive Board unanimously endorsed the suggestion and set up a budget of $350,000 a year for the department. Interest on the *knippel* covered pretty much the whole cost. My successor, Louis Stulberg, asked me to become the department's first head, which I did, serving without pay. Under the Older Americans Act of 1965, we got a three-year grant of roughly $200,000 a year more to expand the department by creating a Friendly Visitor Service to keep in direct touch with our retirees. That service was such a success that when the experimental agreement expired in 1970 and there were no more government funds available, the union voted to continue it alone with union funds.

Our union also originated the idea of asking intellectuals to do research on industrial problems to help the union represent its members more effectively. This too went back to the earliest days of the I.L.G., a recognition in part of the many technical problems that existed in our industry, of our close relation to the consumer and, most of all, of the extent to which the public became involved in insisting that civilized conditions exist in the garment shops. The 1910 Protocol of Peace was a reflection of that involvement. We needed people who could marshal facts, and you could not always find all of them in the shops. The other needle-trades unions, the Amalgamated Clothing Workers and the Millinery Workers Union, followed the same idea. But it remained alien to the building trades and most of the other old-line unions, where intellectuals were always distrusted. When I came to the A.F.L. Executive Council in the early 1930s, the general labor movement looked askance at this thing called research.

I remember Dan Tobin, the president of the Teamsters, saying, "What in the world have these intellectuals got to do with unionism? Where do they come in?"

But in the end even Tobin came around to recognizing that unions needed technicians of every kind, not only lawyers and accountants and specialists in social insurance but research departments staffed by experts from the universities and from other agencies outside the industry. That was indispensable after the New Deal. I remember how shocked I was when Tobin told me he was hiring Dave Kaplan, a graduate of the University of Wisconsin who had done research for the Machinists and who once belonged to the I.W.W., to head up a research department for the Teamsters. Then I knew how much the trend was changing. Our first research director was Alexander Trachtenberg, who later became a leading theoretician for the Communist Party. From the beginning we organized an extremely effective department, which has functioned since 1937 under the superb direction of Dr. Lazare Teper, an economist highly regarded by industry and government.

For us, however, it was not enough to have a generalized research department. The complexity of wage determination in our industry meant that we had to go still further. We created a management-engineering department to give the union some measure of equality in dealing with large employers who introduced scientific principles into their shops and wanted to avoid haggling over piece rates on the shop floor. An experiment had started in 1919 in Cleveland, where the plants were generally large, stable and efficient. By joint agreement a Bureau of Standards, with an impartial board of referees, was set up to establish wage rates on an incentive basis. It worked well until the depression, but the system broke down when it became impossible to maintain the fixed wage floor.

The passage of the federal Fair Labor Standards Act, with its statutory limits on wages and hours, created new boundaries for competition. The pressure was especially severe in the low-end garments, the so-called cotton-house-dress branch of the industry, where a difference of pennies in production cost meant the difference between success or bankruptcy for a manufacturer. The clear line that had ex-isted between silk dresses, expertly tailored, and house-dresses, made by relatively unskilled workers outside the big cities, eroded. Later, synthetics would almost entirely erase it. Our workers who sewed a complete garment, an opera-tion requiring considerable skill, could not compete against those who operated under the assembly-line techniques of section work. In that system each worker sewed a particular part of the dress and had a piece rate designed to achieve a fixed basic earning opportunity of so many cents an hour. We did not encourage the development of section work, be-cause we felt our first obligation was to the older workers in the established production centers like Seventh Avenue. But we knew we could not stop it and we did not try. Instead, we established our own engineering department just after World War II to assure a fair break for the workers in deter-mining rates. Our engineers also were often of great help to manufacturers who did not understand the new techniques and were in danger of going out of business. We were able to protect our members because the slide rules by which piece rates were established were now in our hands as well as the bosses'. And the whole industry benefited.

Unlike the management-engineering department, another of our innovations, the Training Institute, was a good idea that went sour. It grew out of our union's desperate need for qualified officers. Because 80 to 85 percent of our members were women, many of whom left the shops when they got married, it was hard to develop leaders from within the shops. It had been the custom for shop chairmen or mem-bers of a committee establishing piece rates to become officers, but few of these had the background for the highly technical negotiation that were necessary in the union. As early as 1934 we established a few scholarships so that some of our bright new members could go to the Brookwood Labor College in Katonah, New York, but that lasted only a few years. Later we financed fellowships in the Harvard trade-union program. We also passed a requirement that those wanting to be officers in New York had to enroll for special qualification courses to equip them for their new responsibilities.

None of these programs met the need, however. In 1947 I shared with the I.L.G. convention delegates my conviction that labor generally needed new sources of leadership. My idea was that we had to pull in idealistic young people from the colleges who wanted to make trade-unionism a career. In my mind was a memory of one of my first trips to Baltimore in the early days. I met with the head of the most important nonunion shop there and asked why he fought the union. He said his father had taken an oath never to have a union shop because our chief organizer had once come in, supposedly to discuss a grievance, and instead of talking to the employer, he picked up a yardstick and clapped it on the table. "Stop the shop," he shouted. The result was such resentment that the union could not even get a hearing after that. I felt we had to find people with a bit more understanding, a bit more polish.

With the support of the convention, we organized a full-time Training Institute, which would give a one-year preparation course for union leadership. Seven months were spent in the classroom and five in field duty with our locals and joint boards. The first class began in May 1950, with thirty-seven young men and women as students. Eighteen were college graduates, eleven had some college training and eight were high-school graduates. Most applied themselves seriously to their studies and to learning what our union was all about. The dropout rate through all the ten years of the institute's existence was low. About half the graduates served in various posts in the union; the others went off to jobs in business or government. The fact that many of the students thought of the institute as a chance to educate themselves out of the movement rather than as a service to labor was one of my first disappointments in the experiment.

An even greater disappointment came in the early 1960s when some of the institute graduates became the spearhead of a movement to organize a union within our union. They called it the Federation of Union Representatives (FOUR), and they demanded recognition as collective-bargaining agent for the I.L.G. staff on wages and working conditions. To me their demand indicated that they had a total misconception of unionism, one that reflected seriously on the work of the institute itself. What disturbed me was not that they had grievances they wanted to discuss. That, of course, was legitimate. The staff wages in our union always were low by comparison with those in the building trades or the teamsters. The business agents in many locals of other unions earned more than I did as president of a union with more than 400,000 members. And all our other salaries tended to follow that same concept of not wanting the living standards and expectations of our officers to get too remote from the standards of the people they represented. But I recognized that this was an arguable proposition and that many had great trouble sending their children to college or even making ends meet in an inflationary period.

What did bother me was the idea that they in FOUR, as officers of the union, should set up a union of their own and demand recognition from me as if the union were my personal possession. It was different with our clerks and bookkeepers. They were members of a union and the I.L.G. dealt with them in the usual way through collective bargaining. But the officers and organizers of our own union were different. I felt that they, as part of the heart blood of the union, could not form a union within a union, because I was not an employer. If I wanted to be an employer I could have made lots of money, and I had plenty of offers. But I wanted to represent workers. So when some of the youngsters who had come from the Training Institute organized FOUR and asked for a meeting, I said: "Not on their life will I meet with them representing a union. If it comes to the point where the National Labor Relations Board orders me to do it, I will resign rather than be president of a union dealing with a staff union. They are not working for me, they are working for the union. And the union is not myself. The union is membership. I'm employed as well as they, except I have a higher title."

What I found most disheartening in the whole demand was that these young people in whom I and the organization had placed so much hope seemed to have embraced the Jimmy Hoffa philosophy that a union is a business. This makes the top officers of the union—the president and the general executive board—like the board of directors of a quasicorporation, rendering certain paid services. And the other officers of the union—organizers and business agents— are mere employees of the corporation, like salesmen and store supervisors.

The other theory of unionism, the one on which the I.L.G. had always operated, is that a union is a crusade, a move- ment, a banding-together of working people to defend their interests and to promote the general welfare of the com- munity and the world in which they live. The dues paid to the union is not a price for a commodity but a means of "chipping in" to strengthen the common instrument of the working people in the struggle for a better life. By this con- cept, the top leadership is not made up of the "owners" of the union; rather, it is the mouthpiece for the aspirations and needs of the workers. By the same token, organizers and business agents are not paid salesmen and store supervisors working for a salary or a commission, but rather missionaries out to convert the unorganized and defending the interests of the membership they represent.

I had spent time in a Tsarist jail because I was part of a struggle to free people, not because I was paid to agitate.

The founders of our union had starved themselves to sickness and death, faced beatings and crippling by gangsters, and had gone to prison because they felt that this was their duty to their consciences and to their fellow workers. Never did it occur to us that, in undertaking these sacrifices, we were grasping for a "job."

I have to confess that many liberals, including many whom I greatly respected, did not share my view on these points. They felt that as a union we should be the first to endorse and support collective bargaining for our staff. But this would have been a surrender to the materialist spirit and commercialism of our times, a betrayal of the ideals of our organization. We fought the issue through the N.L.R.B., and in the end the staff union collapsed. It was a bitter struggle, but I am glad we did not take the easy way as many other unions did, to their considerable regret. So far as our own organization was concerned, it stood solidly behind my position. By unanimous vote, the 962 delegates to the 1962 convention approved our actions in the FOUR case. The regrettable thing was that no one after that could get up much enthusiasm about the Training Institute. Training in business unionism was not what we had expected to come from it.

Other union firsts were reflected in our accomplishments on the social front, the area in which we tried hardest to enrich the community at the same time that we were bringing dignity and a measure of economic security to our own members. Decent housing in districts that had been slums was among our proudest activities. In 1953 I was able to say at ground-breaking ceremonies for a towering cooperative development at Corlears Hook in the heart of the old Lower East Side:

"Many of us are here today as natives returning to the scenes of our childhood. We are the sons and daughters of this East Side, the children of immigrants who dared the terror of the sea and a strange land to search for freedom.

Fifty-three years ago the I.L.G. was officially organized to war against the sweatshop. Today the garment workers return to their place of origin. We have wiped out the sweatshop. Now we return to wipe out the slum."

We were not the first union in this country to seek to match the huge housing developments built under union auspices in Socialist countries abroad. That honor belonged to our sister in the needle trades, the Amalgamated Clothing Workers, with its cooperatives in the Bronx and adjacent to us on the East Side. But we had plenty of difficulties when we made our first move at Corlears Hook. The banks and insurance companies would not give us a mortgage at the prevailing rate; and rather than submit to their attempt at gouging, which would have pushed up the down payments and carrying charges for our cooperators, I proposed to our General Executive Board that we invest fifteen million dollars of the union's own funds. Up to then we had invested only in government bonds, staying clear of all speculative securities. But here I saw no risk, and an enormous social benefit. The mortgage bonds would carry a guarantee from the Federal Housing Authority, and the board agreed that this put them on a par with the government's own notes. When the four 22-story skyscrapers on their parklike campus were completed two years later, I hailed them as the "profit" of our early strikes, the social dividends of constructive unionism.

Once launched on housing investment, we proceeded to expand. In mid-1957, we committed 2.6 million dollars to underwriting a Puerto Rican project in which we became bankers to the Rockefellers. This partnership between legendary wealth and a progressive trade union was designed to provide excellent housing for the families of Puerto Rican workers, half of them our members, who had once worked for as little as two cents an hour. The project, put up by a subsidiary of the Rockefeller-sponsored International Basic Economic Corporation, was named for Santiago

Iglesias, the Samuel Gompers of Puerto Rico. It marked a long step in the civilizing of the Rockefellers, once a symbol of rapacious capitalism to workers everywhere.

The biggest of our developments was Penn Station South, in the Chelsea section of Manhattan, within easy walk of the garment center. President Kennedy came to New York in 1962 to help dedicate this monument to I.L.G. social inventiveness. Despite its huge size, the project has always had a waiting list years long. That was a measure of how derelict government and private enterprise had been in making livable housing available at rents that middle-income workers can afford to pay. There was a vacuum that we had to fill.

It was also part of our philosophy of union duty to make contributions to philanthropic and labor causes all over the world. We were the pioneers, even when we did not have money to pay our own salaries or day-to-day bills. We did it out of an awareness that we have to be part of the community. And we made that the philosophy of the A.F.L.–C.I.O. and of many of its affiliates. No longer did unions try to live to themselves, taking but never giving. Labor gave enormously to the foundations set up in memory of Franklin D. Roosevelt and Eleanor Roosevelt. It gave in similar spirit in memory of John F. Kennedy. It stopped being a recluse, and it is our joy that we inspired that change.

NINE

Revolving Door to the C.I.O.

THROUGHOUT ALL OF INDUSTRY the spirit of the New Deal brought the same sense of hope and deliverance to workers that we had found so helpful in rebuilding the I.L.G.W.U. In the smoky steel mills and on the automobile assembly lines, where all kinds of brutality had been used to keep unions out, there was a great stirring. The same thing was true in the tire plants and the factories making electrical equipment; everywhere there was an itch to organize. But it quickly became clear that, if strong unions were going to be built in the mass-production industries, the workers had a handicap to overcome over and beyond the fierce resistance from their bosses. That handicap was the worship of craft unionism by the old-line leadership of the American Federation of Labor.

Technically, twenty or thirty unions could claim jurisdiction over particular groups of workers in every big manufacturing plant—the machinists, the sheet-metal workers, the pattern makers, the firemen and oilers, the various construction crafts, and so on through an endless list. Long experience had shown that these unions, each operating on its own, were powerless to organize gigantic enterprises. But, even though they had never succeeded in organizing these plants—and didn't even make any real effort to do so—the craft unions were so jealous of their jurisdictional "rights" that they would not permit the A.F.L. to issue industrywide charters under which everyone could be brought into one comprehensive union of the kind we had in the women's garment industry.

The senselessness of believing that the A.F.L. structure could deal adequately with the problems of industrial unionism had been recognized by many critics within the labor movement for a long time. From 1904 on, resolutions would be offered at Federation conventions calling for grouping of unions on industry lines, but they never got far until 1934. In that year the San Francisco convention adopted a compromise resolution which, for the first time, gave some small comfort to the industrial unionists. It conceded that craft unionism was a flop where the lines of demarcation between crafts were blurred and that new approaches were needed if we were ever going to succeed in reaching mass-production workers. The resolution specifically empowered the Executive Council to undertake an organizing campaign in steel and to issue charters for new unions in the automobile, cement and aluminum industries.

But, by the time the next convention assembled in Atlantic City in October, 1935, the craft unionists were in no mood to move further in the constructive direction suggested by that resolution. On the contrary, they were determined to move backward at top speed. The majority report of the resolutions committee blandly declared that those of us who felt the need for movement either misunderstood the 1934 statement or wanted to set it aside. After that came a lot of legalistic language, all of which added up to a repeal of the earlier resolution and a reaffirmation in extreme terms of the inviolability of craft jurisdiction.

As a member of both the resolutions committee and the Executive Council, I was aghast at the way the original resolution was being twisted. I joined with John L. Lewis of the United Mine Workers, who was the chief spear carrier for the industrial unionists, in submitting a minority report to the convention. Our report stressed the obligation of the Federation to organize the unorganized in the mass industries and the utter impossibility of doing it with traditional methods. We noted that after fifty-five years these methods had brought only 3.5 million workers out of a potential of 39 million under the A.F.L. banner.

> We declare [the minority report said] the time has arrived when common sense demands the organization policies of the American Federation of Labor must be molded to meet present-day needs . . . Continuous employment, economic security and the ability to protect the individual worker [in the mass-production industries] depends upon organization upon industrial lines.

This minority resolution was rejected by the convention, but the vote in its favor was surprisingly strong—better than a third. The fight was not confined to words or even to votes. At one stage, after "Big Bill" Hutcheson, the president of the Carpenters, had raised a point of order to squelch a delegate from one of the tiny industrial unions struggling for recognition, Lewis described the tactics of the old guard as "rather small potatoes." Hutcheson took that as a personal insult, and pretty soon the two men were swearing at one another and Lewis let go a roundhouse swing that landed on Hutcheson's jaw. The C.I.O. as an autonomous force for building industrial unionism was born with that punch.

Before the convention ended Lewis called a small conference at the President Hotel in Atlantic City. I was there along with Charles P. Howard of the International Typographical Union and Sidney Hillman of the Amalgamated Clothing Workers, and several others. The purpose was to keep the unions favoring industrial unionism in touch with one another and to cement their forces for future A.F.L. conventions. Three weeks later a larger meeting was held at the United Mine Workers headquarters in Washington, at which a Committee for Industrial Organization was formed, with Lewis as chairman and Howard as secretary. Its declared purpose was to organize the unorganized mass-production workers under the principles proclaimed in the minority resolution, but it went out of its way to stress that there was no intent to injure established unions.

I have to confess that I had some reservations from the start. I knew we could not count on the A.F.L. to organize the unorganized, but I smelled a rat. I was not sure everyone at the meeting had the same desire that I did to act as a pressure group within the Federation, not as a dual-union movement outside it. Two weeks later my suspicions were reinforced when Lewis suddenly sent a letter to William Green resigning as an A.F.L. vice-president. He gave me no inkling, much less notice, that he was going to quit, even though he and I were the only two members of the C.I.O. founding group who were A.F.L. vice-presidents. Both of us had been freshly re-elected at Atlantic City, and his unexplained action left me to hold the fort alone.

On November 23 Green sent a letter to all the unions represented at the formation of the C.I.O. warning of the danger of "division and discord" that might come from such a development. I presented the whole question to the I.L.G.W.U. General Executive Board for the first time at its quarterly meeting in Cleveland in December, two weeks after the Green letter. I knew the sentiment of the board members was sharply divided. We had some people deeply devoted to the A.F.L. and suspicious of anything that could possibly split it. We had others who felt the Federation was dead on its feet and much in need of the kind of kick-in-the-pants it was getting from the C.I.O. I encouraged a full debate, deliberately not saying anything myself until they had all expressed their views and voted. The vote was 12 to 9—twelve for joining the C.I.O., nine against joining.

After the die was cast, I told them I was glad they had voted as they did. If they had not decided to join, I said, I would have made them do it, not because I believed we should ever have organized a Committee for Industrial Organization—it would have been better to work within the A.F.L. without any separate organization—but, once a C.I.O. was formed, we could not be out of it. We traditionally stood for industrial unionism, and when a committee is organized for that purpose, we've got to be part of it. If the I.L.G.W.U. were not part of such a committee, our members would not understand it, nor would the community in general.

But I insisted that our formal resolution contain a strong statement that we would belong to and support the Committee for Industrial Organization as long as it adhered to its original purposes and principles, meaning that it would limit itself to organizing the unorganized, and *not* become a dual union in competition with the A.F.L. So, in our final resolution we applauded the goals of the C.I.O. and warned that failure to unionize the mass-production industries under its principles would drive millions into company unions or subversive movements. We also defended the right of our union and any other A.F.L. affiliate to advocate, individually or jointly, a change in organizing methods. But the same resolution said: "Our International Union, which more than any other union has fought dual-unionism and opposition movements within its own midst, would strenuously oppose any movement which has for its purpose to act as an opposition to the American Federation of Labor or to promote any dualism."

Despite our statement, it became clearer each day that Lewis was determined to widen the gulf between the C.I.O. and the A.F.L. When Green sent a letter warning of the danger of separation and strife, Howard prepared a polite reply in behalf of the C.I.O. It defended the right of our group to promote its views by educational means, but it emphasized that there was no intent to raid or infringe on the rightful jurisdiction of any established union. Instead of trying to promote dualism, Howard said, our main idea was to steer the A.F.L. away from a course that invited dualism. It was a fine answer until Lewis added two paragraphs referring to the well-known fact that Green, who came out of the United Mine Workers, was privately quite sympathetic to the cause of the industrial unionists. Then, with a brass typical of Lewis, he invited Green to give up his A.F.L. presidency and take over the chairmanship of the C.I.O. at the same salary. "Why not return to your father's house?" Lewis asked.

To nobody's surprise, Green replied that he was already in his father's house and had every intention of staying there. But the whole episode was acutely embarrassing to him and undercut whatever role he might have played in reuniting the two sides. It is true that Green did take a friendlier view of our arguments than the hard-liners inside the Executive Council did. But Green was a weak man, a Federation president in name only, who walked in mortal fear of the real powers in the Council—Hutcheson and Dan Tobin of the Teamsters. At a December meeting of the C.I.O., I expressed my own unhappiness about our seeming to be looking for a fight, and I urged that we move cautiously. Howard concurred, but Lewis would have none of it. He said we would lose our prestige if we didn't charge ahead. And his view prevailed. All of us were too aware of how much he meant to the movement, and we were firmly convinced of the need on strictly trade-union grounds of inducing the A.F.L. to open the door to effective organization of the mass industries.

When the A.F.L. Executive Council met in January 1936, I attended as the only C.I.O. representative still holding a Council seat. Despite Lewis, I still felt it was possible to get affirmative action without a split. There was no question in my mind that the predominant sentiment in the C.I.O. was to stay inside the Federation, not to operate as a rival to it. Early in the Council meeting Green asked me whether I had been consulted about Lewis's insulting letter. I told him quite frankly that Lewis hadn't consulted me either about that or about quitting the Executive Council. Both were purely one-man decisions.

It became evident right away that one faction in the Council wanted blood. My whole effort was to convince the moderates, who seemed to be in the majority, that they would simply be playing into Lewis's hands if people like

Hutcheson, Arthur O. Wharton of the Machinists and Thomas A. Rickert of the United Garment Workers got their way. I was glad to find that Green had not let his anger over the Lewis letter push him into their camp, though I knew he was more servant than master when it came to making decisions. However, he made one ruling that might have altered the history of American labor if it had not been ignored later on.

It came after some Executive Council members suggested that all the unions involved in the C.I.O. should be suspended at once unless the organization was disbanded. Green said his search of the A.F.L. constitution and records showed him no basis or precedent for action by the Council to suspend the charter of any affiliated union. Only a convention had authority to suspend or revoke charters. Just to underscore the point, Green warned the Council that it would be highly inconsistent for the Federation to tell the C.I.O. unions they had to obey the laws and rules of the A.F.L. if the Council itself did not scrupulously follow these same laws and procedures.

The next day Howard came before the Council to speak for the C.I.O. group. He made a conciliatory statement, explaining that the organization of millions of mass-production workers would strengthen the position of the A.F.L. and of all its unions. When Green asked him whether he would be willing to see the C.I.O. continue if he could be convinced it would injure the A.F.L., Howard replied, "No, I would lay down my life to prevent that."

Afterward, two resolutions were presented for action by the Executive Council. One, sponsored by Green, called for appointing a committee of three to let all the C.I.O. unions know that the Federation considered the organization harmful and divisive and that it should be dissolved. Matthew Woll of the Photo-Engravers Union proposed a milder resolution. He wanted a committee that would meet with officers of the individual unions in the C.I.O. and try to persuade them to withdraw from it because of the dangers that might arise from its activities. If the committee failed, it was to recommend additional steps to the Council.

I urged acceptance of the Woll proposal and cautioned the Council against taking any step that sounded like an ultimatum. I told them they had no right to demand that the C.I.O. be dissolved without first establishing through a formal investigation that the committee was violating the rules of the A.F.L. The Council did not go along with my advice. It adopted a statement that was not strong enough to satisfy Hutcheson and his cohorts, but it contained enough dynamite to give Lewis the encouragement he needed for pushing the situation into head-on collision.

The Federation's resolution asked for immediate dissolution of the C.I.O. on the ground that its objectives ran counter to the will of the majority, as expressed in the Atlantic City convention. Failure to respect majority decisions could only lead to discord and division within labor's ranks, the Council said. However, it carefully avoided any threats of punitive action. Rather, it directed its three-man committee to present to representatives of the unions in the C.I.O. the Council's recommendations and viewpoint. The committee was to report back at the next regular meeting of the Council in May.

The United Mine Workers had a convention right after the A.F.L. Council concluded its meeting. It provided just the setting Lewis wanted for widening the breach. He spent days whipping the miners up into a lather of rage at the Federation for its hostile toward the C.I.O. In one of his speeches he said that, so far as he was concerned, the members of the Executive Council would be wearing "asbestos suits in hell" before the C.I.O. was dissolved. After everybody was thoroughly riled up, Green was allowed to speak in support of the Federation. At the end of Green's speech Lewis asked the delegates how many thought the miners and the others in the C.I.O. should "like quarry slaves at night" be scared into dissolving their organization. Only one delegate rose in response to that loaded proposition. When Lewis asked for general support of his own position, the applause was deafening.

But Lewis was still running all by himself. I was not with him and felt that my colleagues in the I.L.G.W.U. and the rest of the C.I.O. leaders were also reluctant to wave red flags at the A.F.L. We wanted to do a job of organizing, and we still hoped that it could be done without splitting the labor movement. So, when the full C.I.O. group met late in February 1936, we prepared a joint reply to the A.F.L., denying once again any intention to act as a competing body outside the framework of the Federation. We defended all our actions as proper and expressed our readiness to meet with the Executive Council committee to discuss all the issues freely. At the same meeting the C.I.O. offered to contribute $500,000 to a drive to organize the steel industry, provided the A.F.L. would raise another one million and would promise that all steelworkers unionized through the drive would be allowed to remain permanently united in one industrial union, instead of being carved up into a multitude of craft unions. All of this, we said, could be done within the Federation.

The A.F.L. chose to cold-shoulder our offer. However, its effect was to needle Green and the Federation into proposing a $750,000 drive under its own auspices, with the money to come from contributions by its affiliated unions. The result was nil. No money was contributed; instead, there were demands from the A.F.L. die-hards that the C.I.O. group be kicked out of the Federation.

The whole trend of official A.F.L. policy made it clear that the people who wanted no compromise with the C.I.O. were in the saddle. The Executive Council committee didn't even get in touch with anybody in the C.I.O. until May 19, four months after the committee was appointed. The C.I.O. was asked to round up all its people on less than a day's notice to meet with the three A.F.L. people, under the chairmanship of George M. Harrison of the Brotherhood of Railway Clerks. I was on my way to a California meeting of the

I.L.G.'s General Executive Board and could not attend. But it wouldn't have made any difference. The meeting was a farce, because the Harrison committee told Lewis and the other C.I.O. representatives right away that it was there to urge them to abandon their activity, not to make any promises about what the Federation would or would not do about organizing along industrial lines. The whole thing was more a restatement of frozen positions than an effort to find a basis for accommodation.

A few days later the I.L.G., along with all the other unions identified with the C.I.O., got a formal letter from the Harrison committee telling us that we were proceeding in opposition to the policies formulated by the Atlantic City convention and demanding that we let them know within two weeks whether we would either dissolve the whole C.I.O. or pull out of it ourselves. There was no doubt that we were heading for calamity, but I still felt we should try to point a path of reason. Not, of course, that we should bow to the committee's ultimatum, much less backtrack on the C.I.O. purpose of establishing a solid foundation for organizing workers who desperately needed help from those already inside the labor movement.

The General Executive Board of the I.L.G. subscribed to that view. It approved a letter to Harrison in which we expressed for the hundredth time the opposition of our union to anything that smacked of dualism and reaffirmed our loyalty to the A.F.L. But we expressed just as strongly our belief that our union and any other had the right to advocate a change in organizing tactics and to promote such a change in a democratic, fraternal manner without upsetting unity in the A.F.L.

In our view, it was not we, but the A.F.L. people, who were proceeding undemocratically. We accused the committee of having failed to provide an opportunity for presenting our side and of having overstepped its authority by issuing its peremptory order. On that basis, the I.L.G. refused either to move for disbanding of the C.I.O. or to sever our connection with it. The final sentence of our letter was particularly important. It said: "Should it, at any time, be proved that the Committee for Industrial Organization engages in dual-union activities, we assure you that there will be no need of any edict or ultimatum, but the Committee will either correct its policy or we will withdraw from it."

But even before our union and others sent our rejections to Harrison, the mental set of the Executive Council had congealed against us. That was made unmistakable when Charlton Ogburn, the general counsel for the A.F.L., produced a remarkable legal memorandum so outrageously at variance with the facts that it could only have been written on orders. Its whole purpose was to reverse Green's ruling that the Executive Council had no authority under the A.F.L. constitution or rules to suspend any international union. No shyster could have done a more slippery job than Ogburn did in distorting the A.F.L. constitution to conjure up a suspension right that never was there. It was all hocus-pocus; and to his credit, Harrison had the guts to tell that to Green and the rest of the Council when the Ogburn memorandum was presented. He said he deplored the formation of the C.I.O. but believed the unions involved were within their rights in establishing it. Unfortunately, his was a lonely voice. The wolf pack was out to destroy us even if it meant inventing legal weapons by turning the law upside down.

Meanwhile, the Amalgamated Association of Iron, Steel and Tin Workers—which had carried the A.F.L. banner rather feebly in the steel industry ever since 1919, when the major producers routed it in a strike led by William Z. Foster—was being batted back and forth between the A.F.L. and C.I.O. Lewis had told the Amalgamated that the C.I.O. was prepared to make it the pivotal element in the campaign for organizing steelworkers into an industrial union, if assurance was given that those organized would not later be parceled out among the craft unions and also that leadership of the campaign would be entrusted to a capable and energetic person in whom all the unions contributing to the drive could have confidence. After a good deal of shilly-shallying, the Amalgamated finally decided it would never get anything but double-talk from the A.F.L. Executive Council. It also feared that the C.I.O. would go ahead all by itself if the Amalgamated continued to hold back. Accordingly, it agreed early in June 1936 to become part of a new Steel Workers Organizing Committee, with headquarters in Pittsburgh and Philip Murray, vice-president of the United Mine Workers, as chairman. Julius Hochman, an I.L.G.W.U. vice-president and the strongest supporter of the C.I.O. on our General Executive Board, was named to represent us on the organizing committee.

Now the noose began to tighten around our necks. Green disavowed any connection or responsibility on the part of the A.F.L. in the steel-industry drive. At a July meeting of the Executive Council, which I did not attend because it conflicted with my participation in an international conference of garment workers in Europe, Green reversed his earlier position about the legality of suspension without convention action. He accepted the specious reasoning of the Ogburn memorandum without reservation and strongly advocated suspending the C.I.O. unions if they persisted in remaining affiliated with the committee.

Harrison was just as strong on the other side. He said all the lawyers he had consulted informed him that the Council had no suspension authority under the A.F.L. constitution. He deplored the fact that his own committee had been given no warrant to develop a peace plan, and urged that time and energy be put into such an effort instead of finding ways to create more difficulties. He revealed that he had met with Lewis the night before and had been assured that the C.I.O. was ready to dissolve if the Federation would agree to the organization of steel, auto, rubber and one other mass-production industry on an industrial basis. Dan Tobin of the Teamsters, who had been among the loudest of the Council members in denouncing the C.I.O., swung around to a suggestion that a conference with Lewis be held to see whether a formal agreement could be worked out. But the rest of the Council wanted a showdown. They directed Green to send each C.I.O. union notice to appear before the Council on August 3 for trial on charges of "fostering and supporting a dual organization and fomenting insurrection within the A.F.L. . . ."

The C.I.O. unions voted unanimously to challenge this dictatorial summons as a violation of the A.F.L. constitution. In a joint letter to Green, they noted that unions could constitutionally be expelled only by a two-thirds roll-call vote at a convention and that suspension in advance of a convention would stack the deck by disqualifying the C.I.O. from sending delegates. The whole maneuver was denounced as part of a conspiracy by a small craft clique to preserve its dead-hand control over the Federation and frustrate organization of the mass industries. In line with this position, none of our unions appeared at the August 3 meeting, but the trial proceeded anyway.

John P. Frey, president of the Metal Trades Department and spokesman for the most reactionary elements in the A.F.L., acted as chief prosecutor. Harrison sent a letter questioning once again the authority of the Executive Council to suspend anybody without a direct convention mandate and repeating his plea for some effort at reconciliation. But he did not bother to come and make his argument in person, probably because he knew how hopeless it was. I did come, fresh from Europe, to urge in behalf of the I.L.G.W.U. that action on suspension be deferred for three months until the next convention in Tampa. When Green asked me whether the C.I.O. intended to organize an independent, rival movement, I told him I did not think it would happen unless they were suspended by the Council. If the Council did suspend, the answer would be exactly the opposite—"Definitely yes." I made it plain that the garment workers would be part of the rebellion if the Council did arrogate to itself the power to suspend. My argument made no impression. The Council voted 13 to 1, with me as the lone dissenter, to suspend the ten unions if they did not pull out of the C.I.O. by September 5.

To me the action seemed as ill-advised as it was autocratic. When Green sent the I.L.G., along with all the other C.I.O. founding unions, notice that it would automatically be considered suspended if it did not end its affiliation by September 5, I responded by resigning as an A.F.L. vice-president. However, I still felt confident that peace could be achieved if the whole issue were presented to the Tampa convention in November with every union free to participate and vote. A month before that gathering I renewed my peace proposal at a convention of the United Hatters, Cap and Millinery Workers, of which Max Zaritsky was secretary-treasurer and moving spirit. That union was itself split on C.I.O. affiliation. Its men's-hat division, the old United Hatters, was strongly pro-A.F.L., a carry-over from the historic role that union played in the famous Danbury Hatters case. The cap and millinery division, under Zaritsky, drew its traditions from the Socialist Party and the sweatshops of the Lower East Side. The affinity of that group for industrial unionism made Zaritsky line up personally with the C.I.O., but the union did not affiliate as an international organization.

Following out the tenor of my talk, the hatters adopted a resolution deploring the fact that the A.F.L. Council's suspension action had muddied the whole question of how best to organize the unorganized. It urged that all the suspended unions be allowed full representation at the Tampa convention. It also urged that subcommittees be established by both the A.F.L. and the C.I.O. to seek an acceptable peace formula before the convention. Green informed Zaritsky on October 13 that the A.F.L. would designate a three-man committee to meet with the C.I.O. "for the purpose of jointly exploring the possibilities of reconciliation and of seeking a formula which might be applied to the solution of differences."

On the basis of private talks I had had with Green at the

time of the hatters' convention, I knew that the A.F.L. was still insistent on dissolution of the C.I.O. I also knew that they had no intention of supporting the organization campaign in steel, which they regarded, in Green's words, as "a red-hot poker." But when the Executive Council authorized appointment of a negotiating committee it seemed to me a made-to-order opportunity for turning the situation around. I urged Lewis to call an immediate meeting of the C.I.O. so we could get the talks under way as far as possible before the November 16 opening of the Tampa A.F.L. convention.

Instead, Lewis informed me that he was setting up a joint meeting of the C.I.O. and the Steel Workers Organizing Committee on November 9 in Pittsburgh. Both Zaritsky and I tried to persuade Lewis to move up the date, but the best we could get was an advance of the date to November 7. When that date came Lewis lost no time in announcing that he did not think any peace could be worked out with the A.F.L. subcommittee. I argued privately with Lewis that we had had a year in which considerable progress had been made and that peace was now the most practical and sensible course. My argument to him was that we came into being to organize the unorganized, not to establish a dual organization.

"They represent the old, we the young," I told Lewis. "They are the past, we the future. It would make a good combination—a union of militancy and drive and interest in the movement on the part of the youthful idealists, together with the background and experience of the old-timers." Lewis was against it. He enjoyed power too much. At the Pittsburgh meeting he pushed aside all suggestions that the A.F.L. offer be treated seriously. He then proposed that he meet directly with Green. When Green replied that he would meet but had no authority to act, that gave Lewis the excuse he wanted for pronouncing the whole exploration futile. I had a great sense of impending tragedy, an awareness that nothing could stop a fateful split. Stubborn men were in command on both sides, and time had run out.

My rejoicing at the re-election of Franklin D. Roosevelt for a second term was dampened by the knowledge that the same labor movement that contributed so largely to his landslide victory was now about to contribute a monumental headache to his efforts to maintain unified national effort for economic recovery. But there was no help for it. The Tampa convention, with the C.I.O. unions barred from seats, duly ratified the Executive Council's illegal suspension order. The required two-thirds vote in support of suspension never could have been obtained had we been there.

Once the organizational tie had been cut, the C.I.O. began to move in earnest. Organizers were dispatched in all directions. Lewis, a superb tactician, charmed Myron C. Taylor of United States Steel into recognition of the Steel Workers Organizing Committee without a strike. The bull side of Lewis's nature, plus the vigor of the sit-down strikers in Flint—aided by a heavy push from the President—forced General Motors to knuckle under. The strides of the C.I.O. were so spectacular that the A.F.L. decided that it had to come alive as well. Both groups began to gain members at an impressive clip. Nevertheless, by the time the I.L.G.W.U. convention rolled around in May 1937, there were signs that the great momentum of the C.I.O. drive was running out. It seemed important to us to make a new appeal for peace with honor in organized labor. We reaffirmed our belief that the Federation's Council had committed "an act of the grossest illegality" when it suspended the C.I.O. unions. We hailed the accomplishments of the C.I.O. in bringing a million and a quarter new members inside labor's fold and underscored our own dedication to the principles of industrial unionism by contributing another hundred thousand dollars to the steel organizing campaign. But we committed our union to "seek by every means in its power to compose this rift in the ranks of organized labor so that the American working class shall not be confronted with dual national movements."

By October, when the C.I.O. held its first national conference in Atlantic City, the industrial scene was beginning to turn very chilly. The New Deal movement that had brought the nation out of the Great Depression was running out of steam. Factory production and employment turned downward again. The atmosphere seemed ripe for another try at peace, even though both sides had split further in the summer of 1937. I told the delegates to the C.I.O. conference that we ought to make a new overture to the A.F.L. to test its willingness to accept the industrial-union concept, whose worth we had proved so dramatically. "Are they interested merely in perpetuating the power of a few individuals, or are they interested in helping to form other policies for the general labor movement and organizing millions and millions, an accomplishment that has been shown to be possible through new methods?" That was the proposition that I felt we should put, and this time even Lewis was ready to go along—though he did so with his usual flamboyant belligerence.

After a good deal of jockeying back and forth, arrangements were concluded for a meeting of committees representing both sides in Washington on October 25. The A.F.L. committee consisted of George Harrison, Matthew Woll and G. M. Bugniazet of the International Brotherhood of Electrical Workers. The first two were very much on the side of peace. Even Bugniazet was a good deal less adamant against the C.I.O. than many of the real hard-liners in the Federation. The C.I.O. committee was headed by Philip Murray, Lewis's trusted lieutenant, the man he had picked to lead the organizing drive in steel. He was also a man of reasonableness with little of Lewis's overbearing manner or contempt for everyone who disagreed with his viewpoint. I served on the committee, along with seven other ranking officers of the C.I.O. Lewis was the only important figure on our side who did not take a direct part in the peace talks.

It quickly became clear that there was one central issue standing in the way of peace, and it did not involve the status of the ten original C.I.O. unions. They could get full restoration of their original charters and jurisdictional rights, even though the A.F.L. had chartered some rival groups in their fields. Nor did it involve the basic principle of industrial unionism. The A.F.L. committee was ready to concede the appropriateness of that system of organization for autos, rubber, cement, aluminum, flat glass, agricultural equipment, food processing and certain other industries. Even in steel, the only question involved border areas of steel fabricating, not the steel mills themselves.

The single issue was how to resolve problems of jurisdictional overlap between the twenty-two newly formed C.I.O. unions and the old established unions in the A.F.L. Our committee insisted that these problems had to be resolved satisfactorily before any of the C.I.O. unions came back into the Federation. We would never abandon the newcomers to take their chances without our protection. In the end we reached an understanding that would have totally guaranteed the integrity of the C.I.O. unions. None would come in till all were cleared to come in. The issue was thus narrowed down to holding exploratory conferences in each of the disputed areas until a method of accommodation was reached. If the subcommittees dealing with the various dual-union conflicts could not agree, the matter would come back to the general conference committee for further study of every possibility for an accord.

We all felt the basis had been established for restoring unity in the labor movement, but announcement of the accord was delayed until Lewis could be informed. I will never forget how Lewis behaved when Murray came back with the report of our committee recommending acceptance. He read it, tore it into pieces and threw it out the window. Murray was standing there, hypnotized. He couldn't say a word. It was like a cemetery in the room. All our efforts were dead. Even the Communists on our committee had been for peace. I had doubted it at the start, but an intermediary set up a luncheon for me at the old Longchamps on Fifth Avenue and Twelfth Street with the party's commissar for labor. It came just as the peace talks were starting, and I told him: "John Lewis doesn't want peace, and you goddam Communists don't want peace either." So he said, "Dubinsky, you're wrong. We instructed our three people on the committee to support peace." It was a slip of the tongue, but I watched the three from then on—Mike Quill of the Transport Workers Union, Joe Curran of the National Maritime Union, and Abram Flaxer of the State, County and Municipal Workers—and there were certain indications that they were trying to help. But Lewis killed it all.

I called a meeting of the executive boards of our New York City garment locals to explain what had happened. I told them I was not for peace at any price, much less for a patchwork peace that would ignore the need for industrial unionism. But here was the A.F.L. conceding industrial unionism and expressing willingness to limit the power of the Executive Council so it could never again perpetrate the kind of arbitrary suspensions it had used against the C.I.O. unions. With such concessions, I felt, it would be destructive to the cause of labor to perpetuate the conflict. "No one has a mortgage on the labor movement," I declared. "It is not the property of any individual or group." That pinned the responsibility so unmistakably on Lewis that the press asked him what he thought about it. "Nothing in particular," he said, "except that Mr. Dubinsky, whom I esteem highly, seems to be giving an imitation of Eliza crossing the ice and looking backward like Lot's wife. I think he ought finally to decide whether he is flesh or fowl or good red herring." I could not let that pass. "May I suggest to Mr. Lewis," I told inquiring reporters, "that I decidedly disagree with him. Peace and accord in organized labor, in my humble opinion, is looking forward and not looking backward. Eliza crossing the ice may not have had a very pleasant journey, but, as I recall, she had to make the trip getting away from none too kind an overseer."

We did not sever our relations with the C.I.O., despite our deep disappointment over the torpedoing of the peace negotiations. So long as it remained a committee rather than a permanent constitutional entity, we could retain some measure of hope that it would not be a dual organization carrying on a suicidal conflict within labor. The economy was getting steadily worse. Roosevelt was eager for peace. He sent warnings that reactionary elements were profiting from the split, making it increasingly difficult to hold the line in Congress against dilution of the New Deal. But Lewis was still bent on enlarging his personal machine. At the very moment that the C.I.O. was having to lay off organizers because of the deepening economic slump, he induced a conference of C.I.O. presidents to issue a call for a constitutional convention, a move that could only solidify the division. The I.L.G.W.U. made a last stab at getting peace talks revived. Again Lewis rendered the task impossible. He insisted that the A.F.L. had to charter all the C.I.O. unions, old and new, and leave any jurisdictional questions for resolution until after they were all inside the Federation. If that didn't please the A.F.L., he said, he would agree to take all the A.F.L. unions into the C.I.O. on the same terms. That formula for moving the civil war inside one federation or the other, without settling anything in advance, was preposterous on its face. But all our efforts to persuade Lewis of that got nowhere.

When the C.I.O. went ahead with its constitutional convention in Pittsburgh in November 1938, our General Executive Board unanimously declared that we could not participate. We reaffirmed our opposition to dualism, but promised to do all we could to promote a reconciliation while remaining independent of both the C.I.O. and A.F.L. My own view was that we were not seceding from the C.I.O., but that it was seceding from its original purpose of organizing the mass-production industries and assuming a new status that could only help to perpetuate the split in organized labor. Not until 1955 did that split end, and I was delighted to be one of the architects of peace—this time back in my old status as an A.F.L. vice-president.

TEN

Partners for a Better World

I FIRST MET Jay Lovestone when he came to the Lower East Side branch of the Socialist Party in 1918 to try to mastermind a left-wing secession of the branch into the Communist Party. He was a young guy, fresh out of City College, with a very effective debating style, but we licked him. Maybe the reason we did was that his strongest supporter in the branch, a painter named Hiltzig, was yelling all the time and ruining most of Jay's arguments by alienating the crowd.

The next year he became a ranking functionary of the Communist Party, operating mostly on an underground basis. He devoted most of his personal attention to trying to take over the United Mine Workers, but his people were more numerous and more active in the I.L.G. The Communists were convinced that if they could capture these two unions, one in the most basic of heavy industries and the other a bulwark of social idealism, they would have a marvelous springboard for taking over all labor and laying the foundation for a revolutionary takeover of America. Lovestone remains convinced to this day that John Brophy of the anthracite miners, who was backed by his faction, really won the 1927 election in the U.M.W.A. over John L. Lewis. The official result of the referendum, as announced by Lewis, was that Lewis won by 121,000 to 67,000. For him to admit it was even that close was practically a confession that his people had stolen the election. But that was before there was a Landrum-Griffin Act to protect internal union democracy and there was no way to challenge Lewis's figures. During the formative days of the C.I.O., when Lewis and Lovestone were on friendlier terms, Jay asked John L. who really had won the 1927 election. Lewis had a good sense of humor. He put on his best Mona Lisa look and said, "John won the election."

Zimmerman was the field marshal for Lovestone's group in the I.L.G., but Jay was the dictator of policy, even though he was rarely in New York. In 1926 he officially became general secretary of the party, the American Stalin; but not long after that he was in hot water with the real boss, the Soviet Stalin. The Lovestone group had been following the "boring from within" tactics that represented the official party line through the so-called second period of the Communist International. The idea was to work inside established unions until the Communists gained control and were in a position to dictate policy. Suddenly, the Comintern in Moscow instructed the American Communists to set up a left-wing Trade Union Unity League to disrupt American unions. The League was to be a rival center opposing the American Federation of Labor; the Communists were put under orders to set up their own separate unions to wage war on A.F.L. affiliates in every industry.

To Lovestone and his associates, this swing away from the Trojan-horse policies they had been following all along in the I.L.G. and the miners' union was not only senseless but suicidal. All they could see for the Communists in such a policy was impotent isolation. Needless to say, we in the I.L.G. leadership were delighted at their predicament. They still held command in New York and were defying our expulsion orders. To have switched over to the position Stalin was demanding would leave them hopelessly in the cold. We were sure they would never get any sympathy from their masters in Moscow, no softening of the party line that would make it easier for their people to survive.

That is exactly how it turned out. Far from providing a way out for their unlucky stooges in the New York locals, the Comintern leaders insisted on their going into a Needle Trades Industrial Workers Union dominated by Ben Gold and his Furriers Union. My conversation with Zimmerman in Chapter Four detailed all the heartache the I.L.G. Communists had to suffer when they refused to go along. For Lovestone the refusal almost meant curtains, not just for his life in the official Communist Party but for life itself. Stalin told him in one bitter 1929 conversation in the Kremlin that there was lots of room in Russian cemeteries, and Jay would probably be occupying some of it right now if he hadn't escaped from Moscow by fleeing to Germany.

From then on, to the Kremlin, he and his associates were "right deviationists" to be shunned by all orthodox Communists. That didn't automatically make them kosher with me, especially since for the next couple of years the Lovestoneites continued to insist that they were really the only true keepers of the Marxist faith, that it was Stalin—not they—who had strayed.

At first the Lovestoneites called themselves the Communist Party U.S.A. Majority Group, then they changed it to Communist Party Opposition. When it became clear that they were genuinely against dual-unionism and also that they were fighting against domination from Moscow, I told Lovestone that they would never get anywhere unless they dropped the name "Communist." Gradually, Jay saw the wisdom of that, and his group became the Independent Labor League. More important, it was not only anti-Stalinist but anti-Communist.

The reentry of Zimmerman and the other Lovestoneites into good standing in our organization began in 1931. The final sealing of the breach came when Jay himself was invited to address our 1934 convention in Chicago. Not long after that he became active in organizing the United Auto Workers. He worked with Homer Martin, that union's first president, in trying to keep the Commies from taking over. We gave one hundred thousand dollars to help the auto workers build their union, more than any other union except

Lewis and the United Mine Workers. My own hope was that Walter Reuther would move to the top in the early days of the U.A.W. He was ten times better than Martin, who did not know his right foot from his left foot when it came to organization. At my suggestion, Jay met with Reuther at the Hotel Woodward in Detroit. I hoped that Reuther, a man brought up in the Socialist tradition, a creative idealist, could win the presidency as a rallying center for all the forces interested in a progressive, democratic U.A.W. Unfortunately, the conference between Lovestone and Reuther proved a failure. This is what happened, as Jay tells it:

"We went over the twenty-point program drawn up by the Independent Labor League. Reuther said, 'I'll accept 95 percent of it.' When I asked what was the 5 percent that he rejected, he pointed to a clause that called for 'a militant, energetic campaign against the operations of the Communist Party faction in the union.' Reuther told me he was prepared to fight the Commies, but he wasn't going to get involved in any Red-baiting. 'I'll take everything except that,' he said. My reply was, 'Well, if you don't accept that, there is no basis for cooperation.' The whole fight was to keep the Communist Party from getting control of the union, so that finished it between me and Reuther."

My own reaction was one of great disappointment, because I continued to regard Reuther as the most hopeful element in the U.A.W. However, there were limits to how much we could mix into its affairs, and I severed connections after getting the negative report from Lovestone. A couple of years later, after the I.L.G. had pulled out of the C.I.O. in protest against Lewis's decision to make it a permanent organization, Martin was flirting with the A.F.L. about bringing the Auto Workers into the Federation. He needed a loan of $25,000, and I was accused of providing him with the money. Actually, I persuaded William Green to have the A.F.L. endorse a loan by the Federation Bank to Martin. But I did tell him our union would underwrite the guarantee. I felt it would help restore unity in all labor if the U.A.W. did affiliate with the A.F.L.

The next time we got involved in U.A.W. affairs was in 1946, when R. J. Thomas was making common cause with George Addes and the Communists, and Walter Reuther was running against Thomas for the presidency. We didn't give any money from the international union, but our locals did help Reuther financially and every other way. I thought surely he was the better choice from every point of view. I was delighted when he won; I always felt he was a man of enormous talent and dedication, and it was a tragedy that in the larger affairs of labor so little came of all that talent. He was great for the auto workers but not as great as he could have been for the labor movement and the country.

The first important assignment Lovestone got through the intervention of our union came just before the United States entered World War II, when he was made labor secretary of the Committee to Defend America, headed by William Allen White. He was supposed to be chairman, but I had a problem with that one. The committee was made up of extremely distinguished people, and I wondered how in the hell can Jay Lovestone, the man who used to run the American Communist Party, be in a committee with them. I suggested that he change his name, but he wouldn't do that. So we made Sam Shore, one of our I.L.G. vice-presidents, chairman of the Labor Division and Jay was secretary, the guy who did all the work. We made him kosher, just as Matthew Woll had made me kosher in the A.F.L. leadership, which had no great love for Jews.

It didn't take Lovestone long to establish himself as a knowledgeable person. Soon after Hitler marched on Russia, General George C. Marshall received a confidential report from the analysts for the War Department predicting that the Soviet Union would be knocked out of the war in six months. Admiral William H. Standley came to the William Allen White committee to tell them about the Army's evaluation. By this time Jay was violently anti-Communist, but he did not underestimate the Soviet capacity to resist. He told Admiral Standley that in six months the Russians would be sucking the Germans in and destroying them. He explained his reasons forcefully, and the Admiral was so impressed he asked Lovestone for a memo to take back to Washington. I don't know what effect the memo had, but from that time on there seemed to be a shift in the American assessment of Russia's role in the war and a considerable increase in the military equipment that was shipped to the Russians.

In general, the position of the Labor Division was that we would do everything we could to help Russia as an ally in the fight against Hitler, but we would do nothing to advance Communism. That was our line of distinction, and we had no difficulty in maintaining it. One day I attended a luncheon with Winthrop Aldrich of the Chase Bank, who was active in the committee; John D. Rockefeller, Jr., and Thomas Lamont of J. P. Morgan and Company were also there. Afterward, while the four of us were standing together, I put my hand on Aldrich's sleeve. It was made not of material but of butter. It was the softest cashmere I had ever felt. I got so excited in telling him how much I admired it that the conversation became quite long. As I left, a newspaperman came up and asked, "What were you discussing with those millionaires?" I said, "They were trying to negotiate a loan from me." Some joke. About a dozen years later the International Basic Economic Corporation, the development company set up by John D. junior's sons to promote higher economic standards in Latin America, did get an I.L.G.W.U. mortgage loan to build the low-rent housing center for workers in San Juan, Puerto Rico, the Santiago Iglesias project, which we put 2.6 million dollars into.

The Labor Division of the Committee to Defend America worked closely with the International Transport Workers Federation, particularly with J. H. Oldenbroek and Omer

Bécu, who did exceptionally fine work against the Nazis. We gave them money for their underground operations. They also established contact with the European labor desk of the Office of Strategic Services, operating out of London, with Arthur J. Goldberg as its chief.

Money raised by American workers provided a lot of help to Norwegian underground forces, headed by Haakon Lie. We also helped Léon Jouhaux, the great French trade-unionist, and the French resistance movement. The Germans got only limited assistance, mostly in the form of aid to Social Democratic refugee leaders outside Germany. Some were connected to the trade unions, and some were friendly but not unionists. The Chinese got funds through coopera-tives. They had very few unions. We provided a great deal of money to the Czech refugees, but jointly with the C.I.O. we blocked funds to the Czech Communist organizations; we stopped about $100,000 from being sent to them by the National War Fund.

A largely unseen war behind the war was being waged between us and the British trade unions over relations with the Soviet trade unions. We stood fast in the belief that it would be a betrayal of a war against totalitarianism to make partnership in that war an excuse for letting organizations that were an instrument of a dictatorial government take on the aspect of legitimate trade unions; we had no doubt that their only goal on the labor front would be to subvert the unions of all other countries into instruments of Soviet dicta-torship. I had no doubt then of the correctness of that view; I have none now.

I am convinced that the British Trades Union Congress was acting not because it genuinely disagreed with our view but in response to pressure from Britain's wartime govern-ment. In fact, Sir Walter Citrine, general secretary of the Congress and head of the International Federation of Trade Unions, admitted as much when Lovestone and I told him that we believed the A.F.L. was right in holding aloof from the Anglo-Soviet Trade Union Committee that had been set up in 1942 as the first unity vehicle. We felt that the A.F.L. was just as right in boycotting arrangements for setting up a World Federation of Trade Unions in 1944 and '45, with the Russians as a principal element in the new structure. We quoted from Citrine's own book *I Search for Truth in Russia* to support our contention that wartime solidarity should not mean erasing the line between free unions and slave unions. Citrine had a very charming smile. He told us quite plainly that it was government policy; we were allies in the war and the aim was to remain allies later. I assured him that we had the same hope, but we were not going to pursue that goal at the expense of the independence of the trade-union movement.

The C.I.O., of course, was delighted to join with the British and the Russians in forming the W.F.T.U. From the start that organization became a mouthpiece for the Soviet bloc, nothing more. When it sought recognition in the United Nations Economic and Social Council in 1945 as the sole voice of world labor, the A.F.L. successfully fought for equal status. Matt Woll and I were appointed to represent the A.F.L., and we used our position to press for an investigation into slave labor, which was so widespread in the Soviet Union that the number in forced labor exceeded the total work force of all the New England and Middle Atlantic states put together.

The Economic and Social Council had no desire to tackle this issue. Even the United States was loath to get into it. Three or four years passed before Washington gave even the faintest nod of moral support to the A.F.L. campaign, which was conducted on a worldwide basis. We had to collect all the information on our own in the face of the most savage hostility by Moscow. Our affidavits finally obliged the United Nations to take up the issue. Toni Sender, a former Social Democratic member of the German Reichstag, who had come to the United States as a refugee, did a particularly effective job of buttonholing U.N. delegates to support our demand for an inquiry into the massive expansion of slave labor behind the Iron Curtain and the Bamboo Curtain.

When the investigation finally was approved, the U.N. study committee under the chairmanship of a noted Indian jurist issued an admirable report that opened the eyes of millions to the extent of this horrible abuse of human freedom by the Soviet Union. That study is still prohibited in all Communist countries, even Yugoslavia. It had an enormous impact in rousing world opinion against Communist forced labor and in compelling the Russians to diminish, even if not abolish, it.

The brutal march of Fascist dictatorship in Europe in the early 1930s touched the hearts of the I.L.G.W.U. membership, and collections in the shops resulted in the sending of $20,000 to the oppressed unions of Italy and Germany in 1933. The next year our convention in Chicago authorized a drive throughout the union, which enabled us to forward $64,000 to the International Federation of Trade Unions in two months. The money went to the shattered and exiled remnants of the unions ground under the heel of Hitler and Mussolini.

But that did not seem nearly enough involvement for us. We saw all too clearly the danger, not only to labor but to the world, of these predatory leaders with their mad aggressive dreams. So we took the initiative in obtaining an invitation for Walter Citrine to come as a speaker to the A.F.L. convention in San Francisco. I accompanied him by train from New York to San Francisco. With us was B. Charney Vladeck, business manager of the *Jewish Daily Forward*, who also was to address the convention—the first time that a speaker from that Socialist paper had ever been invited. On the train we thought up the idea of organizing a central fund-raising agency to muster all of labor's resources in support of the forces fighting Fascism in Europe. We even thought up a splendiferous name, the Labor Chest for Aid of the Oppressed Peoples of Europe. But we were far from sure that we could get the convention to go along. Too many of the

Federation's key people were isolationists; many were slow to see the menace of any totalitarianism except Communism; some were secret admirers of both Hitler and Mussolini.

Our doubts dissolved after Citrine's speech. It was extraordinary. Usually, when anyone delivered a formal talk to the A.F.L. convention—especially if he was a fraternal delegate from Canada or Britain—people drifted out of their chairs or fell asleep. Not so with Citrine. He had wit and style; even more, he had something revealing to say. He told with pathos and insight what was happening in Germany and Italy. He also told, in an objective way, what was happening in Russia, which he had just visited. His speech made a tremendous impression on the A.F.L. delegates. So did the one delivered by Vladeck, a brilliant orator, as effective in English as he was in Yiddish. The result was that the A.F.L. convention voted overwhelmingly to create the Labor Chest. It was the start of the Federation's really substantial involvement in helping to foster free trade unions abroad. I was proud to be named by William Green as one of its chief officers, along with himself and Matthew Woll.

In 1940 the Jewish Labor Committee appealed to me to obtain United States visas for Socialists from Eastern Europe. Their position was always a dangerous one in that tyrannical area, but the Stalin-Hitler pact had sharpened anti-Semitism behind what later came to be known as the Iron Curtain and many of the Socialists had good reason to fear for their lives. I persuaded Green to join me on a visit to Secretary of State Cordell Hull and we got his agreement to let in three hundred of these persecuted people.

I started to hand over the list, but as my eye ran down the names I noticed something that bothered me. Mumbling an apology to Hull, I rushed to his anteroom and placed a call to Jacob Pat, the committee's executive secretary. "What have you done?" I screamed at him in Yiddish. "The list is all of bigshots—political leaders, writers, artists. Where are the plain people? Where are the tailors and the textile workers? Where is Hershel and Yonkel and Mordecai?" The end result was a list that included the poor as well as the illustrious. The Soviet firing squads would not have drawn a line between them. Neither did we.

Needless to say, the fact that I insisted on drawing a line between the Soviet Union as military ally and as practitioner of totalitarian tyranny within its own borders did not endear me to Moscow's American mouthpiece, *The Daily Worker*, not that its enmity was anything new. One day early in 1943 a front-page banner in the *Worker* solemnly informed me and the rest of the world that I was single-handedly to blame for the fall of Kharkov to the Nazis. "Who is responsible for the fact that the Red Army had to evacuate the great city of Kharkov?" the paper asked. Who else but that traitor and kingpin of a "gang of unscrupulous Fascist agents," David Dubinsky.

And how had I engineered this despicable feat? By taking the lead in organizing a mass meeting in Mecca Temple to protest the shameful execution on Kremlin orders of two great leaders of the Polish Jewish workers, the Socialists Henryk Ehrlich and Victor Alter. Ehrlich was the William Green of the Polish workers. Alter was a writer, a theoretician, a dreamer. That's all you could accuse them of—being idealists and dreamers. We had heard just about the time that the United States entered the war that they were to be shot as "Nazi spies." It was preposterous. We sought to intervene in their behalf. So did William Green and Matthew Woll and Mrs. Roosevelt. We got no word on what had happened to them. Finally, when Wendell Willkie went to Russia in 1942, we asked him to make a personal plea to Stalin to save Ehrlich and Alter. On his return, he told us that Stalin had assured him that they were both all right and that his people would look into the case. Green followed up by asking Soviet Ambassador Maxim Litvinov in Washington to find out what happened. Then we learned that they had actually been executed a full year before, that there was no truth to any of the things Stalin told Willkie.

War or no war, I decided that we had to hold a memorial

meeting in New York to protest this outrage. It was not a popular undertaking. The Russian people were fighting for their lives and for our lives, too. I was wholeheartedly with them in that fight. But the principles underlying the fight, the things that differentiated us from the tyrants, had to be kept clear. I got a commitment from Senator James M. Mead of New York that he would come. William Green came. So did James B. Carey, the secretary-treasurer of the C.I.O., who had to defy all the pro-Communists in that organization —and they had never enjoyed more power there than they did in wartime. Joe Curran of the National Maritime Union warned Carey that he would push his nose into his face if he entered the hall, but Carey had the guts to come anyway.

One man I stayed away from was Mayor La Guardia. He was very close at that period to his old law partner, Representative Vito Marcantonio, and to a lot of other Commies. I thought it would embarrass him to be asked. Then a couple of days before the rally I got word that he felt bad that he was not invited. So I asked him to come and he accepted. He weaseled quite a bit in his speech and then he went to wash himself a couple of days later when the Communists called a May Day demonstration. He joined them there so that it shouldn't be a stain on his record that he talked for these two men whom the Communists called "counter-revolutionaries." But it still took a lot of courage for La Guardia to come to Mecca Temple, and I don't want to detract from it. Senator Mead tried to duck out at the last minute. He said he had to be in the Senate that night, and Vice-President Truman called to back him up—at the State Department's request, I suspect. But I told Mead that I would arrange a long-distance phone hookup—there were plenty of phones in Mecca Temple. He couldn't turn that down, because Mead was a little bit obligated to me for being in the Senate at all. So we had our meeting and we had a full house. But we got almost no publicity for it. And Wendell Willkie pleaded some excuse for not coming, even though he knew Stalin had lied about the whole affair. The only ones who gave us credit were the editors of the *Worker*—for bringing down Kharkov. When the Russians retook the city, I asked my staff, "What happens now? Do I get a refund?"

In 1944 the A.F.L. convention authorized the establishment of the Free Trade Union Committee as a permanent arm of the Federation. It represented a broadening in both sponsorship and activities of the work Lovestone had been carrying on in the headquarters of the I.L.G.W.U. He was appointed as the committee's executive secretary, though we continued to pay his salary, the group's office space, electric bills, telephone service and mailing arrangements.

As the war in Europe came to an end, it became increasingly obvious that the question of whether democracy was to revive in the countries overrun by Hitler and Mussolini lay in the trade unions. We got Irving Brown, who had once been in the Machinists Union and on the War Production Board, over to Europe in 1946. He worked closely with Joseph Keenan, labor adviser in the Office of Military Government in Germany, who had come out of the Chicago Federation of Labor and the International Brotherhood of Electrical Workers.

General Lucius D. Clay was the first Military Governor of Berlin, and he had some difficulty at the outset in discerning the difference between a bona fide unionist and a Communist masquerading as one. We had a lot of trouble straightening him out, and the fact that we did was a crucial contribution to West Germany's revival in an atmosphere of freedom. The German trade unions soon took on a genuine democratic nature. Without the efforts of Irving Brown and Henry Lutz, the A.F.L. representative in Germany, the W.F.T.U. would have used the instrumentality of four-zone labor meetings to put a Communist stamp on the future of German unionism. Unfortunately, there were plenty of damn fools and pro-Communists in military government ready to help the W.F.T.U. by interpreting regulations in ways that gave it carte blanche. Everything we fought for might have gone down the drain if our efforts had not made the Pentagon, the

State Department and the White House appreciate the importance of preventing a Communist take-over of the German unions.

In 1947 the A.F.L. gave enthusiastic support to the Marshall Plan as a generous and well-conceived program for promoting European reconstruction. John L. Lewis, who was on one of the "in" sides of his frequent movements through the revolving door of affiliation with the A.F.L., gave us trouble in the Executive Council on the proposed report by the international committee endorsing the plan. He had always been something of an isolationist at heart. He shared with the old America First Committee a belief that the United States should stay out of foreign affairs, even when the world was threatened with Nazi enslavement. He still hadn't got over that feeling after V-E Day, but he was careful to keep any note of isolationism out of his argument against the Marshall Plan. Instead, he insisted that labor was giving something to the Truman administration without getting anything in return for it. "This is not collective bargaining," he said. "What are they going to give you? First get something for it."

My reply was, "We do it because we believe in the Marshall Plan. We don't have to be given anything for it." George Meany spoke in the same vein. Lewis was licked, and the endorsement got official A.F.L. approval. The Marshall Plan did not get the same welcome from the C.I.O., thanks to the continuing strong influence of Communists on its policies. At our urging, President Truman sent Marshall himself to address the C.I.O. convention in Boston in 1947, but it didn't help one bit. They rejected the plan. However, their resistance was much less firm than it appeared. Philip Murray long before had begun to question the possibility of reconstructing European labor in partnership with the Communists. Both he and the British had come to realize that the W.F.T.U. was a tool of Soviet foreign policy and that Moscow's last interest was in building free and independent unions in Germany or anywhere else.

Through the Free Trade Union Committee, we had impressed Murray in the first year after V-E Day by our successful fight against an excursion into slave labor by Brigadier General Frank J. McSherry, who headed the manpower division of American Military Government in Germany. General McSherry was a great friend of Sidney Hillman until Hillman's death in July 1946, but to us he was always bad news; a patsy for the W.F.T.U., he was almost persuaded by it to write rules under which the Communists would have found it easy to take over the postwar German unions. Our objections stopped these rules, to the lasting benefit of all Germans.

The more important contest, however, and the one that did most to open Murray's eyes was the success of the Free Trade Union Committee in torpedoing a proposal by McSherry to overcome a shortage of coal by conscripting German miners. We raised hell about that, but the W.F.T.U. went along with it. Murray sent a scathing telegram of protest against the whole idea. "I didn't know this could ever be presented in a labor organization," he told us when we notified him about it. "I didn't know what we were tied up with."

So I was not too surprised when the Marshall Plan came to life under Averell Harriman and Murray threw out the Boston convention's decision as if it had never been made. When the Russians, who had a majority of the votes on the W.F.T.U. executive board, blocked all moves for labor cooperation in realizing the constructive potential of the Marshall Plan, that was the beginning of the end of affiliation for the C.I.O., the British Trades Union Congress and the Dutch Federation of Labor. After the British pulled out early in 1949, the B.T.U.C. voiced sadly a lesson we in the I.L.G.W.U. had learned the hard way nearly a quarter century before.

"The stream of vilification and abuse which has been poured on the British T.U.C., American labor, and the leaders of those national centers who are not prepared to become subservient to Communist doctrine and dictation is not restrained by any desire to overcome inherent difficulties," a B.T.U.C. statement said. "Any realization that international trade-union unity depends on the good will and good relations between the trade-union movements of the participating countries is completely absent in the tactics we have encountered. From all Communist-controlled national centers—and they speak with remarkable accord—propaganda is regarded either as a strategic barrage to facilitate a given line of tactics or, alternatively, to discredit any individual movement or government which does not wholeheartedly accept the point of view of the authorities."

The disintegration of the W.F.T.U. as anything other than a mouthpiece for the Soviet Union was obvious in July 1948, when twenty-five organizations attended a conference of unions on the Marshall Plan in London. George Harrison of the Railway Clerks and I were there for the A.F.L., with Jay Lovestone acting as secretary of the American delegation. The C.I.O. members were David J. McDonald of the United Steelworkers and Victor Reuther, director of C.I.O.'s international department. There was no problem between us. In fact, the nearest thing to a problem was within the C.I.O. delegation. Victor got up to make a long speech for Socialism. Europe had to go Socialist, he said. McDonald took the opposite point of view. "I'm for capitalism," he said. Fortunately, that side debate didn't last long. Everyone quickly got back on the track that the Marshall Plan represented the best hope for the democratic rebuilding of the war-torn economies of Europe.

Averell Harriman appeared at that London meeting in his capacity as Economic Cooperation Administrator in charge of the Marshall Plan. By coincidence, at that very time there was a break between Stalin and Tito, and Lovestone and I believed that this could have very important consequences in restraining Soviet expansionism. We had a long session with Harriman on the subject, trying to persuade him that the United States should help Tito under certain circumstances. It was hard to convince him, but I think we did.

Later on, at a meeting of the A.F.L. Executive Council in Philadelphia, the sledding was no easier. The great majority of the Council members were Catholics, and Catholics were being persecuted in Yugoslavia. Nevertheless, we persuaded the Council to adopt a resolution urging United States help for Tito, provided, first, that he resisted Russian aggression; second, that he yielded on the Trieste question; and, third, that he stopped providing refuge for the Greek guerrillas. That was the key point; for the civil war in Greece could not have ended as quickly as it did if the guerrillas had been able to find sanctuary in Macedonia. Tito agreed to these conditions, and our government then began to help his Communist regime, after the so-called reactionary A.F.L. took the initiative and made Washington see the wisdom of it.

The International Confederation of Free Trade Unions came into being at the tail end of 1949 as a positive answer to the global needs of workers for democratic organizations independent of external domination. The C.I.O. by this time had become thoroughly fed up with its role as partner of the Soviet-dominated unions of Eastern Europe. The same disgust was felt by the British and the other free unions of West Europe. They were happy to join with the A.F.L. in a new alliance.

To me the I.C.F.T.U. would have justified its existence if its only usefulness was to destroy the illusion that the W.F.T.U. represented anything more than a transmission belt for Moscow. But it did more by building free unions and raising the economic standards of workers in the underdeveloped countries of Asia, Africa and Latin America. I would be less than honest, however, if I did not admit that in many ways it proved a disappointment. Since practically everything in the postwar world involved some measure of disappointment, maybe that should be no surprise. Yet, there would be much more to boast about in the I.C.F.T.U. record if it had not become a victim of personal animosities and power plays.

One of its problems was that the bureaucracy quickly became a world of its own, turning the organization into a do-nothing mechanism for personal gratification and self-importance. This is a disease of all international organizations, and the I.C.F.T.U. quickly fell prey to it. Worse still from the standpoint of American participation, this became the area of bitterest conflict in the perennial feud between George Meany and Walter Reuther—more so after the A.F.L.–C.I.O. merger even than it had been before. The fact that Lovestone and Victor Reuther disliked each other undoubtedly made things even more tortured than they had to be, but the two principals contributed more than their fair share to keeping the pot aboil. The trouble was that the I.C.F.T.U. was also in that pot. The British were very skillful at playing one American leader off against the other, until finally Meany soured on the entire enterprise. One new executive director after another would be installed in an effort to restore his confidence in the I.C.F.T.U., but in no time at all Meany would be as disgusted as he had been with all the others.

Taken in its totality, however, the role of the A.F.L. in foreign affairs, especially in the immediate period after World War II, is one that does great credit to American labor. It was a special credit to George Meany, who came out of the most parochial section of the labor movement, that he did more than any of us to broaden the horizons of labor's interest in helping workers everywhere create free unions and defeat the thrust of totalitarianism, whether with a swastika or with a hammer and sickle as its emblem.

General Clay, with whom Meany had so much trouble at first because he did not recognize the importance of trade unions in denazifying Germany and in keeping it out of Moscow's clutches, became our most enthusiastic booster after a while. At the time of the founding conference of the I.C.F.T.U. in London, he invited Lovestone, George Harrison and me to come to Berlin to see how they were surviving the blockade. We took my wife, Emma, along and got to Frankfurt, where we switched to a military plane. It was a

tense period in Soviet-American relations there, and when we
flew over the Soviet zone one of the plane crew gave each of
us a parachute. He assured us everything would be all right,
but he felt we ought to know how to use the parachute just
in case. Emma asked the captain, "For Lovestone and
Dubinsky, have you got a parachute that goes up, not down?
If the Communists get them, they'll be better off dead."

In Berlin, Clay acknowledged to us that our effectiveness
in countering the Communists in the trade unions had been
an important element in preventing the Communists from
taking over the Berlin labor organization and "everything else
in the city." The Communists had captured the unions as
soon as the war ended, but we gave five thousand dollars to
aid those that wanted to split away from their domination.
The Free Trade Union Committee helped them to get a headquarters, office equipment and surplus army supplies. The
first task of the new Berlin central labor organization was to
mobilize the workers not only on their jobs but in their gar-
dens, so that every foot of ground would be cultivated. We
did that because the food would help, but even more to give
them a sense of involvement in reconstruction. And Clay was
the first to acknowledge that the civilian population couldn't
have held out against the blockade and all the other
harassing moves without the morale instilled by the unions.
Those were the unions which I can honestly say would never
have got off the ground without the help we gave them from
New York.

But coming to Berlin at the time of the airlift was a difficult experience for me. As a Jew, after what the Jews
suffered in Germany, I found it hard to accept that even
these Socialists in the trade unions did not participate in
murdering all these people. Even at the trade-union meetings
I couldn't shake hands with any of them. It took me time
before I could say a word to them. I was almost paralyzed
for at least fifteen minutes before I could talk. But that
didn't stop us from helping to rebuild their unions, from
sending 400,000 CARE packages to Germany, from getting

their property back for them when the mark was revalued and the union treasuries were lost.

There was no similar emotional problem a year earlier when I was received by Pope Pius XII at the Vatican, along with Emma, Jay, and Irving Brown, just after an election in which the Communists had almost taken control of Italy. We had done all we could to help the democratic coalition headed by Premier Alcide de Gasperi and Giuseppe Saragat win the election. The Pope had done a good deal more in his "nonpolitical" way. When our group was ushered into the Pope's presence, we started to mumble little nonsenses. Then I broke the ice by saying, "Father, you did a great job in the elections." His aides looked scandalized. Not so the Pope. He smiled, clasped his hands in front of his chest and turned his eyes heavenward. "When the truth is attacked, one must rise to the occasion and defend the truth," he said.

The seed we planted with a very tiny staff and very little funds through our Free Trade Union Committee may well be recognized in history as the factor that gave democracy a chance for survival in Europe after the war. Without us the Moscow brand of totalitarianism would have replaced the Hitler-Mussolini brand. Stalin's idea was to get control of all the democratic countries through the labor unions. And our military authorities were no match for the Communist cunning, especially since most of the military's early orders from Washington were to give the Communists a free hand in everything that had to do with labor. In some places, like Germany, they even infiltrated the manpower branches of our military government. It was the A.F.L. that alerted the authorities to the perfidy of George Shaw Wheeler, a key assistant of General McSherry, who subsequently defected to Communist Czechoslovakia after having done his best to frustrate recognition of authentic unions in the Allied Control Council.

In Italy, General Mark Clark got instructions from Washington to turn over all the Fascist Party headquarters and

funds to the resistance organizations, the great bulk of them
Communist. So the groups that wanted to put a Moscow
chain on Italian labor started off with a tremendous amount
of money, with the blessings of the United States Army.
Clark was personally against it, but the policy was established from above and he could not fight it. The whole cry
was for "unity," and that gave the Communists a tremendous
advantage to grab control for their own selfish purposes. We
tried to get the Catholics and the Socialists of Italy to
join forces, but we didn't entirely succeed. However,
even though there were two challengers to the Communist-dominated General Confederation of Italian Workers
(C.G.I.L.), they at least served one indispensable purpose:
they kept the C.G.I.L. from flying the flag of all labor and
thus bringing Italy to its knees through paralyzing strikes.

Now, in the revisionist mood that has grown out of unhappiness with the tragic course of the Vietnam war, it has
become fashionable to deride what we of American labor
did in the decade after V-E Day. The current vogue is to
charge that we were not free agents, concerned with the
preservation of freedom all over the world, but fronts for the
Central Intelligence Agency in a cold war designed to
spread American imperialism. The truth is just the opposite.
Whatever some individual unions may have done on their
own, we in the Free Trade Union Committee took the most
adamant position against any C.I.A. intrusion into our activities. In fact, we told General Walter Bedell Smith, when he
was running the C.I.A., to keep hands off. He then filed a
formal complaint with William Green and Meany against
Lovestone, but that didn't change a thing. Our word was
still "Hands off."

Everyone at the top in the C.I.A. and the State Department knew of our opposition to their horning into labor matters. It was based on two grounds. One, we didn't want the
C.I.A. to interfere in any way in the American labor movement. Two, we resented bitterly their getting tied up with
labor forces overseas, because they invariably got involved

with the worst characters, many of them Commie plants, and that interfered with the effectiveness of our own work with foreign labor movements.

By 1950 and 1951 we were refusing even to talk to them, which was what prompted General Smith's complaint against Lovestone. The A.F.L. sent an Executive Council subcommittee consisting of Meany, Harrison, Matthew Woll and me to confer with Smith. Lovestone came along with us, and we gave him total support. We told Smith that the only thing the C.I.A. was accomplishing was to block us in our attempts to have free labor talk to free labor without any intrusion of government.

We made a sharp distinction between C.I.A. undercover funds and the help extended through E.C.A. in the Marshall Plan period. We not only gave money from our own union treasuries to help get democratic unions started but, in accordance with the decisions of the London conference of 1948, used all our influence with Harriman to secure Marshall Plan financial assistance for the workers of Italy, of Greece and of Finland. It was against our policy, however, to act as the conduit for this E.C.A. money. We would never say to Harriman, "Give us so much money, we want to give it to somebody." We would say, "This and this union needs funds." And they would get it from the E.C.A.

Part of the revisionist mythology is that we used C.I.A. money to break strikes. That is nonsense manufactured by the Communists after we defeated their efforts to stop Marshall Plan food from being unloaded at the port of Marseilles, food that was desperately needed all over Europe. The Communist obstruction got so bad that Paris and Washington were prepared to send in French and American troops. We said absolutely not; we of the trade unions would go down there by ourselves and get that food through. We sent in Irving Brown, and he got the cooperation of the workers of Marseilles. An inspiring and decisive role in this situation was played by Pierre Ferri-Pisani, a very courageous man with a wonderful anti-Nazi record. The Nazis had imprisoned and beaten him, even thrown him out of a second-floor window. He was put in charge, and we organized educational committees on the waterfront. And we beat the hell out of the Commies who wouldn't allow the food to come in, and we didn't have soldiers or anybody else. There was no strike at all, and from then on we were very strong in Marseilles.

Our worst battle with the C.I.A. came at a meeting with General Smith in the Waldorf Tower suite of Louis Marx, the toy manufacturer, which Smith sometimes used when he was visiting New York. It was in 1951 when the situation in Italy was extremely critical. The C.I.A. was moving into the labor situation and we resented it. We told them they would ruin things, but they wouldn't stay out. General Smith kept sounding more and more dictatorial at our conference. Finally, Lovestone said to him, "You're a general, but you sound like a drill sergeant." When he protested, I said to Smith, "You're not going to tell us what to do; we are from the labor movement." Then I turned to Matt Woll and said, "Why are we sitting here, let's get out." And that was good-bye.

ELEVEN

Labor in Politics— Politics in Labor

THE FIRST RE-ELECTION CAMPAIGN of Franklin D. Roosevelt in 1936 was the start of the American labor movement's systematic, year-round involvement in politics. It wasn't exactly planned that way, which seems to be the way most long-term changes in our society happen. The C.I.O. was worried that it would be shut out of any leadership role in the campaign, because Jim Farley, F.D.R.'s chief political arranger, wanted to give all the spotlight to Dan Tobin of the A.F.L.'s Teamsters Union, who was going to be appointed chairman of the Democratic Party's labor committee. That meant the A.F.L. would run that part of the show, something John L. Lewis couldn't stand just when the C.I.O. was beginning to get off the ground. The C.I.O. also couldn't stand to have Roosevelt defeated. The N.R.A. had been killed by the Supreme Court; the Wagner Act had just been passed, but nobody could be sure the Court wouldn't kill that too. The Liberty League had been brought into being by Big Business to murder every part of the New Deal. Labor—and, most of all, the struggling young unions that the C.I.O. was building in the mass-production industries—could not afford to let F.D.R. lose.

John L. Lewis and Sidney Hillman went to George L. Berry, the president of the A.F.L. International Printing Pressmen's Union, who had been something of a man in the middle in the civil war inside labor and who also had lots of political ambition of his own. They convinced him that labor needed an independent political instrument to get out the vote for Roosevelt. He agreed to become chairman of something called Labor's Non-Partisan League, but Lewis was the real boss, as he was in everything he got into. The important thing was that they established a bridge for getting C.I.O. and A.F.L. unions to work together in politics, even though they were fighting like cats and dogs everywhere else.

In New York there was a double importance to the League's formation. It gave us a way to break down the resistance of old-line Socialists—me among them—who would not vote for any candidates on the Democratic line. We were strong for Roosevelt, but that still didn't make us stop hating Tammany Hall. Berry came to a meeting at the old Hotel New Yorker and urged labor to set up a local League branch. It was organized then and there, with Luigi Antonini of the I.L.G. as chairman, Alex Rose of the United Hatters as secretary, Andrew Armstrong of the Printing Pressmen as treasurer, and Jacob S. Potofsky of the Amalgamated Clothing Workers as chairman of the executive committee.

As soon as the new officers met to determine how the new organization could help re-elect Roosevelt, they realized that they had a special problem with the Socialists. The relations between the New York A.F.L. and C.I.O. were all right at that time, so there was no need to worry about the State Federation of Labor or the Central Trades and Labor Council trying to destroy the whole idea. The real question was how to get the Socialists, who numbered tens of thousands in and out of the unions, to vote for F.D.R. I told Rose and the others that I myself maybe could do it, but most of the Socialists never could go to vote on a Tammany line. And that was a substantial vote in New York. It could mean the difference between carrying the state and not carrying it if the election was close.

My own identification with the Socialist Party had been getting weaker and weaker ever since the 1928 campaign, when Alfred E. Smith was running for President on the

Democratic ticket. Part of it had begun even earlier when the long struggle with the Communists inside the I.L.G. made me realize that a trade-union leader was always in trouble whenever there was any question about whether the trade union was his first and paramount loyalty. If the demands of a political party got in the way, that was no good, and that was just as much true in relation to the Socialist Party as it was in relation to the Communist Party. So when I was asked to make speeches for Norman Thomas in 1928, I told the Socialists that I couldn't do it, because I really believed it would be better if Smith got elected. The commission he had appointed in 1925 to make recommendations in the garment labor dispute had been of considerable help to our union, and he had always been sympathetic to our problems.

When they heard that I was inclined to vote for Smith and not for Thomas, the Socialist leaders were terribly upset. The reaction of these old friends bothered me so much that I decided not to register, and so, for the only time in my life since I became eligible to vote I didn't, because I still respected the Socialists and I was afraid I might be tempted to vote for Smith. But, even though I didn't register, I did serve as a watcher for the Socialists in the Fourth Assembly District on the Lower East Side. After all, they had a full slate of other officers running in 1928, and it was no secret that Tammany rigged the election count. We used to complain in every election whenever we spotted dirty work going on. It never did any good, but that didn't stop us from complaining. The 1928 election was no exception. After the polls had closed, orders came to stop counting the ballots in our precinct. An hour later we got orders to resume the count. The explanation was plain enough. Tammany was making a survey of how the vote was going in the rest of the city and state. The idea was to find out how many extra votes they had to load onto the totals in districts like mine, where they could do whatever they wanted, law or no law. We Socialist watchers made our usual complaint and nobody paid any attention.

I have no doubt whatever that the stopping of the count in the Tammany strongholds permitted them to throw in enough votes to elect Franklin D. Roosevelt as governor, the stepping-off point for his winning the Presidency four years later. History would have been a lot different if they had not stacked that election, but the experience revived all my old distrust of the crooked Democrats. By 1936, however, F.D.R. had begun to translate into reality many dreams of the Socialists for a more just society. The venom with which reactionaries were ganging up against him made me decide I had to align myself openly with his re-election campaign. Months before Labor's Non-Partisan League came into being I notified my colleagues in the I.L.G. that I was resigning from the Socialist Party, for nothing facing labor was more important than insuring Roosevelt's return for another four years. The test was to develop an instrument that would persuade other lifelong Socialists to cast their votes for him.

So we arranged a meeting at the Brevoort Hotel with some of the Socialist leaders known to be sympathetic to Roosevelt. Louis Waldman, who had been elected as a Socialist Assemblyman back in World War I and who was afterward a Socialist candidate for governor, was there. So were B. Charney Vladeck and Alex Kahn of the *Jewish Daily Forward* and a few others. I was there, along with Hillman and Max Zaritsky, who was then the international president of the United Hatters, and so were the officers of the New York branch of L.N.P.L. At that meeting we decided to turn the branch into an independent political party with its own line on the ballot—the American Labor Party.

The first headache was getting enough nominating petitions to put our slate on the ballot, not only Roosevelt for President but also Herbert H. Lehman for governor. That was not so easy, because both the major parties had cooperated over the years to load the state election law with booby traps, all aimed at blowing third parties out of the political process. You had to get at least fifty signatures in every county to get a new party on the ballot, and the only way to be sure your signatures would stand up under challenge was to get a lot more than that. We made our goal two hundred signatures, even though in many upstate counties they never saw a union organizer and didn't want to see any. Our success in those places was mainly because the Brotherhood of Railway Trainmen did a great job for the American Labor Party. The conductors and brakemen traveled every day to every part of the state; they knew the local people, and the local people knew them. So we got all the signatures we needed—and more. Jim Farley himself passed the word not to interfere with us. The Democratic organization didn't help with the petitions, but at least they didn't try to make our job harder.

As it turned out, much to my surprise, I became an "issue" in that election. The Democrats had agreed to put six labor people on the joint Democratic-A.L.P. slate of Roosevelt electors from New York State. I was one of them, along with Hillman, Zaritsky, Antonini, Armstrong, and Meany, who was then president of the State Federation of Labor. In August 1936, when the campaign was just beginning to get hot, I was on a ship returning from a labor conference in London. My office informed me that an appeal had come from Sir Walter Citrine, the chairman of the International Federation of Trade Unions, for a contribution to a fund to provide medical aid and relief to victims of the civil war that was then raging in Spain. The fund was to be known as "Labor's Red Cross for Spain," and it was to be a purely humanitarian effort without any political identification. I immediately sent a cable instructing that $5,000 be sent right away and that a drive be started to get much more from our own members and from other unions. When the ship docked in New York, I was met by a reporter from Hearst's *New York Journal*, asking whether it was true that I had authorized the contribution. I told him that not only was it true, but it would not stop there. "The labor world has its eyes on Spain," I said. "What happens there may have a direct bearing on labor everywhere." A few days later, on my request, our General Executive Board authorized us to conduct a general drive to raise $100,000 from unionists and others for Labor's Red Cross for Spain.

That provided a field day for all the reactionary forces opposing a second term for F.D.R. With Father Coughlin and the Hearst press leading the attack, they pictured me, both in words and in front-page cartoons, as an agent of the Kremlin who would represent Moscow in the Roosevelt Cabinet. Hardly a day would pass without John D. M. Hamilton, the Republican National Chairman, addressing a rhetorical question to the President about how long he intended to keep Dubinsky as an elector. Even Alfred M. Landon, the G.O.P. Presidential nominee, picked up the refrain. True, I was in good company. Eleanor Roosevelt, Harold L. Ickes, Rexford G. Tugwell, Felix Frankfurter, all came in for the same type of abuse, but I got more than anybody else. The clippings became so numerous that I stopped reading them. I told Hannah Haskel, my secretary, to stack them up on the floor, those that were against me in one pile and those that were for in the other. The "antis" made eight times as high a pile as the "pros"; for just one week they came up well above the level of the desk top.

I had no intention of backing down on my support of Labor's Red Cross for Spain, but I knew enough about politics to worry that I might really be spoiling Roosevelt's chances to win. Proud as I was to be an elector, I didn't want that to become a handicap to the survival of the New Deal and to a victory for the President. So I called Mayor Fiorello H. La Guardia and made him my messenger to let Roosevelt know that I was ready to get off the ticket rather than cause him any more embarrassment. La Guardia came back with Roosevelt's answer: "Tell that little son-of-a-bitch to mind his own business. This is my business; I'll take care of it. Let him stay where he is." I did.

The interesting thing that no one knew was that, almost as soon as the original contribution to Spain was announced, the Communists sent an emissary to me to propose that labor join with them in a united front to raise money in support of the Spanish Loyalists. My response was that I wished them well in their fund-raising efforts, but it would be opportunistic hypocrisy on both sides for us to join forces after all that the party had said about the I.L.G. leadership as "betrayers of the working class." If we worked hand in hand, our members and theirs would both lose confidence in us, and the money would stop coming in to either drive. We concentrated on our own collections, mostly for the widows and orphans of slain Spanish Republicans, and the Communists went their separate way.

In the end, of course, Roosevelt won by a landslide. The American Labor Party drew more than a quarter of a million votes on its line. F.D.R.'s margin was big enough so that he would have won even without our votes, but the A.L.P. total did make the difference between victory and defeat for Governor Lehman. That was a great blessing for us.

All through the 1936 campaign, unions kept asking whether the party was a one-shot affair or whether it was to be a permanent organization. As soon as the election was over we had to answer that question. I felt that it should be permanent, and so did Alex Rose. To our surprise, we discovered that Hillman did not seem very eager. He felt that the A.L.P. had served its purpose of helping to re-elect Roosevelt and should disband. The state executive committee was called to a meeting in Atlantic City and amazed Hillman by demanding in the strongest terms that the party continue.

He apparently decided that if he couldn't kill it by decision he would do it by attrition. He asked us to release Elinore Herrick, who had been serving as the party's executive director, and offered to give us Gus Straebel, an organizer for the Amalgamated, to take her place. That would have been fine, except that as soon as we made the switch Straebel disappeared. Hillman had decided to appoint him regional director of the Textile Workers Organizing Committee. That dropped the party in Alex Rose's lap. As state secretary, he neglected his duties at the Millinery Workers Union and went into the A.L.P. headquarters every day to hold the fort until Straebel came back. It was a busy period. We were already into 1937 and a mayoralty election was coming. La Guardia became terribly interested in the party, because he was about to run for a second term; and newspapermen kept dropping in, looking for stories on what the party intended to do.

After a few weeks, Rose and Andrew Armstrong, the state treasurer, went to see Hillman. When they asked when Straebel would be coming back, he gave them a song and dance about the importance of the textile drive and the impossibility of pulling Straebel off it. The end result was that he told Rose and Armstrong to take care of things, and that was what they did. It didn't take a genius to figure out that the A.L.P. would be for La Guardia in November, even before any formal decision had been made. So Rose began dropping hints to the newspapers. He had a great talent for making a lot out of a little. The A.L.P. kept getting bigger and bigger headlines. When La Guardia saw them, he got very excited. He sent Paul Kern, the head of his Civil Service Commission, to get the party's ideas on appointments to the new labor-relations agencies he was setting up. This evidence that the party was being taken seriously gave us reassurance that we were right to continue.

Another meeting of the state executive committee was called to decide what to do about an executive director to replace Straebel. Then another meeting and another meeting. Somehow we couldn't come up with the right choice until one day Charney Vladeck said, "Why are we knocking ourselves out looking for a director when we have the right one here already?" Of course, he was right. The committee all asked Rose to take over the directorship officially, and that was the best decision the party ever made. Alex was a born political strategist. In the most difficult situations, he knew how to play the party's cards to maximum advantage, even when the cards added up to a bust. Nobody in either the Democratic or the Republican Party could match him. The A.L.P.'s success that year in polling almost half a million votes for La Guardia was a testimonial to his capacity.

In June of 1938, after Royal S. Copeland died and left open a seat in the United States Senate, Rose got a call one morning from a political reporter for the old *World-Telegram*. The reporter said he had nothing to write, and Rose told him he had nothing to tell him. Then, as a joke, he added, "Unless you want me to tell you Hillman is going to run for the Senate." The reporter said, "Oh, yeah," and hung up without another word. Rose thought no more about it until he picked up the *World-Telegram* later in the day and found a four-column headline on page one to the effect that Hillman was in the Senate race. The reporter had let his imagination flow even more vigorously than Rose did. He reported that the White House was using its influence to see that Hillman got the nomination on both the Democratic and A.L.P. lines. There was a lot more buildup. It all sounded very convincing.

Rose felt terrible. When Hillman called him the next morning, he started to explain how it all happened. Hillman didn't listen. "Don't tell me, I'll tell you," was what he said; and he asked Rose to meet him for lunch at the Oak Room of the Plaza. After the lunch Rose came to see me at Mt. Sinai Hospital, where I was recovering from an ulcer operation. It turned out that Hillman was not at all upset by the story. Just the opposite, he was taking it very seriously. He told Rose that he really did have the White House backing. To top it off, on his way to lunch with Alex, Hillman had met John D. Rockefeller, Jr., and he quoted Rockefeller as saying, "Sidney, you're a natural." The lunch wound up with Hillman asking Rose to be his campaign manager. It was all ridiculous, and Rose and I laughed so hard over it that a nurse came in and told me to be careful or I'd open my stitches. Just to make it still funnier, Antonini, who was the state chairman of the A.L.P., had issued a statement, out of loyalty to me, suggesting that I ought to be the Senate candidate, not Hillman. I lost no time in making it clear that I didn't think either of us should be nominated. Things began returning to some degree of sanity at that point. After a few days Hillman met with Roosevelt and Farley at the White House, then announced that he had withdrawn his name as a candidate. The A.L.P. gave its support to the two official favorites of the Democratic Party, Senator Robert F. Wagner, Sr., whose term was expiring, and James M. Mead, running for the Senate seat left vacant by the death of Copeland. Both won in November.

Now that the party was firmly established, we had increasing headaches from two directions. One was the Democrats, who wished we would drop dead. They insisted we were stealing their votes; we were convinced we were appealing to the great mass of independent voters in New York as well as the old-line Socialists. More important, we were acting as a liberal counterweight in the whole political process through our ability to tip the balance—in favor of the Democrats when they had good candidates, against them when they put up clubhouse stumblebums. We could foul up their plans by nominating a candidate of our own or by endorsing a Republican if he was a man of character and independence. The Democrats didn't like that. The State Federation of Labor and the rest of the A.F.L. hierarchy kept edging away from us, partly because they still had strong ties to the machine Democrats and also because most of our leadership was from the C.I.O. By 1938 George Meany was openly denouncing the A.L.P. and telling union labor to boycott it.

The other big problem for us—and in a real sense much the more serious—was the strain created by the never-ceasing efforts of the Communists and their stooges in the left wing of the C.I.O. to capture the A.L.P. apparatus. They might well have succeeded as early as 1940 if the signing of the Stalin-Hitler pact had not forced the New York members of the "Moscow First Society" into what was the politically suicidal position of opposing a third term for President

Roosevelt. Hillman, whose people in the A.L.P. had been working more and more closely with the Communists, suddenly became aware that there was a real danger that the party's state committee would refuse to endorse Roosevelt. As a key adviser to F.D.R. in the pre-Pearl Harbor defense effort, Hillman was as upset as I was over that possibility. He invited Alex and me to meet with him at his home, and we mapped a strategy for cooperation of the Amalgamated, the I.L.G., the Millinery Workers and the rest of our people, to make sure that the anti-Roosevelt crowd didn't take over. By the time the nominating meeting was held in Utica on September 14, 1940, the lefties saw they didn't have the votes so they switched to their favorite tactic of disruption. Midnight of that day was the legal deadline for making nominations. Their idea was to shout and riot until they broke up the meeting. That would keep Roosevelt from getting the A.L.P. line. They made so much commotion that we got expelled from the meeting hall, but we reassembled in the lobby of our headquarters hotel. We got the cops to throw out the worst troublemakers, and we finally managed to get a roll call despite all the yelling. There was a majority for Roosevelt and he got the nomination, but we never could have done it without the police protection.

In June of 1941, when the Nazis invaded Russia, the Commies turned around and became the biggest supporters of Roosevelt and the war effort. The ease with which they could turn round and round simply confirmed the feelings I had always had about their untrustworthiness as allies. Hillman, who had always been more ready to enter into united fronts with them, was delighted now that everybody had to pull together to win the war. When he became chairman of the national C.I.O. Political Action Committee in 1943, Hillman floated a "united front" plan for the A.L.P. that could have no other effect but to deliver the whole party over to the left wing.

By that time, I have to confess Hillman and I had drifted a long way apart. The garment workers were no longer part of the C.I.O. We had gone back to the A.F.L. in 1940. Also there had been a bitter disagreement between Hillman and me over A.L.P. policy in the 1942 elections. Rose and I believed that Senator Mead would be the best candidate for Governor. To our dismay, Jim Farley and Tammany Hall dictated the selection on the Democratic ticket of a nobody named John J. Bennett to run against Tom Dewey. We refused to follow suit. Instead, we put in an independent, Dean Alfange, to teach the Democrats that labor would not blindly follow their lead when they put up a worthless candidate. Hillman, who had no more respect than we did for Bennett, nevertheless argued that in wartime we couldn't split "the progressive forces." Whereupon he pulled the Amalgamated out of the A.L.P., which hardly seemed to me to be consistent with his own doctrine.

Early in 1943 the rift grew deeper when I presided over a protest meeting in Mecca Temple to denounce the murder by the Soviet government of two heroic members of the Polish Bund; they were Jewish Socialists who had been executed for their opposition to Stalinist dictatorship. Mayor La Guardia joined in this testimonial to the martyred Henryk Ehrlich and Victor Alter, but the meeting was held only after the most strenuous efforts had been made to get it called off not only by the Communists but by many in high governmental office who should have known better. The contention was that no one should say anything critical of Moscow while we were fighting on the same side. My answer was that our obligation to condemn Soviet misdeeds was particularly great when we were linked in a battle whose whole point was to keep human liberty alive. Hillman did not share my view. J. B. S. Hardman, editor of *Advance*, the Amalgamated's union newspaper, was eased out of his job not long after he joined me as a speaker at the Ehrlich-Alter rally.

A few months after the rally Hillman came forward with his plan for "unifying" the A.L.P. under a formula that would have transferred control of its state committee to the

pro-Communists who had been trying ever since its formation to capture power. His plan to "democratize" the party
by admitting all left-wing unions on the basis of their
dubious membership statistics and per capita payments
would have shut out any voice the liberal elements un-
affiliated with trade unions had in the A.L.P. leadership. It
was exactly the plan the Communists themselves had been
pushing for a long time, and we would have none of it.

But Hillman did not give up. He was playing for bigger
game than the A.L.P. The whole future of the Political Action Committee in the C.I.O. was tied up with how successful he could be in delivering New York to the left wing. The
relations between Hillman and Phil Murray were cool; Hillman's ties with the pro-Communists kept getting stronger
and stronger, because they were the only people he had outside his own Amalgamated. And the pro-Communists were a
very important factor in the C.I.O. nationally. The Hillman
peace proposal was modified several times in an effort to get
us to go along. He even got a promise from Mike Quill of the
Transport Workers Union and Joe Curran of the National
Maritime Union that they would take a back seat in the new
coalition leadership. But the more eager the Communist
forces were to show their "moderation," the surer we were
that their whole purpose was to draw us into an intolerable
setup. We would provide a respectable front and they would
quickly be running everything.

Finally, it became clear that there had to be a showdown
within the party by putting the leadership fight up to our
members in the 1944 primary. President Roosevelt wasn't
too happy about that prospect. He was running for a fourth
term that year, and the trading of charges inside a party that
was born to help him carried a certain amount of embarrassment for him. He telephoned and asked me to come to see
him. It was all very secret. When I was shown into his office,
the President was not there, but all by itself, in the middle of
his desk, was a single piece of paper. I recognized it right
away; it was an editorial that had appeared in the *New York*

Post, written by Ted Thackrey, who was then its editor. The point of the editorial was that it would be un-American for us to leave the American Labor Party.

When F.D.R. came in, we went into the whole situation. I reminded him of what happened in 1940, how these same Commies had wanted to deny him renomination for a third term because of the Stalin-Hitler pact. I reminded him of all the reasons why our union had got out of the C.I.O. I told him we had no alternative now except to get out of the A.L.P. if these same Commies won in the primary. And I left feeling I had persuaded him, because he told me, "You're right." I came back to New York and assured Alex Rose that the President was on our side, and we developed a whole strategy based on that. We started right away to negotiate with Judge Samuel I. Rosenman about the wording of a letter from Roosevelt, in which he would tell the voters before the primary that he would not take the A.L.P. endorsement if the left-wingers won. The letter would be sent to us and then we would circulate it to all the party's enrolled members, so they would understand what was at stake. We were so sure that the letter would come that Rose told James A. Hagerty, the senior political writer for *The New York Times,* that we would have it in a day or two. Hagerty said, "You'll never get that letter." He was right. We never did get the letter, even though Alex and Rosenman, the President's closest adviser, had agreed on what the never-sent letter would say.

What happened was that Hillman also was asked to visit Roosevelt. He met with him four days after I did, and evidently Roosevelt told Hillman he also was right. That left everything up in the air so far as the members of the A.L.P. were concerned. It was two months before the primary and the only thing to do was to slug it out. Mayor La Guardia lined up behind the Hillman formula. He was on the spot, because his old law partner, Congressman Vito Marcantonio, was the chief spear carrier for the pro-Communist faction in Manhattan. La Guardia was always playing with

Marcantonio, and the excuse always was, "Marcantonio is my boy and I cannot dump him." Then he would add, "Sometime Marc will come to his senses and he'll be all right."

That was La Guardia's alibi for undercutting us before the primary. It never convinced us, and we took newspaper ads to denounce Hillman as two-faced in pretending that the Communists could be kept from taking over if the leftists won. Their fake façade of labor unity carried the day; they came out on top in the primary by a margin of about three to two in the 87,000 votes cast. We were not heartbroken, because the important thing in our view was to be rid of them. We didn't want to stay in the same party with them and provide a front. Even if we had prevailed in the primary, that would not have been the end of it. They would have used their power in the county organizations to disrupt the party until they succeeded in either dominating or destroying it.

A month after the primary we organized the Liberal Party as a rallying center for those labor and liberal forces that wanted a genuinely independent outlet for political action, free of the two major parties and of the Communists as well. Our first question was whether we should advise Senator Wagner, who was up for re-election, to take the nomination of our new party but to reject that of the A.L.P. on the ground that it was Communist-dominated. We came to the conclusion in talks among ourselves that, while we would not be happy about his accepting the A.L.P. endorsement, he should do it. At that time we didn't know what Roosevelt himself was going to do on that question, though we suspected—rightly—that he had already made up his mind to run on their ticket as well as ours. If that was not his intention, he would have sent us the letter we expected before the primary.

But our thinking about Wagner was separate from our conjecture on what F.D.R. might or might not do. We were concerned with the Senator's re-election. We did not want to put him on the spot, nor did we want to create a situation where, if he turned down the A.L.P. on our insistence and then got defeated, we would be blamed for it. We recognized that politicians have a different approach to politics than do people like us. They have to get elected. Whether it was Wagner or Roosevelt, their concern was to be elected. Ours was to provide a place where liberal voters could have a political home and not have to go to the American Labor Party. Recognizing that difference, we interposed no objection to the Senator and the President running on our line and the A.L.P. line at the same time any more than we did to their basic identification with the Democratic Party.

In the first election after the split, the A.L.P. got about 500,000 votes and we got about 305,000. From then on the A.L.P.'s role diminished as it became increasingly clear to everyone that it was a vehicle for the Communists. For all practical purposes its swan song came in 1948, when it served as the New York arm of the Progressive Party, which the pro-Communists organized to kill the re-election chances of Harry S. Truman. They hated him for the Marshall Plan and the Truman Doctrine, both of which helped block Soviet imperialism after World War II. Henry A. Wallace, the former Vice-President, who had nursed a grudge against Truman ever since F.D.R. dumped Wallace in favor of Truman at the 1944 Democratic convention, was put up as a spoiler candidate for the Presidency.

In truth, that year it looked as if Truman could not win, even without the assassination attempt by the so-called Progressives. Many leading Democrats were cold to him. That was easy to understand in regard to the Dixiecrat wing of the party; they disliked him for his vigorous positions on civil rights and for his veto of the Taft-Hartley Act, a veto that didn't stick in Congress. But there was also a great sense of defeatism about Truman among many liberal Democrats, including a lot of unionists in both the A.F.L. and the C.I.O. They were so convinced that he could not beat Governor Thomas E. Dewey of New York, his Republican rival, that a strong effort was made—not by conservatives, but by liberals—to persuade General Eisenhower to seek the Democratic nomination instead of Truman. Nobody was sure what party he belonged to, much less where he stood politically, but he looked like a winner. He won all right, but that was four years later and under the Republican label. He wasn't interested in running as a Democrat.

The lukewarmness of the Democratic Party organization toward Truman persisted even after he became the official party nominee. It quickly became evident to me that he had no chance at all if the unions did not get behind him in a big way with both manpower and money. The A.F.L. was inhibited by its historic "nonpartisan" position from giving Truman its formal endorsement, but most of its unions went through the motions of working for him as the man who had tried to stop passage of the Taft-Hartley "slave labor" law. Most of the unions of real substance in the C.I.O., especially the United Steelworkers under Phil Murray and the United Auto Workers under Walter Reuther, mobilized for Truman, even though few of the top people had their hearts in it. The C.I.O. was moving further and further away from its pro-Communist wing by 1948, and the unanimity with which the Muscovite elements in the C.I.O. lined up behind the Wallace third-party bid helped speed the final break, which came a year later.

To be honest, I had originally shared the belief that Truman's chances of winning were so small that it would be better to draft Ike as the Democratic candidate. The first time I had had occasion to visit Truman in the White House was after F.D.R.'s death, and I came back and told my associates very frankly, "To me, it appears that the hat is too big for him." But when I saw what a fighter he was in the campaign I developed increasing respect for him.

After he got the Democratic nomination, the A.F.L. called a meeting of about fifty of its top leaders in Chicago to decide what the Federation should do in the campaign. The voting was still two months off, but most of the people at the meeting were ready to toss in the towel so far as any chance of electing Truman was concerned. They argued that labor should put all its muscle and money into electing Congressmen pledged to repeal of the Taft-Hartley Act and forget about the main event.

That didn't make much sense to me. "I don't know whether we can elect President Truman," I told the group, "but this I do know: If we get a Republican President, we will need two thirds of the votes in Congress to repeal the Taft-Hartley law. If we elect Truman, all we need is a simple majority. On the basis of arithmetic alone, we have to do everything we can to get him elected."

That didn't convince the rest of them. The A.F.L. stayed officially neutral in the Presidential race, but the I.L.G. and the Liberal Party went all-out for Truman—which was a big help to him, because the Democratic Party was not lifting a finger for him in New York and the left wing of labor was doing everything it could to knife him through the Wallace third-party movement.

I have to confess that I had developed a great dislike and distrust for Wallace long before he ran for the Presidency as a spoiler. It all started in 1944 when he was still Vice-President, but Franklin D. Roosevelt had dropped Wallace from his ticket and was running for a fourth term with Truman as his Vice-Presidential nominee. It was the Liberal Party's first time out after the split with the A.L.P., and we had arranged a Madison Square Garden rally to wind up our campaign for F.D.R.

We realized that the President's health was giving out and that it would be unfair to ask him to come to the Garden as a speaker, though in the closing days of the campaign F.D.R. did tour the Seventh Avenue district in an open car on a raw, rainy day just to prove to the voters that he was still in good shape. Looking at the pictures of that drawn, ravaged face with its brave grin as he waved to our garment workers still brings tears to my eyes. Truman was not well known to our people, and Wallace was still a respected figure, so we asked the President to get both of them to speak at the rally as proof that there was unity in the Roosevelt camp. I went down to the White House with a committee to make the request personally to F.D.R.

He called in Steve Early, his executive secretary, and asked him to get Wallace on the phone while I was sitting there. The President told Wallace he thought it was important for him to accept the invitation, that it would mean a lot to me and it would also mean a lot to the national ticket. When he hung up, the President said: "You've got him. He'll be there, and so will Truman."

Well, we made the necessary arrangements. There was no television in those days, but we bought a half hour of radio time, and radio was expensive. It was our plan to have them both go on, Wallace and Truman, in that half hour. And they agreed. But on the night of the rally I began to get trouble signals. Suddenly, I was told that Wallace had arranged to speak some place in Brooklyn at just the time he was supposed to be in Manhattan for our rally. So I got in touch with Wallace's bodyguard, and he promised that they would be back in time. He told me he would call at 7:30 P.M. to give me a further report, but he didn't call. According to the arrangement, both Truman and Wallace were supposed to walk out onto the platform at nine o'clock. At a quarter to nine, I still hadn't heard from Wallace. But I got word from a detective assigned to guard him. "We are now on Canal Street; Wallace is walking around the streets." I told him to see to it that he got in the car and came right up to the Garden. The detective said, "He's walking around and he doesn't want to get into the car." I went over to Wallace's man at the Garden and I said, "What the hell is this here? What kind of a game is he playing? We need him here. He has to be in this room so they can both go into the hall together. You got to get him." Well, that wasn't so easy. There was no two-way radio to get right through to the Wallace party. So we got the police precinct on the phone and they sent a prowl car out to get the word to Wallace.

In the meantime, Truman came to the waiting room, but I wouldn't let him go out into the hall alone. I kept him sitting and waiting. Nine-fifteen ticked past, then nine-thirty. I went over to Wallace's man on the platform and I said loud enough for many in the crowd to hear, "That son-of-a-bitch won't put it over on me. I'll keep the crowd till eleven o'clock if I have to. I'll pay overtime." I knew what Wallace was up to. He wanted to upstage Truman by coming in after Truman was already on the platform. Then Wallace would get a tremendous hand and show that he really should have been the candidate and not Truman. I wouldn't give that son-of-a-bitch that chance. Not in his lifetime.

A few minutes later Wallace arrived and I took him into the room where Truman was waiting. I took them into the hall together. And in the end when Truman spoke, as the Vice-Presidential candidate, he got very good applause—part of it I think because the word had spread and half the audience knew what Wallace's game was. And I could see Wallace was disappointed that he hadn't been able to pull it off the way he wanted. It was worth the overtime we had to pay to the Garden personnel. After that experience, it was no surprise to me when he let the lefties talk him into being the Progressive Party candidate against Truman in 1948. And his tactics didn't work any better that time either.

In that campaign the Liberal Party became the main recruiter of support for Truman in New York City and New York State. The Democrats here were so overawed by Dewey and so sure that he had the election wrapped up that they did practically nothing for Truman. The rag-tag of the A.L.P. was doing everything it could to pirate what would normally be Democratic votes and turn them over to Wallace. We told them all to go to hell. The Taft-Hartley Act prohibited unions from spending funds out of their own treasury for political purposes. I set out to prove that, far from making unions less effective politically, that prohibition could be turned from a handicap into an asset. I organized an I.L.G.W.U. campaign committee to seek voluntary campaign contributions from garment workers all over the state. That not only brought in $275,000 but also got our people personally involved in politics in a way thousands of them never had been before. Our locals set up permanent registration committees to try to get everybody registered; in some cases whole shops went to register in a group. The response was so spectacular that I felt I ought to send notes of thanks to Senator Taft and Representative Hartley. They had enabled us to save the union's own money and still do more politically than we ever had before.

Through the Liberal Party, we provided the setting for a dramatic wind-up rally in Madison Square Garden a few days before the 1948 election. President Truman spent the day being seen by hundreds of thousands of New Yorkers in the Seventh Avenue garment center and elsewhere. That night he gave heart to his followers all over the country with one of the most rip-roaring of his famous "give 'em hell" speeches. I am certain that the Liberal rally was a decisive element in the astonishing upset that Truman scored less than a week later. I know Truman himself always assured me afterward that it was, and I don't think he was just being polite. In fact, when Alex Rose and I visited the White House a week after the election, he said flatly that our rally at the Garden was the highlight of the whole campaign.

Once Truman beat Dewey, of course, all the political pundits who had been sneering at me and the Liberal Party for wasting our energies in a hopeless cause suddenly started saluting us as political masterminds and miracle workers. The newspapers began running stories touting me as a fusion candidate for Mayor in the municipal elections to be held in the next year. I told the reporters who asked me about it: "I would make a good Mayor, but I am not a candidate." That never was an ambition with me; the union was my life.

TWELVE

The Third Party That Wasn't

OBVIOUSLY, the question came up over and over about extending the concept of the Liberal Party on a national basis. If our party had a useful role to play in New York City and State, why wouldn't it be a good idea to have the same kind of party pulling together labor and other progressive forces in Presidential, Congressional and local races all over the country? This did not necessarily mean trying to go the way of the Labour Party in Great Britain, which much of the time qualifies as the dominant party in British politics. Rather, the idea was to act nationally as a balance-of-power party keeping the Democrats and Republicans honest by throwing our support to one major party or the other, depending on their stance in any particular period. The other half of the idea was that we would run independent candidates of our own when both parties presented hopeless programs and people. That was exactly what we did in New York, and I had no doubt that the same principle could work on a larger scale, provided that there was genuine evidence of grass-roots support from coast to coast. This last proviso was all-important. Without a countrywide base, the whole idea was impractical. It could not be imposed; it had to stem from sustained dissatisfaction, at the local level, with the record of the two major parties, and even then you would need a charismatic leader to bring the whole thing to life.

Part of the reason for my caution on this point was that I knew very well how little chance there was that the main elements of American labor would take a leadership role in such an effort. The Gompers philosophy of practical alliances based on "what's in it for us" has always remained the keynote of A.F.L. political action, despite the magnified force in politics that the Federation became under George Meany, especially after the merger with the C.I.O. On rare occasions Meany has thought that labor ought to have a third party, but that was usually when he was particularly fed up with the Democrats as well as the Republicans. One such occasion was in the spring of 1949, when he was rightfully disgusted with the record of the do-nothing Eightieth Congress, which had come in at the same time as Truman's re-election. On the face of it, labor had every reason to expect some favorable action not only on its pet project, Taft-Hartley repeal, but also on other issues that it considered crucial to the country's economic welfare. The reactionary elements on Capitol Hill had taken a shellacking in November. By A.F.L. standards the number of prolabor Senators had increased from 25 to 44; in the House the number had gone up from 83 to 209. However, the Dixiecrats in Congress undid all that labor thought it had gained by forming a closed shop with the G.O.P., and labor got nothing but disappointment.

Meany was so sore that when he came to New York in May 1949 to speak at a Liberal Party function, he said, "It is quite evident to me that the present Tweedledee and Tweedledum two-party system and its virtues have been greatly overrated." He added that it would be no catastrophe if a third party came into being to serve as a national balance of power, and he suggested that the labor movement itself might take the initiative in forming an independent party when and if events indicated that was necessary to achieve its goals. Despite the vigor of his words, the reality, of course, was that what Meany was saying was part pique, part blackmail, intended to put a burr under the tail of Congressmen who owed their election to us. He never had any genuine enthusiasm for a national third-party movement. In fact, most of the time he would have been happier if the Liberal Party had dropped dead even in New York.

In fairness to Meany, I have to confess that the only time Alex Rose and I, the cofounders of the Liberal Party, thought seriously that a national third party might be a realistic possibility was at a most improbable juncture in United States and world affairs. That fascinating episode in the history of the Liberal Party came in 1944, while the country was still involved in World War II. It centered around Wendell Willkie, for whom we had had no use at all when we were still in the American Labor Party and he ran for President against Franklin D. Roosevelt; at that time we considered Willkie an agent of special privilege, "the barefoot boy from Wall Street," dedicated to enriching the utilities and other monopolies. By 1944 we had formed a very different estimate. I don't mean that Willkie had replaced F.D.R. in our esteem or affection. Nobody could do that. But the constructive role he played in trying to unify Americans during the war and especially his brilliance and persistence in preaching the idea of One World made us realize that he was a person of great integrity, even if he was a Republican.

Willkie made a stab at winning the G.O.P. Presidential nomination for a second time in 1944, but Governor Thomas E. Dewey of New York had things sewed up before the first primary. The Republican machine gave Willkie such a raw deal in the Wisconsin primary that he abandoned hope. He decided not only that he had no chance for nomination that year but that the powers in control of the G.O.P. never, never would tolerate a liberal Republican as their Presidential nominee. That meant that Willkie had no future in the party; he was a political orphan in need of a new home. What better place to turn than our brand-new Liberal Party? All the issues we had raised in our fight with the Communists and their allies in the A.L.P. appealed to Willkie. We had lost in our fight; he had lost in his fight. But we were both fighting for the right things, and neither of us was ready to run up a white flag.

So in May, not long after he failed to win a single convention delegate in Wisconsin, out of the blue I got a call from Willkie saying he would like to get together with me and some of our people to talk about the future. I called Rose and we arranged to meet with Willkie for a private dinner at my apartment on West Sixteenth Street. We invited the three principal intellectual leaders of the Liberal Party—Professors John L. Childs and George S. Counts of Columbia University and State Supreme Court Justice Samuel Null—to join us for a discussion after dinner.

Willkie lost no time in telling us the idea that was burning inside him. It was time, he said, to get started on building a national third party—not for the 1944 Presidential campaign, but for the years to come. In his estimation, both the Republican Party and the Democratic Party were moribund. Once F.D.R. died—and no one could doubt that his health was failing—the Democrats would be as much a prisoner of the reactionaries as the Republicans. That was the way Willkie saw it, and he made it plain that he was more than eager to volunteer to lead a liberal coalition under a third-party banner.

Alex and I told him it would be a mistake to surface too early with such a move. We said the best way to start would be to concentrate on the next municipal election in New York City, which was just a year away. Fiorello La Guardia was winding up his third four-year term, and the anticipation was that he would not run again. We advised Willkie that, if he declared his candidacy for Mayor early in 1945, the Republican Party in New York City would not dare deny him its endorsement. Even if the party leaders tried to blackball him, he would win the nomination hands down. We assured him that he could count on our backing as well. That would mean he would be running on a Republican-Liberal coalition ticket, which couldn't lose. It would embody all the ideas of fusion for good government that La Guardia had stood for. A bold move of that kind would be insurance against a comeback for the old Tammany machine and all the graft and gangsterism it represented. It was just what New York needed.

Willkie was excited by the prospect. He admitted that there could be no better springboard for extending the third-party idea nationally than to start as Mayor of New York City. So, as we drank coffee and brandy at the end of the long evening, we were all inspired with the belief that we had made a historic decision—a decision that would surprise not only the city but the whole country. Through the months that followed, all of us kept the project a deep secret, but our enthusiasm for it grew.

For the Liberal Party, it could mean a marvelous start in local politics. Willkie was at the top of his prestige with progressives. He would be a great asset at the head of our municipal ticket. As for him, the more he saw of the 1944 campaign, the more contempt he developed for the Republican Party machine. He had very idealistic expectations of what the world could become when the war ended, and that made him more anxious than ever to be part of a movement with imagination and inspiration. He even discussed his thoughts in a general way with F.D.R. and came away convinced that he had Roosevelt's good will for what he had in mind.

Then it all ended as suddenly as it began. I picked up a newspaper in October 1944 and read of Willkie's death of a heart attack. It was a crushing moment. The national third-party project died with him. So far as I was concerned, it died for all time. No similar Mr. Right ever came along as a potential rallying center.

But the fact that the Liberal Party remained confined to New York did not prevent it from playing a role beneficial to the nation as well as the city and state. One of the proudest services Rose and I were able to render through the Liberal Party was to keep our old friend Herbert H. Lehman from dropping out of the United States Senate race in 1949. A brave chapter in American political history would never have been written if he had not run. In June of that year ill health forced Robert F. Wagner, Sr., to give up the Senate seat he had filled so well. Governor Dewey appointed John Foster Dulles as his successor, but under the law a special election had to be held that fall.

As soon as the Wagner resignation was announced, Ed Flynn, the Democratic boss in this state, called Lehman and urged him to take the nomination. Lehman was then in honored retirement after his brilliant career as Governor and as postwar administrator of relief and rehabilitation for the United Nations. While Lehman was debating whether to say yes, he read in the press an attack by Cardinal Spellman on Mrs. Eleanor Roosevelt. She had written a newspaper column supporting a bill in Congress that would have given federal aid to public schools but not to parochial schools. In the course of that column Mrs. Roosevelt had a sentence that said the Cardinal's pressure to have Catholic schools included in the money "forces upon the citizens of the country the kind of decision that is going to be very difficult to make."

Her statement was absolutely correct, but it stirred Cardinal Spellman to fury. He denounced the Congressional bill as "infamous" and accused Mrs. Roosevelt of conducting "an anti-Catholic campaign." Forgetting that a churchman, and particularly a Cardinal, ought to be forbearing, he wound up by asserting that Mrs. Roosevelt's record was "unworthy of an American mother." Lehman was shocked by the unfairness of the Cardinal's attack. He realized that he would probably kill his chances of being elected Senator if he spoke out in Mrs. Roosevelt's defense, but he did not hesitate. In a letter to *The New York Times*, Lehman stressed the right of any citizen to express his convictions on controversial issues "without being vilified or accused of religious bias." He said Mrs. Roosevelt's whole life had been dedicated to a constant fight for brotherhood and tolerance, and he voiced confidence that she would retain the trust and affection of people of all creeds despite the Spellman diatribe.

Not long after the letter I got a call from Lehman asking Rose and me to visit him at his apartment on Park Avenue. He showed us a letter from Spellman rebuking him, and he told us he was sure it wouldn't be long before he would be hearing from Ed Flynn and Paul Fitzpatrick, the Democratic State Chairman, to tell him not to run. (A week later he called to say they had made just such a call.) Alex and I spent two hours trying to convince him that he should not pull out of the race for the Senate nomination. We got strong help from Mrs. Lehman. She told him the same thing, even though she worried about the strain a fight would put on his health. His elder brother, Chief Judge Irving Lehman of the Court of Appeals, had died only four years before.

In spite of all our pleading, we got the impression that he was ready to make a withdrawal statement. That impression became even stronger after Flynn and Fitzpatrick began pressuring him. However, we persuaded him to go off on vacation in Lake Placid and let things simmer for a while before making up his mind what to do. Every couple of days Alex and I would call him with whatever encouraging information we could think up. Meanwhile, public sentiment began to rally strongly behind Lehman. Catholics joined with Protestants and Jews in praising him for his guts in defending the right of free speech. Finally there was a public reconciliation between the Cardinal and Mrs. Roosevelt. At once Flynn and Fitzpatrick became as eager to have Lehman run as they had previously been to have him drop out. In the end he decided to run, and the State Democratic Committee made him its nominee. Dulles ran for the Republicans, and at the end of a bitter campaign, Lehman won by only 200,000 votes. Once again our party provided the victory edge for an oustanding Democrat, one who had already served the state with great distinction and who went on to write a brave chapter in political courage in the Senate.

In the next decade the American Labor Party crumbled into nothing, but the Liberal Party became an increasingly consequential political factor. So much so that I got my first certain indication that John F. Kennedy planned to go all-out for the Presidency in 1960 more than a full year before the Democratic nominating convention. In the summer of 1959 he asked Alex Rose and me to have breakfast with him in his home at Georgetown. I can never forget when he came out to greet us with two-year-old Caroline on his arm. She was beautiful, and so was his carrying her. I saw George Meany later that day and told him, "If he runs for the Presidency, all he needs is a picture with Caroline, and all the women in America will vote for him." At the breakfast, we didn't speak of the Presidency but of general politics and labor matters. It was all very vague, except that both of us knew just why we were there. He wanted our help—both in getting the A.F.L.–C.I.O. on his side and in lining up convention votes in New York through the Liberal Party's pushing power with the Democrats.

My own real activity in support of Kennedy began early in 1960. The A.F.L.–C.I.O. was still neutral, and Meany wanted to keep it that way. Many of our people were strong for Hubert Humphrey, who had always been a favorite of ours since he emerged as Mayor of Minneapolis. Others felt that Adlai Stevenson, who had lost twice to Eisenhower, was entitled to another shot at the Presidency. At its midwinter meeting in Florida in February, the A.F.L.–C.I.O. decided that the labor movement should avoid any formal commitment until after the nominating convention. That bothered both Alex and Arthur J. Goldberg. They had no trouble convincing me that we ought to start early to push the decision toward Kennedy, that he was the one with the best chance to win and also the best one to win. Goldberg was then the general counsel of the United Steelworkers. He had just been principal negotiator of the contract that settled the 116-day steel strike of 1959, the longest strike in the history of that basic industry. It had been a frustrating experience for him and had been made more so by the playboy qualities of the union president, David J. McDonald.

Goldberg had other frustrations. With the single exception of Meany, no one had been more responsible than he for the merger of the labor movement. He had been general counsel of the C.I.O. in the premerger period, and he had to maneuver around Walter Reuther, its president, who used to talk unity, but never really wanted it. Arthur was chiefly responsible for drawing up the actual merger compact. It skillfully finessed many tough issues, including what for a while was the toughest of all—a name. A dozen simplified titles were suggested, but Goldberg finally realized that there never could be agreement on anything but the full name of both organizations. He played a similarly important role in drawing up the final constitution, a document that successfully bridged a thousand potentially disastrous differences of viewpoint.

By every right of contribution and capacity, Goldberg should have been general counsel of the merged Federation. But Meany dealt him out. He insisted on giving the top spot to J. Albert Woll, who had become general counsel of the A.F.L. chiefly because he was Matthew Woll's son. Goldberg had to be content with a made-up title as special counsel to the A.F.L.–C.I.O. He was the author of the ethical practices codes, under which we kicked out the Teamsters and other crooked unions. It was the best thing we ever did, but it didn't get us very far. The Teamsters were just as strong— and just as crooked—outside as in. So by 1960 Goldberg had had it. His main interest was in finding a new use for his talents in government, and he had plenty of talents.

Without cutting his ties to the labor movement, Goldberg threw himself full force into the Kennedy campaign. Meany was nominally neutral, but it soon became evident that he had no desire to interfere with the lining up of labor delegates for Kennedy. When Rose talked to Meany about it the first time in March or April, he raised no objection to our activities for Kennedy. But he did make it plain that he had doubts about Kennedy's getting the nomination. "I'd settle for Vice-President for him," Meany told Alex. By the time the Democrats held their nominating convention in Los

Angeles, the union sentiment was overwhelmingly for J.F.K. in his battle against Lyndon B. Johnson for the Presidential spot. I did not go to the convention, though there were almost as many labor leaders there as you would find at an A.F.L.–C.I.O. convention. I was at my summer home in Hampton Bays on Long Island, when suddenly, on the day after Kennedy won the nomination, I got a call from Goldberg.

Naturally, the first thing I asked him was, "What's doing?" He said, "Kennedy wants to nominate Johnson as Vice-President." I jumped. "It's terrific," I said, "it's a winning ticket." That was my instant reaction. "Yes, but your friends don't think so," said Goldberg. I asked, "Who are my friends?" He replied, "George Meany, Walter Reuther, Alex Rose."

"What," I said, "Alex too? I think he's crazy." Goldberg answered, "I think so too, but still and all that's the situation here. They want Hubert Humphrey or Stuart Symington, not Johnson." So I said, "I'm going to talk to them."

I spoke to Alex first, telling him what Arthur had told me and saying, "I think it's terrific. What's the matter with you guys?" Rose responded, "As far as I'm concerned, it's all right with me. But Walter and George Meany want no part of it. Right this second Walter is dictating a statement next door opposing the designation of Johnson." I broke in, "I want to talk to him. Connect me with him." It was so fast that I wasn't thinking straight. Alex slowed me down. "It would be better if you called him direct, not through my room."

I called Walter and he gave me an argument about how terrible Johnson was. I said, "Walter, keep cool. You're making a great mistake. Think it over before you do anything." I didn't want to tell him that I knew he was typing a statement. I had already made one error by asking Alex to connect me. I didn't want to make another now. So all I said was, "Keep cool, think about it, give it time. You may come to the same conclusion that I did." He promised me.

Then I called George Meany, who was on the golf course

when they located him. He had some people with him, Joe Keenan of the International Brotherhood of Electrical Workers and a few others. I began giving him my reasons for favoring Johnson, but he said: "You are there in Hampton Bays, I am here at the convention. I know better." I saw there was no use talking. When he is so set, it is pointless to try to convince him. But my call evidently did some good, because later they had a caucus—the labor people, all of them—and they decided not to issue a public condemnation of the Johnson nomination. That had the effect of removing any obstacle to Johnson's getting the number-two spot.

So far as I was concerned, the case for Johnson was strong. When he was Senate Majority Leader, I had always found him most sympathetic and cooperative on the minimum wage, which was of special concern to our members. A higher federal minimum made it harder for chiselers to steal work from New York and other unionized centers and set up shops in low-wage areas in the South. We had trouble with many Southern Congressmen on pushing up the minimum, but never with this particular Southerner; and his influence was crucial on Capitol Hill.

More than that, I was worried about how Kennedy would win. He had the Catholic thing to beat, and I knew that would be especially troublesome in the South. So it was clear that Johnson could be a great help. Texas would be definitely in the Democratic column, and L.B.J. would gain votes for the ticket everywhere else in the South. And the results showed that it was, as I had said, "a winning ticket." The television debates with Nixon and everything Kennedy did for himself wouldn't have been enough if he had had somebody like Humphrey as his running mate. And I say that even though Humphrey was always a friend, a dependable friend, whom we held in deep affection.

It had seemed most improbable, after the bitterness of the fight at the convention and just before it, that Johnson would ever think of accepting the Vice-Presidential nomination. That's why I was so astonished to learn from Goldberg, first, that Kennedy wanted him and, second, that Johnson would take second place on a Kennedy ticket. It was not a question of Humphrey or anyone else at that point—just whether labor would hold out against a Johnson designation. It would have been a great mistake if they had.

As the campaign developed, Kennedy telephoned me about financial assistance from the labor movement. The important thing unions could do was supply money in a hurry when it was needed to meet a campaign emergency. Walter Reuther and I met with Bobby Kennedy on this question, and we made Goldberg the chief arranger. We decided to take the matter up with Meany, because it was a question not just of our own unions but of the entire labor movement. So we approached Meany and he called a conference, again with Goldberg as the stimulant factor. The moment the ball began rolling, it became apparent that substantial sums could be collected.

More than a million dollars was raised, and Arthur was the effective solicitor of those funds. Up to then there had been a lot of talk, a lot of *schmooze* when it came to raising money for campaigns. Where our union was involved, we always spent a lot of money. We collected a lot of money from our members, because the law prohibited us from giving money from the union treasury. The goal was a million dollars, and we collected more than that. And it all started with the call I got from Jack Kennedy right after the convention.

The normal I.L.G.W.U. campaign spending ran between $300,000 and $400,000 a year, including our contributions to the Liberal Party. We were the backbone of the Liberal Party. In my time, we did not support the Democratic Party—ever. We supported Democratic candidates, like Roosevelt and Truman and Kennedy, but they were also our candidates on the Liberal line. We spent most of the I.L.G. money ourselves, not only in New York but through our organizations around the country. The money went for Congressmen and Senators and for local candidates, as well as for Presidential candidates.

In 1936, when (as part of the American Labor Party) we began to be a factor for the first time, we gave $30,000 or $40,000 to the Roosevelt campaign. And even though in the end F.D.R. was elected by a landslide over Alf Landon, there was great nervousness on the part of Tommy Corcoran when he came down to see us for money. It was the first time our union financially supported a Democratic candidate, and what we gave was a sizable sum in those days before television pushed all campaign spending into the sky. It is true the United Mine Workers gave $500,000 and later John L. Lewis used that donation to try to blackmail Roosevelt when the President didn't do everything Lewis wanted him to do in the General Motors sit-down strikes.

We in the I.L.G. never felt that we were buying a candidate with our funds. It would never occur to us to say that one who had supped at labor's table had to pay the cashier on the way out, let alone leave a big tip. We were satisfied if they stuck to the progressive principles they campaigned on. We had disappointments, but not too many of them. And that was partly because we always recognized that a President has to carry the people along with him. That means making compromises and sometimes doing things he doesn't like and we don't like.

As it developed, the first tension between organized labor and John F. Kennedy arose even before he got into the White House. It revolved around his choice of a Secretary of Labor and, from my view, the issue showed labor at its stupidest. Historically, the old American Federation of Labor always took the view that the Department of Labor was labor's department and should be headed by a labor man in just the same way that the Department of Commerce was business's department and always had a chief who was business-minded. In line with that conception, when Franklin D. Roosevelt was elected in 1932, the A.F.L. moved to have the presidents of all its affiliated unions sign a petition urging the appointment of Daniel J. Tobin, president of the Teamsters. Union, as Secretary of Labor. Every single union president did sign except me, though I was the newest president of all and came from a union that most of my colleagues in labor's top drawer considered a *mishmash* of alien radicalism.

Frankly, it did not seem right for me as a Socialist to petition a Democratic President on whom he should pick as his Labor Secretary. But there was another factor in my thoughts as well. I felt that if a labor man was going to be selected, it should be one with progressive ideas in tune with the emerging spirit of the New Deal and not a tired union hack whose principal distinction was his loyalty to the Democratic Party. I was somewhat surprised that the only other Socialist who headed an international union in that period, Max Zaritsky of the Cap and Millinery Workers, did sign for Tobin. F.D.R. chose Frances Perkins instead, but he later made Tobin his chief labor contact and Tobin did help the President a lot within the labor movement in spite of his turndown for the Secretaryship. Labor did get one concession right away to make up for the passing over of Tobin. Edward McGrady, who was then general organizer for the A.F.L., became Assistant Secretary of Labor under Miss Perkins.

Labor continued after that to hold to the argument that the top job ought to go to a top union official. Oddly, the first one who gave it to them was the Republican Eisenhower. He appointed Martin P. Durkin of the Plumbers, and that turned out to be a mistake both for Eisenhower and for Durkin, who resigned in disgust after his ideas on Taft-Hartley revision were brushed aside by the President. We were a lot better off with Jim Mitchell, and so was the administration. Mitchell came from industry, but he understood labor.

When J.F.K. was elected, labor renewed its demand for appointment of a labor man. Kennedy had his own man in mind. He wanted Arthur Goldberg, and Goldberg very much wanted the job. He had earned it by his hard work for Kennedy in the campaign, and he had more than earned it by his service to the labor movement. To my way of thinking, he was doubly qualified, because his unique apprenticeship had given him a thorough understanding of the needs and practices of labor and an equal understanding of the many ways in which labor's great power could be abused to the detriment of the community. The months of frustration in the 116-day steel strike and the economic slowdown that it helped to bring in 1960 made Goldberg feel that he wanted to get into a post in which he could make some effective contribution to improved public protection in labor disputes. He felt that both labor and management were losing their way and that government had a duty to help point new directions for both, especially in fields where strikes and the economic settlements that came out of strikes had a direct impact on the economic well-being of the total community.

Once the votes were counted, Kennedy lost no time in letting Goldberg know he was eager to have him in his administration. He first offered to make him Solicitor General, a tribute to his legal scholarship, but Arthur was not inclined to take it. And I happened to agree with him, because I felt that would make him a lawyer's lawyer, removed from any voice in determining public policy. Then Kennedy approached him to be Secretary of Labor. In the meantime, some influential members of the A.F.L.–C.I.O. Executive Council began the old agitation that the job should go to a labor man, and they made it clear that they did not consider Goldberg a labor man. In their eyes, he was a lawyer, a hired hand. The old anti-intellectualism was back at work. Technicians were needed by unions, but there had to be a wall between the book-pushers out of the academies and the elected officials who came up out of the work place. The fact that Goldberg had been a master architect of labor unity and of the ethical-practices codes that restored labor's good name was of no account. Neither was the fact that almost alone he had mapped the strategy that brought the steel strike to a successful conclusion. Dave McDonald, of the steelworkers' union, hadn't even been present when he worked out the final terms with Vice-President Nixon, Secretary Mitchell and R. Conrad Cooper, executive vice-president of United States Steel.

George Meany was in Geneva, attending a meeting called by the International Labor Organization, when the anti-Goldberg cabal was organized. Six or seven A.F.L.–C.I.O. vice-presidents got together on their own in Washington to talk about the subject. And they gave several names to Bob Kennedy, all union presidents, people they would prefer to see appointed Secretary of Labor. Jack Kennedy had already talked with Goldberg about taking the job. Now he let him know that he wanted Arthur with or without the Federation's official blessing. Goldberg said he did not want the job on that basis; he would accept only if he were also the candidate of the labor movement. That meant it was up to Meany to say whether he was or was not acceptable.

One night I was working in my office at about eleven o'clock when my private telephone rang. Very few people knew that number. One of them, it turned out, was the President-elect. He told me of his dilemma and asked how he could reach Meany by telephone in Europe. So I said to him: "Mr. President, my advice to you is: Don't call the A.F.L.–C.I.O. office, because everyone will know right away that you are calling on this here thing. Tomorrow I'll supply you with the telephone number to talk to George Meany."

I can't pretend the Kennedy call came as a surprise. Arthur, as a very close friend, had been keeping me closely informed about the whole affair. I wanted to be of any possible assistance. So did Walter Reuther, who did not agree at all with the group that was trying to sidetrack the nomination. Walter was in touch with me six times a day. Suddenly, in the midst of it all, I got a call from Bobby. He asked, "Have you got a good name for Secretary of Labor?" I said,

"Yes." He said, "Who's your candidate? What's his name?" I said, "Arthur Goldberg." Bobby gave a sigh of relief. "He's my candidate, too," he said, "but the labor movement doesn't want him." So I said, "Sit tight, sit tight, don't rush." That was my answer, and the three-way communication between Dubinsky, Reuther and Goldberg never stopped.

When Jack Kennedy got the number and called Meany with his problem, Meany told him, "I'll be back in three days. Hold it over." Meany arrived in New York on a snowy Sunday morning. The storm was so bad that he could not leave for Washington until Monday afternoon. He was not in contact with me. He knew he had a problem and the labor movement had a problem, but he was not in contact with me. I thought, "If he's on strike with me, then I'm on strike with him." And I didn't call him, either at his hotel in New York or after he got back to his office. On Wednesday Meany called off the strike and telephoned me from Washington.

"Dave," he said, "we have a problem."

"What's the problem?"

"The President wants to appoint Arthur Goldberg, and the labor movement is against it."

All innocence, I asked why.

"Because he's not a labor man," said Meany.

At this point I decided that it was time to stop the poker-playing. I trotted out the names of all the revered Socialist lawyers who had played an indispensable role in the early days of the I.L.G.

"George," I said, "you come from New York. Morris Hillquit—was he a labor man though he didn't have a union card in his pocket? Was there anyone more labor conscious, more devoted to labor, than Morris Hillquit? And Congressman Meyer London, who was beloved by the cloakmakers in the earliest years of our union, or Judge Jacob Panken? They didn't have cards, but they were union; no one could doubt that."

Meany seemed to find that a convincing argument, but not convincing enough. After I finished, he said, "Yes, but Goldberg is going to take the appointment from Kennedy without labor's approval."

I knew that was not the case, but again the part of wisdom seemed to be to play the innocent. "Oh, if that's true, then it's a different story," I said. "He should not take it without the labor movement. If he's ready to do that, then I'm not for him." So I told Meany I would call Goldberg myself and ask if he would do a thing like that. It was a safe enough proposition, since Arthur had informed me himself that the President, disgusted with the whole business, wanted to swear him in, but Arthur wouldn't go ahead without Meany's assent.

I went through the motions of another call to Goldberg and then called back Meany. I said, "I just now spoke to Goldberg, and he said the President wants to swear him in today, but Arthur says he can't do it. If you don't give your consent, he won't take the job."

"Well," said Meany, "now we'll settle it."

The settlement involved Goldberg and the President agreeing to take Jerry Holleman, the head of the Texas A.F.L.–C.I.O., as his Under Secretary. That was the compromise, and the next day Arthur was officially named, and Meany was there beaming as Kennedy made the announcement at his home in Georgetown.

By way of footnote, one other part of my conversation with Meany is worth recalling. Before we got into the back-and-forth about whether Goldberg would accept the appointment without a go-ahead from labor, Meany told me that "the committee" had held a meeting and drawn up a list of labor people they would prefer to see as Secretary of Labor. So I said, "Am I a member of the Executive Council? I never knew that you appointed a committee to make such nominations. I was never called to a meeting. What kind of a meeting, for whom did they speak?"

That put him on the defensive. "I didn't appoint any-body," Meany said. "They had a meeting on their own." I decided to press my advantage. "I saw the names they rec-

ommended," I said. "Where is my name? Why is my name
not there? Am I not as good as"—this one or that one; I
picked the first two that came to mind. He couldn't answer
me. One result of the whole conflict was to make Meany
much less interested in having a labor man at the head of the
Labor Department. When Goldberg left to go to the Supreme Court, he was succeeded by Willard Wirtz, a law
professor and arbitrator. That was fine with Meany. In the
Nixon administration, the President decided as a gesture to
the hardhats, who were backing him on the Vietnam war, to
give the job to Peter J. Brennan, president of the New York
Building Trades. Meany did not push the appointment and
never cared much for it. When Brennan reversed his lifelong
positions on labor issues to become a Nixon team player,
Meany's coldness turned to outright contempt, and he boy-
cotted the Labor Department altogether. Now he has turned
180 degrees away from labor's historic view that the Secretary of Labor ought to be from labor. He would much rather
see a businessman or a neutral in the job. For a labor movement that likes to boast of its independence from government, I think that is the right attitude. A Labor Secretary
can't serve two masters.

The high regard in which I held Kennedy was strengthened by his conduct throughout the tug-of-war over the
Goldberg appointment. At one point, when it looked as if the
stalemate would not be broken, the President told Arthur he
was ready to name him as Attorney General. It was not the
right place for a Jew in this period when racial issues were
so tense. I advised Goldberg not to take it, and he was of the
same opinion.

The last time I saw J.F.K. was at the A.F.L.–C.I.O.
convention at the Americana Hotel in New York a week
before his assassination. Meany had designated me a member of the three-man escort committee to greet the President
outside the hotel and bring him to the grand ballroom.
Kennedy, as usual, was without a hat. The minute he saw
me, he whispered, "Tell Alex I left the hat in the car." Alex

Rose made it a practice to send every President at least one hat and he was always terribly disappointed—whether it was Truman or Kennedy or Johnson or Eisenhower—when they showed up at any union function without a hat. With the Democrats, of course, he was especially insistent. Kennedy was his worst customer. He practically never wore a hat, even with formal clothes.

As far as I was concerned, he was a great President, one who would have made a lasting mark had he not been cut down too soon. But one thing I did not admire was the freedom he gave a little clique headed by Bobby to undercut his Vice-President, Lyndon Johnson. Bobby's group considered L.B.J. an embarrassment to the administration, and they were trying hard to persuade the President to dump him from the 1964 re-election ticket. By the time the mid-term Congressional elections rolled around in 1962, it was already evident that the oust-Johnson group had made great headway.

The Liberal Party was scheduled to hold its annual dinner shortly before the 1962 balloting, and Alex and I felt that would be a good time to show our friendship and regard for Johnson. We needed a principal speaker anyhow, so we decided it would help us and help him to invite him to come. He was delighted. A few days before the dinner, Johnson called to say he would like to visit a garment factory while he was in town. I arranged for him to go through one of our leading firms on Seventh Avenue, the Schrader Dress Company, and I went along as guide. In fact, I gave the Vice-President an exhibition of my skill as a cutter of lace material when we inspected the cutting room. Abe Schrader, the president of the company, was enormously pleased at the visit. He explained to Johnson that he had almost failed to get into the industry at all. Schrader had tried to qualify as a cutter but was rejected by the Local 10 examination committee. He appealed to me as manager of the local, and I asked the committee to give him another test. This time he passed.

From then on, Schrader prospered. He became a manu-facturer and made a great success. When he told the story to Johnson, he summed it all up in these words: "You see, Mr. Vice-President, what can happen in America. Two immi-grants from Russia, one becomes president of a great union and the other a poor millionaire." It became one of Johnson's favorite stories. Ever after, whenever we met, he would ask, "How is your friend, the poor millionaire?"

Johnson and I pushed our way through the crowds along the garment-center streets at lunchtime while the *schmooze* was on. When Johnson got to dinner that night, he de-scribed his tour and topped it off by recalling that one garment worker had yelled to another as we passed them on the sidewalk, "Who is that tall guy with Dubinsky?" When he heard it was the Vice-President, the I.L.G. member pre-tended that he felt I was slumming. "You mean Dubinsky goes with the Vice-President?" was his comment. That got a good laugh. Johnson went on to deliver an excellent speech, one that was very well received and that did a lot to build up his spirits and his popular standing.

But the people in the White House who were out to knife him didn't give up. So Alex and I felt we had to try again. We heard that Johnson was coming to New York for some political affair, so we arranged a meeting of the Liberal Party's Trade Union Council at the old Astor Hotel. It was supposed to be right after lunch, but in the morning I got word from Alex that Johnson had decided not to come, even though he was in the city. When I checked to find out why, it turned out that the Democratic politicians here had ad-vised him to stay away for fear he would be booed. Alex and I called him right away and persuaded him that nothing of the sort would happen. We warned him that the worst thing he could do would be to stay away, because it was known that he was supposed to be at the meeting. If he did not come, everybody would feel he was scared.

Under the program, it was planned that I would speak just before Johnson. I started about ten minutes before he was expected to arrive, but he didn't come on time so I had to spin out my remarks for at least twenty minutes. When he finally did come in, he got a tremendous hand. He asked me not to interrupt my speech, even though I had spoken much longer than I intended. That never was any problem for me. I gave Johnson an introduction like he never had before. Maybe he got some to match it when he was President, but never as Vice-President. I told of his relations with our union and with the Liberal Party and, most of all, I told of what he had done for us on several occasions on the matter of a higher minimum wage when he was Senate Majority Leader.

It is true, I told our officers, that he never made any promises to me when I urged his support. But, instead of promising, he divulged his keen interest in the poor people and the misery of their lives. He had his own experience of it in his own home town and in his young days, and he knew that the poor people ought to get consideration and they ought to have a better chance in life than they were having now.

And when Johnson started his speech, he spent a lot of time on that same topic. Then he told a very interesting story about Maury Maverick, who was then the Mayor of San Antonio. Johnson recalled how, when Maverick was first running for Congress as a liberal Democrat bucking the organization, the I.L.G.W.U. sent him a check for two thousand dollars to help his campaign. Texas had a poll tax of one dollar at that time, which kept many Mexican-Americans and other poor people from registering to vote. Maverick turned our check into two thousand silver dollars, and he spread them out on a table in his office and gave one to each supporter who needed money to qualify to vote. That made Maverick happy. It made the poor voters happy. And it helped him get re-elected as Congressman and later as Mayor of San Antonio.

But the contribution also got him into trouble. He was accused of violating Texas law by taking money from a New

York union to buy re-election in San Antonio. Maverick called Johnson as a character witness in his trial. Johnson was already Majority Leader of the Senate, and his testimony undoubtedly helped Maverick beat the case. But Maverick did a good job in his own defense. He said that, for years and years, Texans complained that Yankees exploited the South; they built factories there and capitalized on the labor and resources of the South to make huge profits, which they then took North, leaving Southerners as the victims. Here was a Yankee reversing the process—giving to, not taking from, the South, so that poor citizens could exercise their democratic right to participate in the election.

Maverick wound up his testimony by saying, "I think I'm entitled to praise for my activities in turning around the old practice. Instead of allowing the Yankees to take and exploit our people, I exploited a Yankee. Now you're going to send me to jail for that crime?"

Well, that made a terrific impression, and so did Johnson's presence, and as a result the whole case was thrown out. After Johnson got through telling the story, he said, "This is the accomplishment of your little president, Dubinsky. Don't tell me what he does only in New York. Dubinsky did it in San Antonio and he deserves the credit." And again he got a thunderous ovation from our people just when he felt his career was touching bottom.

On the day after the meeting with our activists I received a call from Lady Bird telling me how much she and her husband appreciated the effusive reception he had received. "We'll never forget what you did for Lyndon." I was greatly touched. Ever after there was a close personal bond between me and both Johnsons, so much so that, one night during his Presidency, when I attended a formal dinner at the White House and lingered so long that I could not get a plane or train back, Mrs. Johnson offered me a bedroom at the White House to sleep over. Naturally, I wouldn't intrude. I'm not used to sleeping in the White House. I wouldn't be able to sleep, no matter what kind of a good bed it would be.

I decided to take a chance on getting a hotel room, but as I prepared to go out I ran into Nelson Rockefeller, then New York's Governor, who had been a guest at the same dinner. He asked, "Where are you going?" I told him my problem, and he solved it by taking me back to New York in his private plane.

The one slight strain in relations between President Johnson and me did not arise out of the Vietnam war or minimum wages or any other cosmic issue. It involved something closer to his heart and to mine. Before the wedding of the President's daughter Luci Baines, we read in *Women's Wear Daily* that a nonunion firm was making her wedding gown. A reporter from *Women's Wear* called me and asked, "How is it that your friend, the President, is letting his daughter be married in a gown made in a nonunion shop?"

Naturally, not wanting to bother the President, I called up Lady Bird and suggested that it would be unfortunate if her daughter's gown were made in that particular shop, that it would be much better if it were made elsewhere. She and her secretary listened very sympathetically. They realized it would be very embarrassing to us, to have his daughter's dress made nonunion. But it also would be very embarrassing to the President, since he was so well known as a friend of labor. The I.L.G.W.U. and its employers had spent millions of dollars to popularize the union label. Mrs. Nelson Rockefeller sewed in the first label in 1959. Two years later Mrs. Eleanor Roosevelt sewed in the *eleven billionth* label. That is how successful we had been in making American workers conscious that the label stood for decent standards, skill and creativity in design.

In this particular case, however, I wasn't so much interested from the standpoint of the union as I was in trying to spare the President embarrassment. And Johnson understood that and wanted to do everything he could to set the matter straight. But when you are dealing with questions of style and of a woman's personal preferences, politics cannot be the only consideration.

Evidently, there was a conflict within the First Family. This particular firm had been chosen because it had an outstanding reputation for excellence in designing wedding gowns, and Luci Baines plainly had her heart set on being married in one of its gowns. How could the White House resolve this touchy problem? Here is Dubinsky, with the support of the labor movement, pulling in one direction and Luci Baines, the bride-to-be, in the other.

Finally, I got assurance that they would withdraw the original order and have the dress made by a union manufacturer. We gave them a good house and they had a gown made there for Luci Baines. But it was not the gown she got married in. They made two dresses, one in the union shop to satisfy me and my conscience and whatever pressure there was of public opinion, and the other in the shop Luci Baines had wanted in the first place. And the second was the one she wore, though that was never publicly revealed.

Proud as I am of the record of the Liberal Party and of the I.L.G.W.U. in national politics, I recognize that our greatest influence—and, in my estimation, our most useful contributions—were in New York City and State. It was always there that the vast majority of our members were concentrated. It was also there that a union or a party standing for political decency and idealism could do most to keep the major parties responsive.

In 1954 it was the urging of the Liberal Party (and skillful behind-the-scenes coaching by Alex Rose) that induced Averell Harriman to snap out of a period of indecision and announce that he was a candidate for governor on the Democratic ticket. Rose, with my blessing, was the key figure in putting together a coalition that won Harriman the Democratic-Liberal nomination and then won him the election by 14,000 votes over Senator Irving M. Ives. Without our intercession, the Republicans would have had an easy victory.

In 1961, when Mayor Robert F. Wagner, Jr., decided to stand up against Carmine de Sapio and the rest of the old-line bosses, we provided much of the guidance that enabled him to defeat them. In the process, I regret to say, we also helped start Abraham D. Beame on the road that eventually made him mayor. Rose advised Wagner to put on his ticket career technicians from the civil service as a means of showing how nonpartisan he was. Beame, who had won respect as Budget Director, became the Wagner running-mate for Controller. The Wagner-led ticket swept through, first to nomination, then to election.

Four years later the party bosses tried to pick themselves out of the gutter by a deal that would cement their shattered ranks. They met at the home of Representative Charles Buckley, head of the Bronx Democratic machine. Frank D. O'Connor, District Attorney of Queens, agreed to shelve his ambitions to be mayor, in favor of Beame, the choice of Assemblyman Stanley Steingut and the rest of the Brooklyn organization. The *quid pro quo* was a promise by the assembled leaders that O'Connor would stand for president of the City Council on the Beame slate and then would get the nomination for governor in 1966.

Even without knowing about the trade-off inside the organization, we in the Liberal Party were worried about the reemergence of the bosses and about the possibility that they would take over again if Beame won the 1965 mayoral race. The city was in bad shape anyway. Even under Wagner, whom we liked and respected, things had gone downhill. There was a general feeling—which I shared— that it was time for a change that would sweep out all the cobwebs in City Hall and throughout the municipal bureaucracy. What was needed, all the reformers agreed, was another La Guardia. But who was around to match the Little Flower of the 1930s and early 1940s?

There were only two possibilities—Senator Jacob K. Javits and Representative John V. Lindsay, both Republicans and both reluctant to try to buck the Democrats in a city so overwhelmingly Democratic in voter enrollment. Javits we knew well and admired. We had supplied the votes that sent him to Washington for the first time as a Congressman in

1946. But he refused to run for the mayoralty. Finally, the good-government forces persuaded Lindsay that he ought to run as a Republican-Fusion candidate in the La Guardia tradition.

To me, he was pretty much a stranger. He came from the Silk Stocking district on Manhattan's East Side, and he had a lot of high-hat qualities that did not appeal much to our people. But he had a good voting record in Congress, especially on civil rights, and his willingness to make the race showed that he had guts. When the time approached for the I.L.G. to decide whether it wanted to join in supporting him for the Liberal Party nomination, I was in the hospital with a minor ailment. I designated Louis Stulberg, our secretary-treasurer, and Charles S. Zimmerman, manager of the Dress Joint Council, to serve as members of an eight-man committee that would interview Lindsay on behalf of the Liberal Party. I wanted their appraisal so that our union could make an intelligent judgment on whether he should be our man. They came back with a favorable report.

That was good enough for me. But it wasn't good enough for some of our other top people. They didn't like the idea of breaking with the Democrats. Two of our vice-presidents, Luigi Antonini and Israel Breslow, spoke sharply against Lindsay at the citywide meeting of the Liberal Party, even after it had been decided that the I.L.G. would back him rather than Beame. They insisted that a Lindsay victory would mean turning the city over to the Republican reactionaries. It bothered me that they persisted in their opposition after we had made a collective decision. It was one of a number of things that made me start thinking about resigning as president. "When I can hear you tell me that I do not speak for the organization on politics, I know it is time to get out," I told the dissenters. "Once that starts, good-bye." And less than a year later, at the age of seventy-four, I cut short my term and stepped down.

But my disappointment that the union was no longer a united force politically didn't stop me from putting all my energy into getting Lindsay elected. Instead, it made me fight harder; and, believe me, I had plenty of pressure to fight against. All the people I was closest to in Washington —President Johnson, Vice-President Humphrey and George Meany—called and tried to persuade me to back Beame. But the more I saw of Lindsay, the more I liked him. He had plenty of guts, and I did too. I was damned if I would go out with a defeat when people in our own organization were stabbing us in the back. And they thought they had us licked. Our enemies were already dancing on my grave. Not only dancing, but they already had me buried. But they forgot that little fellow, Dubinsky. They left a little hole; they didn't cover me up. That little fellow, Dubinsky, he'll slip through the eye of a needle. And I did.

The Liberal line gave Lindsay an opportunity to attract the support of tens of thousands of independents and Democrats who would never have voted for him as a Republican. With their help he came through, even though the Democrats swept the other citywide offices. I am glad he won, and not just for my sake. Some say he killed New York; I say he saved it at a time when it could have torn itself apart with fighting between black and white. Perhaps he was not a practical man; the civil-service unions certainly played him for a sucker. He had no head for union relations. In that field he was a disaster when he was tough, and even more of a disaster when he was giving away the city's money with both hands. But he did fight the power brokers; he had a sense of humor and he had a heart; he enriched the city's cultural life; he gave it a style to match its greatness. I am proud that the Liberal Party elected him the first time and that it did it alone the second time in 1969, when the Republicans threw him over. (That was before he threw them over by switching to the Democratic Party in protest against what Nixon was doing to the country.) Lindsay left the city in terrible shape, but I am not sure anyone could have done much better. It had just been running downhill too long.

Resigning from the I.L.G. presidency didn't mean pulling

out of the Liberal Party for me. By request of the state executive board, I stayed on as first vice-chairman and continued to play an important role. It wasn't the same for the I.L.G., however. Our union had always been the backbone of the party and the biggest element in filling its pocketbook. But my successor, Louis Stulberg, who I had always believed was as devoted to independent political action as I, didn't want that. He started pulling the union out of the Liberal Party almost as soon as he got in. He made it more and more a standard part of the regular Democratic organization. Part of it was that Stulberg never had the same high respect that I did for Alex Rose, a respect Rose fully justified over the years by his great political skill. But maybe an even bigger part was Stulberg's eagerness to come out from under the Dubinsky shadow, to show that he was master of the union in his own right, a role he never could play in the Liberal Party.

The break came in the very first election after my resignation, the contest for the governorship in 1966. The Democrats were locked into supporting O'Connor by the deal the leaders had made a year earlier when he stepped aside to let Beame be the mayoral candidate. O'Connor had won the City Council presidency while Beame was losing to Lindsay. In August, eager to avoid any similar split on the governorship, O'Connor came to Alex Rose's office twice and offered to make the Liberal Party an equal partner in his administration if we joined the Democrats in nominating him.

We had a Liberal Party policy committee meeting late in May. Stulberg and Gus Tyler, the assistant president of the I.L.G., were the only ones who favored O'Connor. The rest of us were all against him. We regarded him as too much of a boss-dominated candidate, and we didn't want to see that in Albany any more than we did in City Hall. However, when it came to the governorship, I did not feel that the Liberal Party could line up behind the Republican candidate as we had done when Lindsay was up for mayor.

This was true even though the G.O.P. candidate was one

for whom I had considerable admiration, both as a person and as a politician—Nelson Rockefeller, seeking re-election to a third term as governor. I had first taken that stand when Rockefeller made his debut in elective politics in 1958 after serving as wartime Coordinator of Inter-American Affairs and as Under Secretary of Health, Education and Welfare in the Eisenhower Cabinet. That year he was try-ing—successfully, it turned out—to take the governorship away from Averell Harriman.

I had lunch with Dolly Schiff, publisher of the *New York Post*, a few weeks before Election Day. Her editor, Jimmy Wechsler, was strongly for Harriman. She had started out being for Harriman, too, but I could see that Rockefeller's charm had got to her and that she was looking for an excuse to commit the *Post* to supporting him (which at the last minute she did).

Mrs. Schiff posed this question to me: "I know how highly Rockefeller regards you. I also know how friendly you are toward him. How is it that you don't support Rockefeller rather than Harriman?" My reply was that I would not hesitate to support a good Republican, especially one as good as Rockefeller, for the Senate or for judge or even for mayor, but I would never support a Republican for governor or for President, no matter how much I liked him personally. The reason to me was very clear. A governor has to be the leader of the party in his state, just as a President is the leader of his party in the nation. And their obligation to their party is greater than their obligation to the citizens as a whole on matters in which politics is paramount. To me, the G.O.P. always had been and always would be the party of Big Business in the worst sense, and I wanted no part of it even if its nominee was ready to run with Liberal endorse-ment.

The truth of that maxim was brought home to me when Kennedy was President in 1961 and labor was conducting a drive to raise the federal minimum wage to $1.25 an hour. I was called to the White House, since I was always in the forefront of pressure to boost the minimum, to confer with some of the President's staff on problems they had in getting enough votes in the House of Representatives. Their counts indicated that they were short four or five Congressmen. To get over the hump on Capitol Hill, I was assigned to get statements in favor of the higher wage floor from Governor Rockefeller and also from Jim Mitchell, the former Secretary of Labor, who was then a candidate for governor in New Jersey. The second part of my assignment was to ask Rockefeller to make a personal appeal to two Republicans whose votes were needed. I met the Governor the next day and laid the problem out as frankly as I could. When I asked him to put his prestige on the line publicly by issuing a statement for a higher minimum, he was very troubled. "Dave," he said, "you know I cannot do that even though I'm for the bill in my personal capacity." I told him I understood and asked if he would try privately to get the two G.O.P. Congressmen to swing. He agreed unhesitatingly. When I called Mitchell, there was no problem about getting a statement. He was a candidate, not an elected governor, and thus did not have to have the same regard for party regularity that Rockefeller did.

The only time he could be as free as Mitchell—or even almost as free—was in the period just before his own re-election campaigns. In 1970, when Nelson was preparing to run for a fourth term, he came up with many good proposals and got the conservatives in the state legislature to swallow them. I was riding in his car one day a few months before the election and I told Rockefeller it would be a good idea if governors were elected every year, then we could count on always getting progressive programs for the benefit of the people, even from the Republicans.

The point of this long detour was to explain why, when we learned that the Democratic bosses were determined to go through with the deal to make Frank O'Connor their candidate for governor in 1966, I didn't think the right and easy way out for the Liberal Party was to give its endorsement to Rocky. Instead, Alex and I tried to enroll Bobby Kennedy as an ally in trying to shift the Democratic nomination to someone with more independence and more substance than O'Connor.

Rose had a meeting with Kennedy at the Hay Adams Hotel in Washington one morning and asked, "Why don't you take the initiative?" We gave Bobby five names of people who would be acceptable to us as alternatives to O'Connor. They were Eugene Nickerson, then the Nassau County Executive; Bob Wagner; State Controller Arthur Levitt; Presiding Justice Bernard Botein of the Appellate Division; and Sol Linowitz, the former head of Xerox. "We'll back any of those," we told Kennedy.

He replied rather sadly that he thought we were right in wanting to find a stronger candidate than O'Connor, but that for him to get into it would mean another fight with the organization, something he did not want. He had barged into New York from Massachusetts only two years before to take the Senatorship, and almost at once he had become involved—at our instigation—in a donnybrook to dump the party machine's choice for Surrogate in New York County, a treasure house of patronage. That fight for good government had been successful, thanks to teamwork between us and him, but it had left deep wounds, which he had no desire to reopen by bucking the organization again so soon. "If I start another fight now," he told Alex, "the word will go out all over the country that Bobby Kennedy can't get along with the organization, that I have to have everything my own way."

Once he gave his reasons for keeping hands off, Alex and I knew there was no way to stop O'Connor from getting the Democratic designation. But that didn't make us any happier about his running. L.B.J. personally called me to use my influence to get O'Connor the Liberal nomination. It was midnight when he called me. I was in the bathroom and he kept me on the phone a half hour arguing why we should take O'Connor. I had a miserable time because I hated to refuse the President anything, and he knew it. But I couldn't accommodate him on that any more than I could when he had called the year before to urge that I back Beame on the mayoralty. I had to stand by my guns.

Our problem, though, was to find someone of stature who was independent enough to run on our slate alone against both O'Connor and Rockefeller, a formidable prospect. We found the man we wanted in Franklin D. Roosevelt, Jr. We hadn't thought much of him in 1954 when he had the strong backing of the state C.I.O. and many other groups in the contest against Harriman for that year's Democratic gubernatorial nomination. He had been a popular Congressman and at the start a good one, but he became too much of a playboy and we were delighted when our efforts to push Harriman resulted in his beating young F.D.R. and then going on to win the election. At the insistence of Herbert Lehman, Roosevelt got the nomination for Attorney General as a consolation prize, and much to his own surprise but not to ours was the only one on the statewide Democratic-Liberal ticket to lose in 1954.

However, by 1966, F.D.R. junior was a changed man, much more serious than he had been twelve years before. He got much valuable guidance from Joseph P. Lash, the newspaperman and biographer of Eleanor Roosevelt, who was a devoted friend. Franklin himself showed a tremendous awareness of the issues, along with much of the personal charm that had made him so appealing a political potentiality at the start of his career just after World War II. I joined Rose in backing him for the Liberal nomination and I was impressed with the way he conducted himself right through the campaign. It was a painful experience, nevertheless, because my involvement with F.D.R. junior put me in opposition to the officialdom of the I.L.G.W.U. Stulberg lined the whole organization up behind O'Connor and pulled the union out of the Liberal Party for good. In the end Roosevelt got more than 500,000 votes on our line, an extraordinary accomplishment. Without our pulling away votes that O'Connor might have got, Rockefeller would have lost his bid for a third term. But we had the satisfaction of defeating a cynical deal that had given the Democratic line to a hack—a nice man, a friendly man, but still a hack. We did the right thing in running our own candidate.

There was only one period when we gave real thought to winding up the Liberal Party, and that was not because we were dissatisfied with what it had accomplished but because we felt maybe the need for it had passed. It was at the tail end of 1961 after we had picked Wagner up off the floor and helped him to rout the machine when they wanted to deny him renomination for the mayoralty. We began to believe that after a century of corrupt rule Tammany Hall had been smashed for good. A strong reform movement seemed to be taking shape within the Democratic Party under the leadership of Lehman and Mrs. Roosevelt as patron saints and Thomas Finletter, the former Secretary of the Air Force, as active chief.

Not long after the election Harry Van Arsdale, the president of the Central Labor Council, came to see me. He had never had any involvement in the Liberal Party; but when his friend Bob Wagner got into trouble with the Democratic organization early in the year he decided that the unions ought to come to his rescue by organizing an independent party of their own, the Brotherhood Party, to support him. Van Arsdale and the other local A.F.L.–C.I.O. officers put a lot of effort and money into their party, but the result in votes was miserably disappointing. His purpose in visiting me was to get some pointers on why the Liberal Party always seemed to do so well in getting out an independent vote. I almost knocked him off his seat by suggesting that perhaps the best way for him to find out would be to take over the whole Liberal Party, subject, of course, to approval by our state executive board and members. He never took the offer seriously, but I was not joking. I could see many advantages in having a direct tie between the Central Labor Council and the Liberal Party.

Not long afterward and totally independent of my action, Alex Rose surprised even me by proposing to disband the party. At a meeting of the policy committee, he expressed the view that the Liberal Party had reached a high-water mark in its history by its role as principal architect of Wagner's nomination and election in defiance of the dictates of the Democratic machine. The Wagner ticket had rolled to overwhelming victory, and now the Mayor was promising a clean sweep of all the bosses in both the local and state organizations. On that basis Rose argued that it would be a good time to dissolve.

The more he talked, the less convinced I was that we should go out of business. First of all, I wasn't all that sure Tammany would stay dead. But, even more, I felt that the reason we formed the party in the beginning was still valid: the independent liberals and progressives and especially my old Socialists must have a political home outside both the old-line parties. I argued in opposition to Rose, and so did most of the others. We debated for two weeks, and in the end everybody but Charlie Abrams, the urban planner, voted to continue the party. It didn't take long to discover that we had not made a mistake. Tammany was not dead. By 1965 we were back in a life-and-death struggle with the bosses, and it looks as if that struggle will never end.

THIRTEEN

Ringing Down the Curtain

I ENJOYED LIFE because every day was a battle. The only times I worried was when there was nothing to worry about—and that was not often. Self-confidence I had plenty of, but I also had the Dubinsky luck, a quality I came to trust increasingly as it carried me through one close call after another.

When I was courting Emma as a youth of twenty, we walked through Central Park with another couple, and when we came out on Fifth Avenue, I ran across the avenue without looking at the traffic to see what street we were at. A car zoomed down on me, knocked me over and stopped with me underneath. Emma and our friends started wailing. Here we had had such a good time, and now I was dead. But I'm a hard guy to kill. In a minute I was crawling out from under the car. The only thing hurt was one leg, so we climbed into a taxi and went to our double apartment of two rooms, one for me and the other for Emma. Almost from the time we arrived until five o'clock in the morning, the ambulance chasers were after me. They came in herds, with everyone anxious to take the case.

Well, of course, I was supposed to be a smart guy, and I figured that whoever did represent me would insist on getting probably 50 percent of the judgment. That seemed too much, so I decided to be my own lawyer. I had to spend two weeks in bed, and I lost two weeks' wages, but the claims examiner did not come looking for me until after I was back at work. When he couldn't find me at home, I knew that weakened my case, so I settled as fast as I could for seventy-five dollars, which looked like a lot of money to me at that time.

My brother was sick and away at a sanitarium in the country. I sent him twenty-five dollars. Emma was a poor girl and needed a coat; I gave her twenty-five dollars. The other twenty-five dollars was to cover my medical expenses. Those were the days when you could get a doctor to make a house call for two or three dollars. What bothered me was that I lost two weeks' pay as a cutter. That meant about fifty dollars. But I was satisfied that my brother should have something and Emma should benefit, and I didn't feel too badly that all I had was twenty-five dollars for the torn suit, the doctors and the rest of it. True, when I went back to the shop, I was still half crippled, and a cutter can't sit down at his work. He has to keep standing, and the pain did affect my cutting speed. But the foreman took pity on me and tolerated it. The peculiar thing is that everyone told me—and they were right —that I could have collected a few hundred dollars if I had put the case in the ambulance chasers' hands. They were good collectors, but as a young fellow I didn't want anyone to make a profit out of my accident. Later on, I have to confess, I wasn't any more disposed to leave anything to lawyers. I always checked their advice against my own instinct.

When we moved into our summer house in Hampton Bays, Long Island, about the time I reached sixty-five, it was plain that I had to have a car and know how to drive it. I bought a second-hand British Ford Zephyr and learned how to drive it well enough so that even Emma got over her original fears and was willing to drive with me. I started out ultra cautious, but a couple of years of experience gave me more confidence than I should have had. I came into a sharp curve a half mile from my house. The next thing I knew, the car was in a skid and turned over. The neighbors put in an emergency call and within two minutes the Police Department and the Fire Department were both there with emergency equipment. The car was sitting on its roof, and everybody rushed up sure that they would drag me out badly banged up, if not dead. When they did pull me out, my cigar was still lit and I kept right on puffing. I told them the steering wheel was too loose and that's what caused the accident. Whether that was right or not, by the time the car was turned back on its wheels it was so smashed up that it had to be scrapped.

The most extraordinary example of the Dubinsky luck, however, did not involve danger to life or limb. One birthday not long after the Hampton Bays accident, my three girls—my wife, my daughter and my granddaughter—went to Arthur King, the New York jeweler, and asked him to design a gift set for me. The main piece was a hand-carved sapphire ring, with matching gold cuff links and tie tack. Ryna, my granddaughter, made the selection, and all three were very proud of their gift, as they had every right to be, because of its beauty. The ring became my favorite piece of jewelry and never left my finger.

One hot day I went out to my motorboat moored in front of the Long Island house and pulled the rope cord to start the motor. While I was pulling, my ring slipped off and I saw it sink into the four-foot-deep water beside the boat. I jumped in at once and hunted around on the bottom, but the water was murky and all I could find were broken shells and stones. The bottom was full of them. Finally, I took careful note of the spot, about fifty feet out from the steps leading to the beach, and went to the local police station for help. A policeman came back with me and put on a bathing suit and glass breathing mask. He had a glass-bottomed box with magnifying lens to help in the search and he set four poles in a twenty-foot square to mark the area where I was certain the ring must be.

The officer looked for an hour with no results. When he gave up, the neighbors took over and we all looked for an hour more. Finally, everybody said it was hopeless, but I refused to give up. I had a snorkel in the house, and I hoped

I could stay down long enough to turn over every shell and stone until I found the ring. But when I bent down, the snorkel was too short to reach the surface and no store in the town had a longer one. That same weekend, before I had a chance to go into New York for another snorkel, a terrible hurricane hit Shinnecock Bay, one of the worst in many years. It swept away everything in the water, including the boundary sticks the officer had posted to mark the area. Several boats were torn from their moorings and smashed up.

Even I had to recognize that the chances of ever finding the ring were now zero-minus, but I wouldn't give up. For eight weeks after that big storm I combed the bottom in front of our house, morning, noon and night. Finally, when we were about to close the house in early fall, I told myself there was no sense to the whole thing. I put up a stick as a monument to the lost ring and vowed never to look for it again. I was sure it was somewhere in Portugal by that time.

But the next morning, when I got up at six o'clock to go to the steam room in the basement, some impulse made me walk over to the water's edge. I had never seen the tide so low. I decided it couldn't hurt to look just one last time.

There were a lot of stones on the beach, but suddenly I spied among them a little piece of brass, probably a quarter of an inch at the most, sticking out among the rocks. It was at least a hundred feet away from where the ring had dropped two months before. I stretched my hand down for the piece of brass anyway. It was my vanished ring. I began to jump and shout like a maniac, "The Dubinsky luck, the Dubinsky luck." I splashed through the water toward the house, still shrieking with joy. When Emma, who was inside the house, rushed to the window and saw me leaping and hollering, she was scared to death. I rushed up to the house, waving the ring and still repeating over and over, "The Dubinsky luck, the Dubinsky luck."

But I would not pretend it was luck that sustained me in my union career. It was the union itself. As we fought our enemies and pushed toward new frontiers, I was always borne up by the vision of a great union—great not only in numbers and resources, in contributions to the labor movement and the wide national community but great also, and especially, in enriching the spiritual as well as the material life of the individual worker.

If the burdens of serving such an ideal were great, so too were the satisfactions. I loved heading the I.L.G.W.U.—it was the consuming interest of my life—but when I passed my seventieth birthday I realized it was time to think of getting out and allowing new leadership to take over. It had for many years been part of my philosophy that the complexity of modern unionism made it necessary always to have an orderly plan of succession established in advance, not only at the top of the international union but in every joint board and local. The head even of a local must be expert in a thousand things that are foreign to the knowledge and experience of the worker in the shop.

In line with that thought, I did more than encourage orientation courses for all candidates for union office and create the Training Institute to involve bright young people from outside the union. I also established the "crown-prince principle," so that each major official in our union would have somebody standing by who was familiar with the organization's practices and problems and who could step in if he retired or died. The term, I realize, is not a good one, because it sounds as if both the international union and all its joint boards and locals were little empires, where the "king" passed the throne to his successor with no democratic right of the people to choose their own new leaders.

But my feeling, based on all my experience before and after we started the crown-prince system, is that it contributed to greater democracy in the union; it did not frustrate it. It was not a substitute for elections. These continued to be held as required by the constitution, with any member in good standing free to run against any established officer for any office, however high or low, in accordance with uniform rules uniformly applied. The aim of the system was straightforward and simple. It was to assure that there would be no break in the availability of expert leadership, steeped in the traditions of our union and thoroughly familiar with the duties they would have to fulfill when a leader stepped down or was removed by death in the middle of his term. This was very much in the interest of the workers, partly because it prevented chaos and also because it discouraged a scramble for power in which cliques were formed and deals made to the detriment of the organization.

Needless to say, I had set the pattern for the crown-prince idea by indicating my own personal preference for a successor as early as 1956. That choice was Louis Stulberg, who had demonstrated his dedication to the union ever since he emerged as a general organizer in the Middle West in 1924. He had come to New York early in 1927 and applied for a card in the Cutters Union, Local 10, which I then headed. We were moving into the bitterest part of the fight with the Communist wreckers and I was delighted to have Stulberg in New York even as a rank-and-file worker in a shop.

In 1928 came the I.L.G.W.U. convention in Boston, and the division among the anti-Communist forces over whether to continue Morris Sigman as president or to call back Benjamin Schlesinger. I felt the needs of the union could best be met by Schlesinger's election. As I ran down the delegate roster to line up support for him, it became clear that Stulberg could be of great help. Because of the esteem in which he was held in Ohio, the Toledo local had designated him as its convention delegate despite his transfer to Local 10. The Midwest was strong Sigman territory, and I knew that the delegates from Chicago and Cleveland would be in his corner unless Stulberg joined me in trying to swing them over to Schlesinger.

I called Stulberg in and asked him how he stood in the contest. He told me he was for Sigman and I spent a couple of hours urging him to change his mind. I explained that no one appreciated more than I the tremendous role Sigman had played as strong man in the civil war against the Communists, but that he was not as good a man as Schlesinger to undertake the monumental task of reconstruction that lay ahead for the I.L.G. Stulberg still would not budge, and I was furious.

I shoved my left hand, palm upward, in front of him. Pointing at it with the index finger of my right hand, I shouted: "Until grass grows in the palm of that hand, you will never become an officer of this union if I have anything to say about it." Evidently I didn't scare him, because he voted for Sigman at the convention and so did most of the Middle West delegates. Fortunately for the union Schlesinger won.

After the convention Stulberg went back to his old job as a cutter in New York and did a good job in the 1929 strike, so good that I asked his foreman to have him come in to see me at the union office. It was the first time we had met since the Boston convention, and I offered him a position on the Local 10 staff as a business agent and assistant manager. He started to laugh and I asked what the hell he was laughing about. He asked to see the palm of my hand, which puzzled me even more. Then he reminded me of my threat, which I had completely forgotten.

He agreed to take the job temporarily, and from then on we did not part company. In 1947 I designated him as manager of one of our most important locals, and the same year he was scheduled for election as an international vice-president at our convention in Cleveland. However, just before the convention, I ran into opposition from some of the members of the General Executive Board to a proposal I wanted to put before the delegates for an increase in the per capita dues to help the union cope with postwar inflation. When it began to look as if they would defeat me on the issue, I quietly prepared a declaration of resignation from the presidency and made arrangements to go home.

When Stulberg heard what I had in mind, he came to me with Charles Kreindler, one of the vice-presidents, and urged me not to quit. Stulberg told me that it had always been his ambition to be a vice-president, but that, if I left, the whole complexion of the union would change in ways he did not like and he would refuse even to run. In fact, he would return to New York to complete contract negotiations then under way involving his new local, after which he would sever all his connections with the I.L.G. I was very moved by his statement. Apparently, word of his position also affected the General Executive Board. They sent a delegation begging me to stay, and the dissenters withdrew their objection to the assessment I considered necessary for the union's financial health.

Stulberg moved into the direct line of succession with his election as executive vice-president in 1956. Three years later I relinquished the post of general secretary-treasurer, which I had continued to hold along with the presidency, and Stulberg was named to that position. However, despite the high confidence I had in him, I did not feel my retirement at that time would be desirable. A number of problems were beginning to surface that I felt I should dispose of, rather than leave them as millstones around the neck of my successor.

The first of these menacing situations involved an antitrust suit that was brought by Attorney General Herbert Brownell in the Eisenhower administration against Local 25, our blouse local, in New York along with the major employer groups under contract with it. The indictment struck at all the basic provisions on which stable labor-management relations in the garment industry had rested ever since they were formulated in the middle twenties by a distinguished citizens' panel appointed by Governor Alfred E. Smith. Their recommendations had withstood many challenges, even to an exhaustive case before the Federal Trade Commission shortly before the indictment of Local 25. To my mind, this was a politically motivated attempt by the Republicans in control of the White House to besmirch the reputation of our union, especially since the charges against the local were accompanied by unsubstantiated allegations of racketeering. Even after these allegations evaporated, the Justice Department persisted in action that threatened to tear the foundations out from under the collective agreements on which the livelihood and the security of workers depended, not only in our industry but also in the rest of the needle trades. With the stakes so high, I felt it my duty to set aside my personal desire to have more time for my family and myself and to see to it that our union was vindicated.

Another problem as the union entered the 1960s was created by the union-within-the-union formed by some of our organizers and business agents. I considered it a direct challenge to a vital trade-union principle, one that posed a potentially serious threat to the internal unity of our union, similar to the bitter experience we had with the Communists in the twenties. It was followed by the scurrilous investigation launched by Representative Adam Clayton Powell to smear our union's outstanding record in civil rights and the promotion and practice of racial equality. Along with these three threats to the very essence of our organization went the unfulfilled mission, which I regarded as of paramount importance, of merging our forty-one retirement funds so that I.L.G.W.U. members working in any shop in any city in any branch of our industry could freely transfer from one job to another without losing any of the accumulated eligibility rights that would entitle them to the dignity and security of a pension in their old age. I was resolved not to retire myself until I had achieved this measure of protection for all our members.

It was not until early 1966, just after I passed my seventy-fourth birthday, that all the elements in the jigsaw puzzle fell into place exactly as I had hoped they would. First, the indictment against Local 25 was thrown out of court, and the integrity of our union and its contractual relationships was fully sustained. We defeated this trumped-up charge just as we had defeated similar frame-up attempts earlier in our history. Second, the false charge of racial discrimination leveled against us by the Powell Committee collapsed under the crushing weight of our union's long record of dedication to the cause of civil and human rights. So impressive was that record and so flimsy were the charges that the committee never even filed a report with the Congress. Third, a decision by the United States Court of Appeals had the effect of liquidating the problem of the union-within-the-union, thus ending this effort to divide and disrupt our organization.

On the affirmative side, we did succeed in unifying the pension funds into a single I.L.G.W.U. National Retirement Fund—a major landmark in the pursuit of social security under the union label. While that six-year merger task was being accomplished, another significant challenge arose in our industry, and this, too, was satisfactorily met before I stepped down. Giant firms with diversified production, like Jonathan Logan and Bobbie Brooks, began to dominate the industry, dwarfing the old established shops in coats, dresses and sportswear. Through their use of advanced technology and mass-marketing methods, they imperiled both the standards and the survival of many enterprises in which tens of thousands of our members worked.

At our 1965 convention we took long-range action to deal constructively with this new situation, not by seeking to obstruct progress but by adapting our own structure to permit the old and the new manufacturing approaches to coexist without damage to our members or to consumers. We established a Master Agreements Department in the international office to deal with those giants that cut across traditional industrial and organizational lines. We strengthened job security for our people by developing the idea of levels of employment—a device under which expanding firms shared their increased productivity equitably with their old workers and their new ones. It was not a cure-all, but the first few pacts we negotiated under the new arrangement convinced me that it represented a useful start on which other leaders could build.

Finally, with no emergencies hanging over the union, I felt that I could indulge my desire to retire. The first person I told, after pledging him to secrecy, was Stulberg. He had been standing patiently in the wings for ten years since I had designated him crown prince, but when I informed him that I was calling a special meeting of the executive board to announce my retirement and to urge that they name him as the new president, Stulberg begged me not to do it. "What will you do when you retire?" he asked. I told him I planned to make a trip to Europe and Israel with Emma. "But you're not going to stay there forever," Stulberg said. "What will you do when you get back?" I replied that I had my house on Long Island and I would enjoy taking it easy. He persisted in his objections. "Dubinsky," he said, "you'll go crazy with nothing to do. In my opinion, you're making a terrific blunder. I think you ought to stay. Maybe if you stay long enough, we'll both go out together."

But no amount of persuasion on his part could change my decision. The only other person I took into my confidence ahead of time was President Johnson. When I did break the news to the General Executive Board on March 16 at a meeting in the Americana Hotel in New York, the vice-presidents were as insistent as Stulberg had been that I remain in office. They appointed a special committee to persuade me not to go through with my decision. Most were in tears at the thought of my leaving. "In an organization or in human life," I had to remind them, "nothing is permanent or forever." When Stulberg again joined in the entreaties that I reconsider, I said, "I didn't have a life; I had a union life. I don't want to die in my boots. I'm not waiting for a free funeral. I want to be free." They still wouldn't take no for an answer, so I recalled that five years before they had tried to get me to ease up by going on a three-day week. That lasted just one week. "You know my nature," I said. "If I'm president, I can't only be president from morning till night. It has to be from morning till next morning."

In the end, they knew it was no use. Stulberg was chosen

and sworn in by me as president two days later. He insisted that I not sever my connection with the union totally and I suggested that the best place for me to serve, one that would not create any potential conflict with him in his proper role as chief executive in charge of administering the union, would be to create a new department to deal with the problems of retirees, with me as its director. The opportunity was perfect because we had piled up a *knippel* of several million dollars collected from manufacturers for failure to pay health and welfare contributions on work illegally done for them in nonunion shops. Stulberg and the board welcomed my proposal that the money be used to establish a retirees-service department, to underwrite pensions for old-timers who failed to meet the technical requirements for a pension, and generally let retirees know the union had not forgotten them.

I volunteered to be administrator, because I knew that, after my lifelong involvement in the movement, I would feel miserable if I did not have something constructive to do. Under the regular rules of the officers' pension system, when a retired officer continued to serve the union in a new capacity, he was entitled to 100 percent of his old pay, rather than the 60 percent pension. However, I declined to accept any pay beyond the $1,445 a month I received as pension. I took leave assuring my old colleagues that I would always be happy to supply any advice, help or guidance they might request but I would not butt into the affairs of the union. I also told them that I intended to continue as a vice-president on the A.F.L.–C.I.O. Executive Council, a post to which I had been re-elected only a short time before, and to remain active in the Liberal Party, of which I had so long been first vice-chairman.

At first everything went swimmingly. There was an avalanche of tributes from all quarters. President Johnson said, "The exit of David Dubinsky from the leadership of the Ladies Garment Workers Union is akin to detaching this country from its traditions." George Meany said, "David

Dubinsky does not need the title of president of the
I.L.G.W.U. to make his impression on the trade-union movement and on America. Even without it, there will be a
'D.D.' stamp on the future of American labor." There were
thousands more, but in some ways the one that moved me
most came from a man whose name meant nothing to most
people. He was Gus Sedares, who had been president of
FOUR, the union-within-the-union, which I fought until it
gave up the ghost. Sedares had gone to work on a federal
antipoverty project in Trenton, and I never expected to hear
from him again. Imagine my surprise when I got a postre-
tirement letter from him saying, "The union will be of much
paler substance without you, but it is certain that the institution will continue to grow because you have so firmly built
over the years."

With greetings like that, I left happily on a two-month
vacation trip to Great Britain, France, Italy and Israel. I had
already told Stulberg that I thought it would be a good idea
to establish the quarters of the new retirees-service department outside the main headquarters of the union, close
enough to be handy but not so close that it would seem that
I had never gone away. Accordingly, arrangements were
made for an ideal office on the second floor above the
Chinese restaurant of my old friend Sou Chan, just two
blocks away from the main office. Stulberg furnished it with
great care. There was plenty of space, and I was extremely
satisfied.

However, I cannot pretend that I found retirement a
pleasure. It is true I went into it with my eyes wide open. I
knew when I quit what had happened in other unions where
the president retired and the second man took his place. I
saw how miserable these former leaders felt. I also was well
aware of the experience of David Ben Gurion, the founder of
the State of Israel and its prime minister for so many years,
who had been most unhappy in retirement. I had got to
know him just when the Jewish state in Palestine was coming into being shortly after World War II.

We first met at a meeting of the Jewish Labor Committee, and I told him that, even though I was sympathetic to the creation of Israel, I was not a Zionist and I did not care much for the way some former Communists were now rallying to the Zionist cause because it was the fashionable thing for American Jews to do. "Now listen, Dubinsky," he said to me. "Why should we fight? If I had come to the United States in 1911 when you did and you had come to Palestine in 1906 when I did, today you would be the prime minister and I would be the president of the International Ladies Garment Workers Union."

The relationship that grew out of that meeting and the enormous respect that the whole world came to have for Ben Gurion made me very sensitive to another conversation I had with him shortly after my retirement. He was attending an official reception given in his honor by Mayor Lindsay at Gracie Mansion. As I shook hands with him, Ben Gurion pulled me close and whispered in my ear, "Why did you retire?" I whispered back, "Why did you retire?" From the look he gave me, I could see we were both in the same boat, two men who had decided it was a mistake to move to the sidelines. Frankly, I never in my life thought it would happen to me, remembering all the crying and begging at the time I gave my resignation, with everyone insisting that I stay, pestering me to change my mind. Never in my life did I expect things to change so fast. And probably neither did Ben Gurion or many others who stepped down of their own accord. I learned: Once you're out, you're out.

The important thing is that the union goes on, strong in spirit as it moves past its seventy-fifth birthday. Stulberg was forced by steady deterioration of his health to step down nine years after my own retirement, but the new president, Sol C. Chaikin, is a dynamic and dedicated representative of a new generation of leadership that combines youthful vigor with fidelity to I.L.G. principles. The challenges change. So do the tools needed to meet them. But one thing cannot change: the conception of trade-unionism as morally clean in a way that no business is. Business is profit; the union is idealism, commitment, service. Without the faith of our members, we lose what we have built. That will not happen to our union.

INDEX